The Province of the Book

# The Province *of* the Book

## Scholars, Scribes, and Scribblers in Colonial Tamilnadu

A.R. VENKATACHALAPATHY

permanent black

*Published by*

PERMANENT BLACK
'Himalayana', Mall Road, Ranikhet Cantt,
Ranikhet 263645
perblack@gmail.com

*Distributed by*

ORIENT BLACKSWAN PRIVATE LTD
Bangalore Bhopal Bhubaneshwar Chandigarh
Chennai Ernakulam Guwahati Hyderabad Jaipur
Kolkata Lucknow Mumbai New Delhi Patna
www.orientblackswan.com



ISBN 978-81-7824-452-5

Typeset in Agaramond
by Guru Typograph Technology, Dwarka, New Delhi 110075
Printed and bound by Manipal Technologies Limited, Manipal

MIX
Paper | Supporting responsible forestry
FSC™ C043100
www.fsc.org

*for*

KANNAN

# Contents

# Preface and Acknowledgements

In the beginning was the word. And then came print, adding immensely to its fascination. This book is an attempt to combine my academic inclinations and my fascination with print. In the process I have accumulated many debts.

On a rather sultry forenoon in the summer of 1990, walking in to be interviewed for admission to the Centre of Historical Studies (CHS), Jawaharlal Nehru University (JNU), I was confronted by a frighteningly distinguished group of historians. That I could not put precise names to the haze of faces helped mitigate my delirium. Though questions began to fly at me from every direction, I found myself put at ease by my own fluent answers. In fact, I was soon beginning to wonder if it was a delusion that my enthusiastic responses had dazzled the committee! The interview had gone on for a reasonable time when what turned out to be a last question was thrown at me: 'Who taught the history of Tamilnadu in your MA?' I had only been a distance education student, I mumbled sheepishly. This seemed to quell the inquisition.

Fancying that a job in banking would provide me the financial security with which to pursue a literary career (those were the days!), I had, well before taking to history, enrolled for a B.Com. This disabling choice notwithstanding, in my first year of college I ventured into the archives to try tracking the inspiring figure of V.O. Chidambaram Pillai (VOC; 1872–1936), the early nationalist who launched the first swadeshi shipping company. Soon enough, in the musty corridors of the Tamilnadu Archives, Clio seduced me. By the end of my efforts with commerce I was sure I wanted to be a historian. Dissatisfied with the state of the social sciences in Tamilnadu, I chose to acquire a postgraduate degree in history via a correspondence course while working at the Maraimalai Adigal Library in Chennai. By the time I reached JNU, I had published some books in Tamil—an edited volume of VOC's letters; a monograph on the 'riots' following his arrest in 1908; a monograph on the 1921 strike in the Binny Mills, Chennai; an edited volume of Maraimalai Adigal's diaries—and contributed to journals such as the *Economic and Political Weekly* (*EPW*).

To my surprise and relief the CHS not only admitted me, they even said I was at the top of their list. Bliss was it in that dawn . . . I explored the beautiful JNU campus, its bookshops, its library. I read, talked, argued, drafted pamphlets. Given the social stigma attached to studying history in Tamilnadu ('Going all the way to Delhi to study history!' was my neighbour's comment), the pride of place that history commanded in JNU was exhilarating.

With no idea of the demands of tutorial writing—a particularly rigorous CHS regimen that I am eternally grateful for—I hopped from class to class, auditing courses and attending lectures. It was the last year of teaching for Professors Romila Thapar and Bipan Chandra. Thapar's surgical precision when lecturing, and Chandra's evangelical zeal in preventing misguided sheep from following the 'satanic' Subalterns, were both in their different ways impressive. And Neeladri Bhattacharya's engagement with the latest in scholarship alongside his insatiable enthusiasm for every new idea were inspirational.

Wanting to keep the questioning to the terrain I was most comfortable in, I had bluffed at the interview that I wanted to work on the Tamil Renaissance. I had no intention of continuing with my earlier work on early nationalism, or on the social history of the Dravidian movement, having wanted to start on something new and fresh. I had spent the preceding three years—the single greatest education of my life—as assistant librarian of the Maraimalai Adigal Library. Founded with Adigal's personal collection as the nucleus, the library had been nurtured by the legendary publisher V. Subbiah Pillai and the great bibliophile R. Muthukumaraswamy into arguably the finest collection of Tamil imprints in India at the time. As the person in charge of the library, like a starving cow fallen on a millet field, I spent those years exploring its enormous riches. There could have been no better place to begin thinking about the history of the Tamil book. The chronological edition of Subramania Bharati's poems had been recently published by the Tamil University, Thanjavur. Reading Bharati's poems in that sequence, along with the rich appendices, helped me contextualize the inspirational poet and his work. I had started mulling over the publishing history of Bharati's writings. In the event, I wrote a paper for Professor K.N. Panikkar's seminar course on why Bharati, the most important Tamil writer of the twentieth century, had failed to make a living as a writer. Out of this seed grew a doctoral dissertation on Tamil publishing.

With K.N. Panikkar as a sympathetic supervisor, I wrote what someone said (as a compliment, I think) was 'a very un-JNU-like dissertation'. The manuscript was completed in late 1993 and submitted in the first week of January 1994.

Reflecting now on the times when the original thesis took shape, it seems an important moment in the history of the book. I had read my first proofs at 16. By the time I enrolled in JNU I had published a few books—'seeing through the press' then meant sitting in dingy letterpresses, reading smudged galley proofs, waiting for the foreman to make the pages, and signing 'strike' on the machine proof. I had spent days squeezed in such inky presses gulping cup after cup of sweet tea. My workplace had been essentially a working museum of print. The great nineteenth-century editors Arumuga Navalar and U.V. Swaminatha Iyer would have recognized it for what it was! By the time I finished my dissertation, desktop publishing (DTP) had made its first tentative entry into Tamil book publishing. I was now given the whole proof at one go and returned to an airconditioned computer room to ensure that the corrections had been carried out. The practice of authors arriving from all over Tamilnadu to Chennai to see their books through the press—a practice dating back to the times of U.V. Swaminatha Iyer (1855–1942) and Veeresalingam Pantulu (1848–1919)—had ceased. Combined with the couriering revolution, the DTP revolution had begun to change the logistics of Tamil book publishing. The boom in English publishing in India had begun too, and Vikram Seth's whopping advance—probably big enough to have bought the entire Tamil book industry—for *A Suitable Boy* had made headlines. Little did I realize then that alarming elegies to Gutenberg were just round the corner. By the time my thesis was evaluated and I was pondering its publication, I was beginning to wonder if book history was more requiem than record.

Print history in India was a rather antiquarian pursuit then. Professor Panikkar introduced me to Roger Chartier's works. At a time when *The Great Cat Massacre* was the academic rage, I also discovered the early Robert Darnton and his book histories. My thesis, though titled somewhat blandly, 'A Social History of Tamil Book-Publishing, *circa* 1850–1939', had its argument pegged on the weakness of the Tamil middle class and its incomplete hegemony—a notion signifying the times when Subaltern historiography was ascendant, if not the orthodoxy. By the time my thesis was examined, book history had taken wing in India. I had written papers in *Studies in History* (1994) on reading practices, and on the domestication of the Tamil novel in *The Indian Economic and Social History Review* (1997); these got some hearteningly positive citations, as did my various presentations and the manuscript dissertation itself. I also wrote monographs (one on the novel and reading practices, another on chapbooks), and a series of essays in Tamil on book history. And I taught a course on print culture, in the late 1990s, at the Manonmaniam Sundaranar University, Tirunelveli.

The early twenty-first century saw the publication of studies by a new generation of scholars: Francesca Orsini, Charu Gupta, Veena Naregal, Anindita Ghosh, Priya Joshi, Rimi B. Chatterjee, Ulrike Stark, Nandini Chandra, Rochelle Pinto, and others. The renowned bibliographer Graham Shaw and the distinguished folklorist Stuart Blackburn joined the fray, not to mention the great Darnton himself with two essays on book history themes in India. The subject found a new institutional location in Jadavpur University, where a series on book history was launched under the editorship of Abhijit Gupta and Swapan Chakravorty. Now, writings on South Asia increasingly factor in the modality of print when analysing cultural change. Sascha Ebeling, Bhavani Raman, and V. Rajesh have extended our understanding of the nineteenth-century Tamil cultural world. No cause and effect relationship is implied here; my sequencing is more in the nature of the Indian practice, when sniffing trouble ahead, of securing anticipatory bail.

Works of history are largely dictated by their sources. The present study, except for the chapter on the colonial state, is based almost entirely on a wide variety of non-governmental sources. This is as it should be: the questions that I am interested in scarcely concerned the bureaucracy that generated the voluminous records now housed in the Tamilnadu Archives. I mined a range of contemporary periodicals to cull data on the world of Tamil letters. Articles, advertisements, and book reviews were especially useful, as were the catalogues of publishers and libraries. The private papers of Tamil scholars yielded a rich harvest. The papers of U.V. Swaminatha Iyer and Maraimalai Adigal need to be singled out here. Over his long life, spanning a good part of the nineteenth and twentieth centuries, the great Tamil scholar–editor U.V. Swaminatha Iyer handled a mammoth correspondence. With the meticulousness that is the hallmark of his editions, he seems to have preserved every scrap of paper he received. He also appears to have gone out of his way to collect the letters of his master and other contemporaries. The result is a breathtaking collection consisting of thousands of letters. Similarly, the Adigal papers, though weak in correspondence, are more than adequately compensated by the diaries, an address book consisting of information on about a thousand of his readers, and the cashbook of his press.

A major repository that needs singular mention is the archive of the Saiva Siddhanta Works Publishing Society Ltd (or Kazhagam, as it is generally known). The first Tamil publishing house with a corporate organization (established in 1920), Kazhagam has been closely associated with the spread of the Tamil classics and, in its long life, has shared in the vicissitudes of Tamil publishing. V. Subbiah Pillai, its co-founder, preserved the correspondence received by the company from Tamil scholars. The outcome is an astonishing collection of thousands of letters, apart from statutory documents such as annual reports and balance sheets. The Maraimalai Adigal Library, which functions under the aegis of this company, houses a wealth of printed and other materials (including hundreds of pre-1900 imprints, rare letters, etc.) collected under the expert guidance of R. Muthukumaraswamy, its librarian and arguably the most knowledgeable of Tamil bibliophiles.

Biographies, autobiographies, memoirs, and similar literature have also been extensively used. The autobiographical writings of U.V. Swaminatha Iyer, running into a few thousand pages, have been indispensable, as also the editorial prefaces of C.W. Damodaram Pillai. Physical aspects of the books published during the period of study, as distinct from their content, also yielded data. Fictional works of the period were mined for information.

The surviving book collections of Tamil scholars and writers such as U.V. Swaminatha Iyer, T. Chelvakesavaraya Mudaliar, Maraimalai Adigal, T.K. Chidambaranatha Mudaliar, S. Vaiyapuri Pillai, and Pudumaippithan were surveyed to get a feel of the mental universe of readers of the period.

Following Tawney's advice to historians—to wear heavy boots—I trudged through book markets in the various towns of Tamilnadu to get a sense of diffusion patterns. Fieldwork was especially useful for the reconstruction of the world of popular publishing. Over 400 chapbooks, ballads, and such other popular reading materials were located and, consequently, Chapter 5 offers perhaps the only account of any length on Tamil popular publishing.

It is customary to note the importance of interviews and the material gleaned from those who were interviewed. I am not sure I want to do that. I would like instead to stress that this is an insider's account of the world of Tamil publishing and letters. As author, editor, translator, proofreader, and even publisher I have been part of this world for the last quarter of a century. Authors who have never seen a royalty cheque in their life, hacks and ghost writers eking out a meagre living, publishers who complain of poor rates of return on investments, printers who never meet deadlines, pressmen and women compositors looking forward to Saturday afternoons for their wages—these have peopled the world I lived and grew up in. It would have been pointless to conduct formal interviews with them; and even when I tried, the interviews usually drifted towards the latest gossip in the trade. Insights gained and information gathered when reading proofs, amidst the deafening noise of old cylinder machines, were more useful. I am conscious of having in this informal way picked the minds of many of those involved in Tamil publishing. I must especially thank my mentors Mamani and the late Tha. Kovendhan, and my publishers, editors, and printers Vellaiyampattu Sundaram, Me.Tu. Rajukumar, K.M. Venugopal, Vaigarai, M. Balaji, and Kannan.

My thanks to the various libraries and archives which permitted me to consult their holdings: Maraimalai Adigal Library, Chennai; Tamilnadu Archives, Chennai; U.V. Swaminatha Iyer Library, Chennai; Roja Muthiah Research Library, Chennai; Gnanalaya Library, Pudukkottai; C. Vijayaraghavachari Memorial Library, Salem; Gandhi Kalaimandram, Rajapalayam.

The original research for this book was conducted with the support of a modest, if indispensable, junior fellowship granted by the Indian Council of Historical Research, New Delhi. Perforce, therefore, I could only initially consult repositories in the province. However, over the subsequent many years I have used the opportunity to travel abroad for conferences, lectures, and visiting fellowships to consult libraries across the world. The India Office Library (now the Asia, Pacific, and Africa Collections of the British Library) is the single most important resource for a history of the Tamil book. I found its collection of Tamil chapbooks unique. The over 600 nineteenth-century Tamil imprints transferred from the Leipzig Mission to the Frankeschen Stiftungen, Halle, were also crucial. I owe thanks to the Nehru Memorial Museum and Library, New Delhi; the National Archives of India, New Delhi; the National Library, Kolkata; the Library of Congress, Washington, DC; the Regenstein Library of the University of Chicago; the Cambridge University Library; Bibliotheque Nationale de France, Paris; Det Kongelige Bibliotek (the Royal Library of Denmark), Copenhagen; the Widener Library and the Houghton Library (which houses the earliest surviving Tamil imprint, the 1578 edition of *Tambiran Vanakkam*) of Harvard University; and the Sterling Memorial Library of Yale University. The library of the Madras Institute of Development Studies deserves separate mention.

One of the saddest moments of my life was a visit to the Kottur Arangaswamy Mudaliar Library, Mannargudi, in the summer of 2000:

the silent voracity of termites eating away the finest collection of early Tamil novels epitomizes the apathy towards our cultural patrimony.

Four libraries relocated during the time I took to revise: the Roja Muthiah collections moved to Chennai from Kottaiyur; the Maraimalai Adigal Library moved from Mannady in north Chennai to the Connemara Public Library; the Bibliotheque Nationale de France to the François Mitterand site; the India Office Library from Blackfriars to St Pancras.

I thank R. Pathmanabha Iyer, A. Murugaiyan, Barney Bate, Steve Hughes, and Sarah Hodges for being especially supportive during my trips abroad.

A. Sivasubramanian at Tuticorin and S. Pothi Reddy at Madurai provided both hospitality and company for essential fieldwork. I spent an interesting day at the Gujili Bazaar with Tha. Kovendhan. A. Srivathsan accompanied me on my trip to Srirangam and Tiruchy. Steve Hughes joined me on an exciting trip to Karaikkudi and Pudukkottai. P. Athiyaman and B. Mathivanan have been generally around whenever I needed assistance.

The late T. Dayanandan Francis permitted me to consult the surviving records of the Christian Literature Society, Chennai. V. Srinivasan let me have a look at his grandfather 'Alliance' Kuppuswamy Iyer's diary and also consult his biography in manuscript form.

Parts and versions of this book have been presented to various academic and literary audiences at Nagercoil, Tirunelveli, Chennai, Mysore, Hyderabad, Pune, Kolkata, Delhi, London, Cambridge, Paris, Copenhagen, New Haven, New York, and Toronto, and I invariably received enthusiastic reactions and constructive criticism.

K.N. Panikkar, the late S. Ambirajan, M.S.S. Pandian, and Sumit Sarkar (as examiner) provided extensive comments on the dissertation version of this book. Barney Bate, Venkatesh Chakravarty, Steve Hughes, Sarah Hodges, Janaki Nair, and Sumathy Ramaswamy commented on earlier versions. Ramachandra Guha and Paula Richman provided pointed comments that helped greatly. If I have taken an unconscionable amount of time to finalize the book, it has not been for want of expert advice.

M.L. Thangappa double-checked translations and S. Thillainayagam helped with the proofs.

In earlier versions Chapter 3 was published in *The Indian Economic and Social History Review*, Chapter 5 in the *South Indian Folklorist*, Chapter 7 in *Studies in History*, and the epilogue in Nalini Rajan (ed.), *Digital Culture Unplugged: Probing the Native Cyborg's Multiple Locations* (London: Routledge, 2007).

One fallout of the delay has been the difficulty of choosing a grand title for the book. All possible combinations of 'empire', 'nation', 'power', and 'culture' having been exhausted, I have had to choose the provincial one that appears.

All translations from Tamil sources are by me. Quotations from English have been indicated as being such. In the footnotes I have provided translations of Tamil book and article titles wherever possible, except in the case of names and proper nouns. The past, present, and future of the book being too serious a cultural matter to be left to experts, I decided against cluttering the text with diacritics that would weary the general reader (and exhaust the publisher's purse). Tamil names appear as they are usually spelt in English texts in Tamilnadu.

I first got to know Kannan as the son of my friend, the late Sundara Ramaswamy, the distinguished Tamil writer. Over the years he has become a friend, collaborator, and comrade in arms. Kannan has been an important player at a crucial time, during which Tamil publishing has been transforming itself. Our dialogues between the past and the future of the book have taken place in the present. This book is dedicated to Kannan.

This is a book about books and I wanted it to be published by a connoisseur of print. Who better than Rukun Advani of Permanent Black, a press named after writer's ink! After several exchanges during which we discussed his editorial suggestions and alterations, I have a better appreciation of why he has such a formidable reputation.

Anitha has been the mainstay of my life over the last decade. The final submission of this manuscript was further delayed but enormously enlivened by the arrival of our little daughter Kannal.

Chennai
25 January 2011

CHALAPATHY

Because entrepreneurs who will take up publishing as a business have not yet emerged, there is still some difficulty [for Tamil authors] . . . Surprisingly, our entrepreneurs have not taken sufficient interest in [book publishing]. Books are, of course, being published now. And a vast number of people do indeed buy and read them. If the book trade were systematically carried out, people would have better books to choose from [. . .] There is no doubt at all that good profits will accrue from book publishing if it is pursued with enterprise.—**Subramania Bharati (1916)**

In this age, when printing machines have become legion and the business in paper has expanded, novels have started to proliferate like termites.—**Review in *Lakshmi* (1924)**

Brother, listen to me. Take up some other occupation: never pursue this wretched profession of writing. Show me *one* person [in Tamilnadu] who has grown rich writing books and essays. How does it matter to us that Shaw and Chesterton have become millionaires by writing?—**Kalki (1931)**

Two books sell the most in our society: one, the almanac; the other, the railway timetable.—**C.N. Annadurai (1950)**

# Introduction

## The Birth of the Tamil Book

> And in this Year we expect to receive, if it so please God, a set of Malabarick Types, by the Ships that shall come from Europe, that we may likewise publish the Word of Salvation among the Malabars, in their own Damulick [Tamil] Language, and introduce the desirable Use of Books for their temporal and spiritual advantage. We may remember how much the Art of Printing contributed to the manifestation of divine Truths, and the Spreading of Books for that End, at the time of the happy Reformation, which we read of in History, with thanksgiving to the Almighty God. O Living god, grant that the Christians here in India, and the Multitude of Gentiles, may, with Hearts full of Gratitude, become sensible of this great Benefit, and receive with Joy that Word of Life which is, and shall be laid before them, printed in their own Languages . . .[1]

Bartholomaeus (or Bartholomew) Ziegenbalg and John Grundler, the first Protestant missionaries in India, writing in 1713 from the shores of Tranquebar on the Coromandel coast to their benefactors, the Society for Promoting Christian Knowledge (SPCK) in London, leave no one in any doubt about the power of print. The writings of the Danish missionaries at the start of the eighteenth century abound in such references. Here are a few other examples:

> As soon as the Effect of the Portugueze and Malabarick Printing Press shall appear, by furnishing the Heathen with a sufficient Number of

[1] Bartholomew Ziegenbalg and John Ernest Grundler, Tranquebar, 7 April 1713, in *A Letter to the Reverend Mr Geo. Lewis* . . . (London: J. Downing, 1715), p. 26.

> printed copies of the Word of GOD, and other Treatises concerning the Christian Faith, and the Duties of our holy Religion, we shall have a fresh and signal occasion to Praise the Lord's Most holy name, for this new and singular Instance of his mercy, and to return our hearty thanks to all those, who have spared neither Pains nor cost to further and promote the fame.[2]
>
> The Single Instance of your having presented a printing Press, with a Font of Portugueze types, to the Malabarians, will make the Remembrance of your concern for them as lasting as the Books themselves published from thence.[3]

Two centuries after Ziegenbalg's prophetic utterances, Subramania Bharati, the great Tamil poet, reviewing a 'remarkable' book in his newly launched Tamil weekly, *India*, wrote:

> *Sivagnana Bashyam*. We read this book with great eagerness . . . Like Jews awaiting the Messiah, scholars well versed in Tamil had long wondered when this book would be published. Even the present reviewer, who cannot claim much scholarship in Tamil, had from a young age wistfully sighed, 'Alas, it is said that the rare work of Dravida Mahabashyam by Sivagnana Munivar is kept under wraps by the Thiruvavaduthurai Mutt! How great might this work be! When will it ever see the light of day!'[4]

The publishing history of this masterpiece of philosophical and literary exegesis, a work written by one of the greatest pre-colonial intellectuals of India, is a revealing case of how print, for all the revolutionary potential attributed to it, is constrained by social and cultural situations—which can determine when it appears, whether or not it circulates to the audience for which it was intended, whether it is bowdlerized, abbreviated, or in the form intended by its author, and so on.

*Sivagnana Bashyam*, or *Dravida Mapadiyam*, or *Sivagnana Mapadiyam*, is a commentary on *Sivagnana Botham*—the founding

[2] *A Brief Account of the Measures taken in Denmark for the Conversion of the Heathen in the East Indies* (London: J. Downing, 1715), pp. 11–12.

[3] Ibid., p. 26.

[4] *India*, 22 December 1906.

text of the philosophical school of Saiva Siddhanta—and was written by Sivagnana Munivar. A resident monk at the revered Saivite monastery of Thiruvavaduthurai Mutt (a name that will frequently crop up in our narrative), Sivagnana Munivar died, according to tradition, in 1785, at the age of 32. Well versed in philosophy, theology, logic, grammar, and literature, he was the archetypal pre-colonial scholar who could dazzle with his erudition and wide-ranging scholarship. His devastating polemics were greatly feared: in one celebrated exchange with Vaishnavite scholars he pointed out no less than twenty-two errors in a single quatrain of the great Kamban, and later, having made his point, went on to answer his own criticisms! The author of over a dozen works in various genres, Sivagnana Munivar's magnum opus was his detailed prose commentary on *Sivagnana Botham* by Meikandar, the thirteenth-century founder of the philosophical school of Saiva Siddhanta. Sivagnana Munivar's exegesis of Meikandar's terse text of 12 sutras, containing no more than 40 lines and 160 metrical feet, runs to over 500 pages. An intellectual *tour de force*, Sivagnana Munivar's work demolishes rival religious–philosophical schools in order to assert the superiority of Saiva Siddhanta. The commentary cites from nearly a hundred texts in both Tamil and Sanskrit.

This extraordinary commentary, for reasons still not entirely clear, was kept under lock and key at the Thiruvavaduthurai Mutt for well over a century.[5] It is said that only three scholars—Meenakshisundaram Pillai, Arumuga Navalar, and Sabapathy Navalar (they will figure in Chapter 1)—had read it during the century or so after its *arangettram* (a ritual debut; for more on this, see Chapter 1) in 1775. In the late nineteenth century, one Muthukumaraswamy Thambiran, who began his spiritual career as a resident monk in the Thiruvavaduthurai Mutt, became the pontiff of Suryanar Koil Mutt, a monastery located barely 10 km from the Thiruvavaduthurai Mutt, in the fertile

[5] C.W. Damodaram Pillai, ruing the fact of *Sivagnana Mapadiyam* not seeing print, saw this as a blemish on the reputation of the pontiff of Thiruvavaduthurai. Rubbishing the conjecture that it was not being printed as it could fall into the hands of the uninitiated, he asked: if the original texts themselves were in print, why not the commentary? *Kalithogai* (Chennai: Author, 1887), Preface.

Thanjavur Kaveri delta. Earlier, over many years as a novitiate, he had gained the complete trust of the mutt's pontiff, and now as the pontiff of a mutt himself, persuaded his former master to part with the manuscript for a few days, so that he might imbibe the text more thoroughly. Having attained the impossible, he took the manuscript to his own mutt and split it up so that it could be copied clandestinely by a few of his trusted resident monks. When the task of copying was very nearly complete, the Thiruvavaduthurai Mutt got wind of this betrayal of trust and demanded the manuscript's immediate return. Consequently, despite the assiduity of the copyists and much burning of midnight oil, the concluding portion of the commentary on the sixth sutra remained incomplete in the copy. Muthukumaraswamy Thambiran's intentions are not clear, and it is possible that he may only have been making a copy without intending to go to the press. In any case, he did not publish the manuscript in his own lifetime: his mutt sent the manuscript to the press only in 1921, three years after his death. But in 1906, within months of each other, two editions of *Sivagnana Mapadiyam*, both incomplete, appeared in print—evidently based on the clandestine copy. How this manuscript copy was smuggled out and copied remains a mystery. One was published by Swaminatha Pandithar of Jaffna, Sri Lanka, the other was printed in Madurai. However, it is the 1921 edition, published by the Suryanar Koil Mutt, that is considered authentic and reliable, despite the missing portion of Sivagnana Munivar's commentary on the sixth sutra. A hundred years later, scholars are still debating whether we have the full text or not.[6]

The irony of the above printing history of one of the greatest commentarial Tamil texts is accentuated by the fact that the seedbed of 'this great Benefit'—the coastal fortified town of Tranquebar, which produced over 300 printed titles during the eighteenth century and was arguably the most prolific printing press using movable type outside Europe at that time—was barely 40 km from Thiruvavaduthurai Mutt, where Sivagnana Munivar was a resident monk.

[6] This account of the publishing history of *Sivagnana Mapadiyam* is based on T.N. Ramachandran, *Sivagnana Munivar* (New Delhi: Sahitya Akademi, 1999), pp. 51–7.

Tamil's tryst with movable type had in fact begun nearly a century and a half before Tranquebar, on the western coast of India.[7] As early as 1554, barely a century after Gutenberg, a catechism called *Cartilha e lingoa Tamul e Portugues*, by Vincente de Nazareth, Jorge Carvalho, and Thoma da Cruz, had been printed in Lisbon, the Tamil having been transliterated into the Roman script. The uses to which Roman letters could be put within a South Indian context were obviously limited: immigrant missionaries could read them, but a more thorough dissemination of 'the Word' required that it be made available to local readers in their own script. So we find that by 1577 Tamil types had been cast and the *Doctrina Christam*—in Tamil titled *Tambiran Vanakkam*—published at Goa. With this Tamil became not only the first language to be printed in Indic characters but also the world's first language to appear in non-Roman characters. A new edition of *Tambiran Vanakkam* was published the next year in Quilon, on the southern Malabar coast, with improved types.[8] The press then moved a little north of Quilon, to Cochin, where three more works were printed, including *Kiristtiani Vanakkam* (1579) and the Tamil translation of *Flos Sanctorum* (1586). Two modern-day Christian scholars, Xavier S. Thani Nayagam who surveyed Christian repositories of Tamil in the West, and S. Rajamanickam who reprinted all the three works, hint at the possibility that the last named was printed in Punnaikayal, on the southern pearl fishery coast in the east.[9] Their

[7] The early history of Tamil printing is a veritable minefield. Many of the early imprints have not survived. Scholars have therefore had to take recourse to contemporary missionary documents. So the linguistic demands on the scholar are considerable. This passage is based on the writings of Georg Schurhammer and G.M. Cottrell, Jr, Xavier S. Thani Nayagam, S. Rajamanickam, Graham Shaw, and B.S. Kesavan. For the best summary of early Tamil printing, see Stuart Blackburn, *Print, Folklore, and Nationalism in Colonial South India* (Delhi: Permanent Black, 2003), chs 2 and 3.

[8] The only surviving copy is in the Houghton Library of Harvard University. There are at least two facsimile editions of this imprint. K.J. John (ed.), *Thampuran Vanakkam: Christian Doctrine in Malabar Tamil* (Calicut: University of Calicut, 2005); Tamizhnaadan, *Tamil Mozhiyin Muthal Achu Puthakam* (The First Printed Book in Tamil; Salem: Salem District Contemporary Painters and Writers Association, 1995).

[9] Xavier S. Thani Nayagam, 'The First Books Printed in Tamil', *Tamil*

surmise is based on the fact that Henrique Henriques, who well deserves the sobriquet 'Father of Tamil Printing', was based in Punnaikayal. However, Graham Shaw is probably right to refute this surmise and declare that 'The claim that Punicale (Punnaikayal) . . . was also a centre of printing at this period [the sixteenth century] is without substantiation.'[10] We may consider Ziegenbalg's assertion to the SPCK that 'the Art of Printing was altogether unknown upon the [Coromandel] Coast' as clinching evidence.[11] However, considering that the history of printing is a field prone to 'frequent confusions that have been perpetuated or intensified by simple borrowing',[12] Punnaikayal remains mistakenly on the map in the secondary literature on Tamil printing.

According to Graham Shaw, of the 1671 books printed in South Asia (including 427 in Sri Lanka) between 1556 and 1800, 266 were in Tamil. Tamil, furthermore, constituted 40 per cent of the 672 books printed in the Oriental languages during this period. Tamil was followed by Sinhalese (139), Persian (100), Bengali (84), Armenian (23), Hindustani and Konkani (20 each), and the other 12 languages totalling only 20 books. It pleases the Tamil devotee no end to note that only one Sanskrit book was printed during this period. In short, Tamil had a head start over every other vernacular and maintained its lead for the first two and a half centuries.[13]

If in the first instance it was chance that brought print to India—the printing press sent by the Portuguese king in 1556 was intended for Abyssinia but landed instead in Goa as the king had meanwhile changed his mind—the second instance, the arrival of a press in Tranquebar, was no less fortuitous. The printing press dispatched from

---

*Culture* VII (3), July 1958, p. 295; S. Rajamanickam, *The First Oriental Scholar* (Tirunelveli: De Nobili Research Institute, 1972), p. 179.

[10] Graham Shaw, *The South Asia and Burma Retrospective Bibliography, Stage 1: 1556–1800* (London: The British Library, 1987), p. 5.

[11] *An Account of the Success of Two Danish Missionaries* . . . , in *The Propagation of the Gospel in the East* . . . pt III (London: J. Downing, 1718), p. 8.

[12] Georg Schurhammer and G.M. Cottrell, Jr, 'The First Printing in Indic Characters', *Harvard Library Bulletin*, VI (2), Spring 1952, p. 147.

[13] Shaw, *The South Asia and Burma Retrospective Bibliography*, p. 13.

Europe by the SPCK was captured near Brazil and had to be ransomed before it could reach the Danish factory at Tranquebar in 1712.

Here, in Tranquebar, early Tamil publishing may be said to have taken root. The Tamil translation of the New Testament (1714), the first full translation of this text in any South Asian language, was executed by Ziegenbalg and made a significant contribution to Orientalist knowledge, a fact still not sufficiently acknowledged by historians. After Ziegenbalg, missionary stalwarts such as Fabricius, Schwartz, and Rottler laboured in Tranquebar.[14] Graham Shaw has counted as many as 338 imprints, many of them Tamil, issued from Tranquebar during the eighteenth century.[15] By the end of the century, however, Tranquebar was left behind. The scene now shifted to the British colonial administrative city of Madras, the first of the three presidencies to acquire a press—derived from the sack of Pondicherry in 1761. At the request of Fabricius, Governor Pigot handed over the press to the Vepery Mission on the condition that government printing take priority. The Vepery press, under the dynamic leadership of Fabricius, made significant strides, its work including a revised edition of the full translation of the Bible (1777–96) and the Tamil–English dictionary (1779).[16] Another false start in the history of Tamil publishing was Thanjavur. Under the modernizing king Serfoji II, a printing press was established in 1807. But this short-lived press published less than ten books, and these only in Marathi and Sanskrit. Even though it acquired Tamil fonts from Tranquebar in 1811, nothing at all was published in Tamil. By 1814 the press had effectively ceased to function and become by the late 1820s more a museum piece.[17]

A far less inauspicious beginning was made with the establishment in 1812 of the College of Fort St George—or the Madras School of Orientalism, in the description of Thomas Trautmann, who has

[14] J. Fred. Fenger, *History of the Tranquebar Mission . . .* (Tranquebar: Evangelical Lutheran Mission Press, 1863), pp. 315–17.

[15] Shaw, *The South Asia and Burma Retrospective Bibliography*, p. 14.

[16] This press later became the Diocesan Press and was active until very recently; the dictionary remains in print to this day.

[17] Indira Peterson's biography of Serfoji II is due out soon. I am grateful to her for permitting me to read the relevant chapter.

thrown new light on this extraordinary intellectual enterprise.[18] Francis Whyte Ellis, the brains behind the college, had created Telugu types and probably adapted existing Tamil fonts. During his time the college published a number of Tamil works—including his own incomplete translation of Thirukkural, Beschi's grammar of high and low Tamil, as well as Beschi's dictionary. Though the absolute numbers were not large, the initiative was of great significance. For the first time, nearly 250 years after Tamil first saw print, non-missionaries and natives had begun engaging with printing technology and were becoming familiar with the protocols of print. Ellis employed and worked with a number of native scholars, many of high accomplishment and ability. Some of them, evidently drawing from their experience of working with print technology during their time at the college, especially Tandavaraya Mudaliar, Kottramangalam Ramasamy Pillai, and A. Muttusami Pillai, pursued serious and a not inconsequential amount of editing and publishing. This was arguably the first moment in the transition from the writing and copying of manuscripts to the editing of printed works in Tamil.[19] Soon, there were native organizations such as the Madras Yupukta Grandha Karana Sabha ('the Madras society for the composition of useful works', founded in 1847) publishing books in Tamil as well as Telugu.[20]

Until the activities of the College of Fort St George, Tamil publishing was almost exclusively tied to missionaries and missionary knowledge production. Except for fragmentary details about the printruns of Bibles—the figures sometimes amounting to several thousands—we get scarcely any information on aspects of Tamil print culture. Few of the printed artefacts have actually survived in

[18] Thomas Trautmann, *Languages and Nations: The Dravidian Proof in Colonial Madras* (New Delhi: Yoda Press, 2006); Thomas Trautmann (ed.), *The Madras School of Orientalism: Producing Knowledge in Colonial South India* (New Delhi: Oxford University Press, 2009).

[19] See A.R. Venkatachalapathy, '"Grammar, the Frame of Language": Tamil Pandits at the College of Fort St George', in Trautmann (ed.), *The Madras School of Orientalism*. Also see Sascha Ebeling, 'The College of Fort St George and the Transformation of Tamil Philology during the Nineteenth Century', in ibid.

[20] *Reports of the Madras Yupukta Grandha Karana Sabha, 1853 & 1854–55.*

India, curious considering that the paper then used was, unlike most modern paper, 'acid free', and therefore much less subject to decay. The few that have survived are copies scattered in missionary and colonial archives elsewhere in the world. John Murdoch, writing in 1865, says many of the anti-Christian tracts published twenty years earlier were 'rarely to be met with'.[21] Perhaps this has a story to tell—of how limited the effect of print was on Tamil society in the first two and a half centuries or so of its advent into the language. One historian puts it rather emphatically: '*No book* was published in India, by Indians, until c. 1800.'[22]

'The coming of the print did not immediately precipitate a battle of [the] books', observes another historian of the book in India.[23] Why was this so?[24] The new technology of movable type had come into a society suffused by a scribal culture. Even by generally impressive all-India standards, Tamil had a long history of writing, literacy, and scribal culture. The earliest rock-cut Tamil Brahmi inscriptions date to the third century BCE, and by the first half of the Common Era stone inscriptions on temple walls and accompanying copper plates proliferated in the Tamil country. Stone inscriptions in Tamil count for the largest numbers of any language in India. Writing on less permanent material took the form of inscribing with an iron stylus on palm-leaf (*olai*) manuscripts (*chuvadi*); palm-leaf

[21] John Murdoch, *A Classified Catalogue of Tamil Printed Books with Introductory Notices* (1865, rpnt. Madras: Government of Tamilnadu, 1968), p. 134.

[22] C.A. Bayly, *Empire and Information: Intelligence Gathering and Social Communication in India, 1780–1870* (Cambridge: Cambridge University Press, 1999), p. 5. Original emphasis.

[23] Abhijit Gupta, 'The History of the Book in the Indian Subcontinent', in Michael H. Suarez and H.R. Woudhuysen (eds), *The Oxford Companion to the Book* (Oxford: Oxford University Press, 2010), p. 39. See also Graham Shaw, 'South Asia', in Simon Eliot Jonathan Rose (ed.), *A Companion to the History of the Book* (Malden, MA: Blackwell, 2007).

[24] This is discussed in Bayly, *Empire and Information,* pp. 238–9; Anindita Ghosh, 'An Uncertain "Coming" of the Book: Early Print Cultures in Colonial India', in *Book History*, vol. 6, 2003. While Bayly emphasizes the then existing information order, Ghosh points to the continuing importance of oral and pre-print traditions.

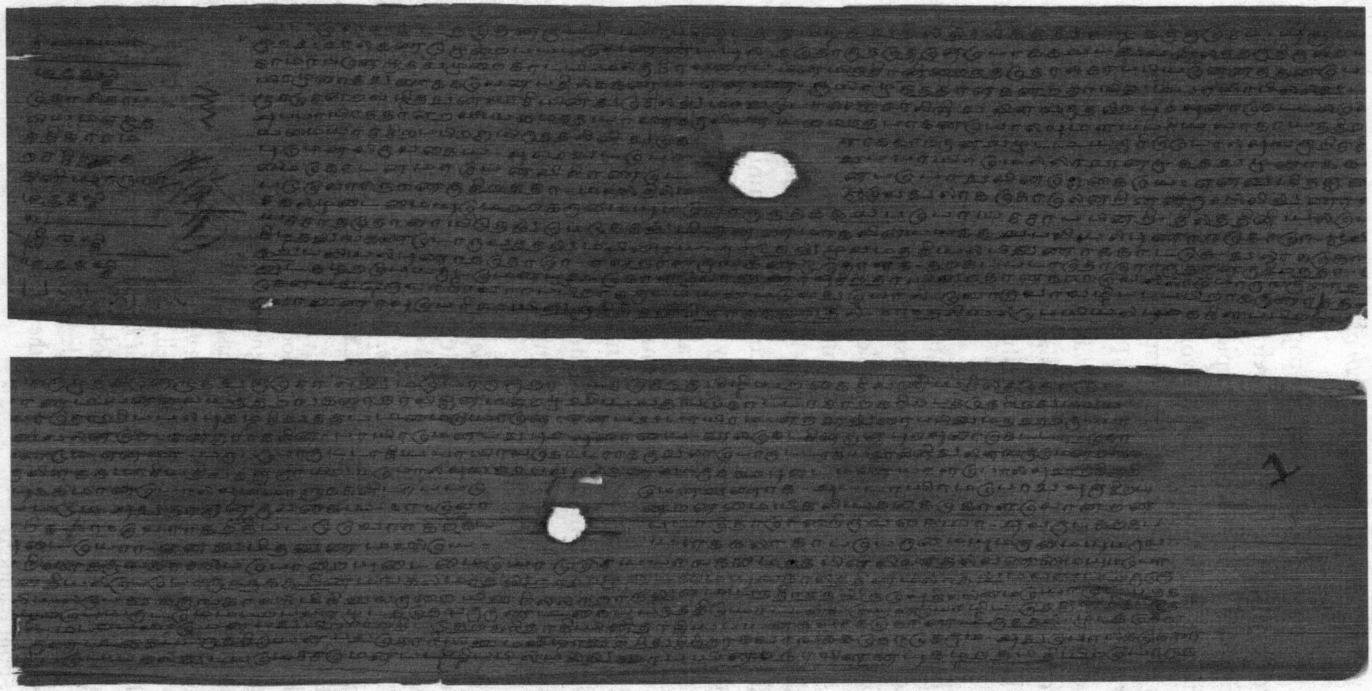

Fig. 1: A palm-leaf manuscript of *Tholkappiyam* spliced into two. The perforations are for the string which ties the manuscript. Note the absence of page numbers, punctuation, word and paragraph breaks, etc.

slats in fact constituted the sole form of popular writing material. And a large variety of texts—literary and non-literary, religious and secular—were written out, copied, and recopied on such slats for purposes of pedagogy and preservation. Thousands of such manuscripts continue to turn up in every corner of the Tamil country to this day. This scribal economy was reproduced for well over a millennium.[25]

Though paper had become available in India by the thirteenth century, it had made very little inroad in Tamil society. The assertion by A.C. Burnell that 'bigoted Hindus of the South consider this material [paper] to be unclean and therefore unfit for writing any book with the least pretence to a sacred character' seems to show no documented or experiential foundation.[26] All the same, once print became entrenched, the palm-leaf manuscript did take on a sacred character and came to be associated with the domain of religion. For instance, *Akilathirattu Ammanai*, revealed by the millenarian Vaikunda Swamigal (1809/1813–51) of the Ayya Vazhi cult in the Tamil-speaking regions of South Travancore, a work undoubtedly within the domain of religion, was not printed until 1939, nearly a century after its composition. Vallalar Ramalinga Adigal's (1823–74) resistance to the printing of his poems, on the other hand, had little to do with any perceived profanity of print: he had edited a few books prior to the publication of his *Thiruvarutpa* (Songs of Grace). Ironically, the publication of his first volume of poems in 1867 triggered a massive tract war involving the major figures of the time, ran into a few thousand pages, and continued for many decades. In short, the situation in relation to the use of paper *vis-à-vis* palm-leaf

[25] Scribal culture is now receiving much scholarly attention. See Velcheru Narayana Rao, David Shulman, and Sanjay Subrahmanyam, *Textures of Time: Writing History in South India, 1600–1800* (Delhi: Permanent Black, 2001); Bayly, *Empire and Information.* A special issue of *The Indian Economic and Social History Review*, XLVII (4), October–December 2010 is focused on this subject. Also see Bhavani Raman, 'Document Raj: Writing and Scribes in Early Colonial South India' (unpublished manuscript, 2010).

[26] A.C. Burnell, *Elements of South–Indian Palaeography* (1874, facsimile rpnt. New Delhi: Asian Educational Services, 1994), p. 11. Burnell co-authored *Hobson-Jobson.*

slats was not simple or straightforward, and it seems clear that there were contending positions.

The materiality of the palm-leaf book, constructed as it was of bundles of slats, precluded in the Tamil realm the possibility of the codex format, which had in much of the West long replaced scrolls. (This also explains the absence of calligraphy in Tamil.) The relatively smooth transition from manuscript to print in the West meant, in the absence of the codex in the Tamil context, that print faced a stumbling block at the very outset.

The difficulty was not of course only technology. The scribal economy operated in a society which supported a smallish literati. There was here a pedagogical system restricted by caste, a state which had not progressed from territoriality to governmentality, and an absence of networks of transport and communication as well as the related changes associated with modernity. By the mid-nineteenth century that world was crumbling. Governor-General Metcalfe's minute of 1835 abolishing the licensing of printing presses helped the 'natives' to set up print shops. It was in this world that print began to take root, and it is from this moment that a history of the Tamil book becomes really possible. Initially at least, the locals saw printing merely as a vehicle. The metaphor of print-as-vehicle, '*achu vahanam*', indicates this. (This metaphor became naturalized and continues to be in use as a term to describe print.) Terms such as '*janopakaramai*' (for the benefit of the people), '*lokobakaramai*' (for the benefit of the world), and '*pracittam seital*' (to make public) are used in this period to refer to the objectives of printing, its transformative potential not being foreseen. As late as 1925 an English printer trained at Cambridge University Press and heading the missionary Diocesan Press in Madras, based on his perspective that printing in each county reflects something of its national characteristic, patronizingly remarked that in India 'printing is still regarded as a foreign innovation; the Indian printer is content to follow the standards set by other countries; his best work is simply a copy, and he has made no attempt to develop a distinctively Indian style.'[27] Soon, however, Tamil print began to

[27] W.H. Warren, *Author and Printer* (Madras: Christian Literature Society, 1925), p. 1.

encompass not only pedagogy but also to move from a scribal culture to the printing of new expressive texts.

This monograph explores the history of the Tamil book from the time it really takes off. It asks: What sustained, materially and ideologically, publishing in colonial Tamilnadu? How did the material foundations of publishing pass from patronage to the market, and why was this passage so tortuous? What cultural forms pushed Tamil publishing into the market? When and how did the institutions of author, publisher, and printer emerge? Were popular publishing and popular reading practices silenced by mainstream middle-class publishing? How far did the colonial state figure in the emergence of a modern print culture? How were printed artefacts received? What were the reading practices and modes of reading associated with print?

The history of the book in India, especially in the Tamil context, has for long been the preserve of antiquarians and bibliographers. Invariably, their concerns have centred on the origins of printing, missionary contributions to its growth, its impact on education, etc. As a result, they have got bogged down in debates on which was the first Indian language book to be printed and where, who gets to take credit for it, where were the types cast, and the like. A.K. Priolkar's work was one of the first of this kind.[28] Based on meticulous documentation, it studied early printing in India with special reference to the role of Christian missionaries and the East India Company. J. Mangamma focused on Telugu publishing with an emphasis on the role of Company agencies like the Text Book Society.[29] B.S. Kesavan's multi-volume history of printing in India, despite its bulk, lacks an overall argument; Kesavan is content to use the 'contributions' approach and his work is an enormous pile of useful information

[28] A.K. Priolkar, *The Printing Press in India: Its Beginnings and Early Development* (Bombay: Maratha Samshodhana Mandala, 1958).

[29] J. Mangamma, *Book Printing in India: With Special Reference to the Contribution of European Scholars to Telugu, 1746–1857* (Nellore: Bangorey Books, 1975).

poorly organized.[30] The bibliographies produced by Katherine Diehl and Graham Shaw remain invaluable resource material.[31]

Mylai Seeni. Venkatasamy's history of nineteenth-century Tamil literature is exceptional.[32] Though structured like a medieval work of Tamil grammar, which precludes the possibility of an overarching argument, it nevertheless provides penetrating insights into cultural practices of the time. Venkatasamy marshals a wide range of evidence on the penetration of print culture into Tamil society in the nineteenth century and provides detailed accounts of print's impact on orthography, schooling, hermeneutics, religious debates, and the Tamil literary world. His early teachers and peers were men of letters active in the age of patronage, and as a result Venkatasamy offers a sensitive portrayal of the nineteenth-century Tamil cultural sphere.[33] Bible studies, as in other languages, have made a significant contribution to our understanding of print history and cultural translation.[34]

A major shortcoming of the extant scholarship summarized above is its emphasis on 'printing' rather than 'publishing'. The two terms

[30] B.S. Kesavan, *History of Printing and Publishing in India*, 3 vols (Delhi: National Book Trust of India, 1985–97). This is not to gainsay the importance of the rich visual material these volumes provide in terms of facsimiles of early, and not easily accessible, imprints.

[31] Katherine Diehl, *Early Indian Imprints* (New York: Scarecrow Press, 1964); Shaw, *The South Asia and Burma Retrospective Bibliography*.

[32] Mylai Seeni. Venkatasamy, *Pathonbatham Noottrandil Tamil Ilakkiyam, 1800–1900* (Tamil Literature in the Nineteenth Century; Chennai: Santhi Noolagam, 1962).

[33] Ma.Su. Sambandam, *Achum Pathippum* (Printing and Publishing; Chennai: Tamilar Pathippagam, 1980) though like Kesavan adopting the 'contributions' approach, is also sensitive to contemporary cultural debates, of which he provides a partisan view. Also see his other works: *Achu Kalai* (The Art of Printing; 1959); *Eluthum Achum* (Writing and Print; 1981); *Tamil Ithaliyal Varalaru* (A History of Tamil Journalism; 1987); *Tamil Ithaliyal Chuvadugal* (In the Tracks of Tamil Journalism; 1990); *Tamil Ithaliyal Kalanjiyam* (A Compendium of Tamil Journalism; 1990).

[34] Sabapathy Kulandran, *Tamil Kiristhava Vedagamathin Varalaru* (A History of the Tamil Bible; Bangalore: The Bible Society of India, 1967). For a more recent work which provides greater analytical detail, see Sarojini Packiamuthu, *Viviliyamum Tamilum* (The Bible and Tamil; Madras: Gurukul Lutheran Theological College and Research Institute, 1990).

are often used synonymously whereas 'printing' is the focus. It is crucial to disentangle these two terms. Simply put, 'printing' is a technology while 'publishing' is a wider social practice. 'Printing', being only the chief technological aspect of the wider activity, when used synonymously with 'publishing' relegates the larger historical role performed by the publishing of a book. Coming as it does at the end of the technical process of multiplication, the book, apart from becoming 'a commodity involved in economic exchange, is a cultural object, a vehicle of ideas, an element in social and intellectual conflict.'[35]

The tendency to focus on 'printing' has a long history. Francis Bacon referred to the invention of the printing press, along with that of gunpowder and the compass, as revolutionary. This was unfortunate, in a sense, as many historians began to see the printing press as an autonomous agent, independent of the social and historical context in which it operated. This is nowhere more evident than in studies on the Tamil 'renaissance'. In this historiography, the technology of print helped 'discover', in the late nineteenth century, a number of ancient classics, which led to the Tamil 'renaissance', which in turn is credited—as well as discredited in another stream of scholarship—with begetting the non-Brahmin movement, fuelling cultural nationalism, and inciting identity politics.[36]

This proposition explains little and begs numerous questions. Why, for instance, if the first Tamil book was printed as early as 1577, was it not until the late nineteenth century that Tamil books began to be available in significant numbers? Why did no indigenous Tamil literary producer resort to print until the early 1800s? Why was the urgency to preserve ancient classics via print felt only in the nineteenth century and not, say, in the sixteenth? Why had C.W. Damodaram Pillai, the nineteenth-century scholar-editor, to hunt (without complete success) for palm-leaf manuscript copies of the grammatical text

[35] Robert Darnton, *The Business of Enlightenment: A Publishing History of the* Encyclopedie, *1775–1800* (Cambridge, Mass.: Harvard University Press, 1979).

[36] See, for instance, Eugene F. Irschick, *Politics and Social Conflict in South India* (Bombay: Oxford University Press 1969); Kamil Zvelebil, *Tamil Literature* (Leiden: E.J. Brill, 1975); Nambi Arooran, *Tamil Renaissance and Dravidian Nationalism* (Madurai: Koodal Publishers, 1980).

*Ilakkana Vilakkam*, which had been written after the arrival of the printing press in Tranquebar?

Antiquarian interest, strongly fuelled by a fascination for the printed word, is largely to blame for the limited interest this scholarship holds for social and cultural historians. The credit for shifting the concerns of book history away from the antiquarians must go to French historians. Lucien Febvre and Henri-Jean Martin set the trend, studying the book in the context of the Reformation and the Renaissance.[37] Elizabeth Eisenstein's arguments for the impact of print culture, and the revolutionary agency that she attributed to print within larger historical change, have proved to be both influential and controversial.[38] French historians, borrowing from economic historians, have used quantitative methods to study the book, both as an economic object and as a cultural sign. This has further shifted the focus from the great works theory of intellectual history to a wider understanding of the reading and writing practices in society as a whole.[39]

Robert Darnton's earlier works,[40] written from the perspective of a social history of ideas, marked the next step in book history and may be said to have defined the field. Through a publishing history

[37] Lucien Febvre and Henri-Jean Martin, *The Coming of the Book: The Impact of Printing, 1450–1800* (London: New Left Books, 1976, orig. French edn 1958).

[38] Elizabeth Eisenstein, *The Printing Press as an Agent of Change: Communications and Cultural Transformations in Early-Modern Europe*, 2 vols (Cambridge: Cambridge University Press, 1979). For the abridged version, idem, *The Printing Revolution in Early Modern Europe* (Cambridge: Cambridge University Press, 1983). For a summary of the criticisms and Eisenstein's combative response, see her Afterword to the second edition (2005). For the influence of her work, see Sabrina Alcorn Baron, Eric N. Lindquist, and Eleanor F. Shevlin (eds), *Agent of Change: Print Culture Studies after Elizabeth L. Eisenstein* (Amherst: University of Massachusetts Press, 2007).

[39] Roger Chartier and Daniel Roche, 'New Approaches to the History of the Book', in Maurice Aymard and Harbans Mukhia (eds), *French Studies in History*, vol. 2 (Delhi: Orient Longman, 1990); Robert Darnton, 'History of Reading', in Peter Burke (ed.), *New Perspectives on Historical Writing* (Cambridge: Polity, 1991).

[40] Robert Darnton, *The Business of Enlightenment*; and *The Literary Underground of the Old Regime* (Cambridge, Mass: Harvard University Press, 1982).

of the French Encyclopaedia, he sought to study how a great intellectual movement, the Enlightenment, spread through society. Fixing the book trade in the social and economic systems of pre-revolutionary Europe, he asked if the material basis of literature and the technology of its production have much bearing on its content and spread. Darnton's conclusions were contrary to the *Annales* formulation that the Enlightenment did not upset the long-term, deep-running currents of traditional culture. Darnton then extended his work, from the perspective of what could be termed an intellectual history from below, via a series of fascinating studies on the literary underground of the Old Regime. But, by the late 1970s and the early 1980s, social history was under attack from both structuralists and culturalists. The latter felt disquieted by the formulation that culture was a third level which derived from the more deep-seated economic and social spheres. This notion of culture as third level was also a critique of a certain version of Marxism which emphasized the deterministic nature of the material base over culture, the latter being seen to be part of the superstructure.

> [O]ur understanding of [cultural] practices which serve to organize economic activity and which create ties among individuals must not be limited to their material ends or their social effects alone. All practices are 'cultural' as well as social or economic, since they translate into action the many ways in which humans give meaning to their world. All history, therefore—whether economic, social or religious—requires the study of systems of representation and the acts the systems generate.[41]

This disciplinarian breakthrough led to interesting results, especially in book history. Darnton forsook 'grubbing at the archives' and went on excursions into the alien territory of past *mentalités* through a series of arresting studies on some episodes in French cultural history. These ranged from a bizarre massacre of cats to police dossiers on authors.[42] Roger Chartier, by concentrating on reading practices,

[41] Roger Chartier, *The Cultural Uses of Print in Early Modern France* (Princeton: Princeton University Press, 1987), p. 11.

[42] Robert Darnton, *The Great Cat Massacre and Other Episodes in French Cultural History* (Harmondsworth: Penguin, 1984).

differentiated uses, and plural appropriations of the same books by different groups, questioned the social history understanding of popular culture. Through his studies on the cultural uses of print in early modern France, he attacked the presupposition that exclusive relationships existed between specific cultural forms and particular social groups, as well as the notion of pure and homogeneous cultures in society.[43]

While these debates did have an influence on Indian historiography, it was arguably Benedict Anderson's work which gave a new strength to the interest in print. Anderson argued that book publishing was one of the earliest forms of capitalist enterprise, and proposed that the explosive interaction between capitalism, print technology, and linguistic diversity was the basis for 'imagining' nations, an overtly political manifestation of capitalist transformation.[44] In conjuncture with the 'late Subaltern' moment, the aftermath of 'imagined communities' saw the proliferation of numerous excellent studies directly addressing print in colonial India: Francesca Orsini on the construction of the Hindi public sphere and subsequently on popular fiction in colonial North India; Veena Naregal on language hierarchies, print and the public sphere in Maharashtra; Anindita Ghosh on how print transformed the Bengali language; Rochelle Pinto on print and politics in Goa; Priya Joshi on the reception of the English novel in India; Rimi Chatterjee on the history of the Oxford University Press in India; and Ulrike Stark on the famed Naval Kishore Press of Lucknow. These scholars have enriched and invigorated the field.

The main part of this book comprises seven chapters, this introduction, and an epilogue. Chapter 1 argues that the basis of Tamil book publishing in the second half of the nineteenth century was the patronage of pre- and early-colonial social classes, which was being eroded by the socio-economic transformation effected by colonialism

[43] Chartier, *The Cultural Uses of Print.*

[44] Benedict Anderson, *Imagined Communities: Reflections on the Origin and Spread of Nationalism* (London: Verso, 1983; rev. edn 1991).

in Tamil society. An attempt was made to reach out to the market and the people, but a period of transition intervened, when literary producers were caught in the dilemmas of transition. Pulled between the old-world charm of patronage and the prospects of an incipient market, theirs was a traumatic experience. Chapter 2 makes this argument by tracing the publishing careers of Subramania Bharati and M.V. Ramanujachari. Chapter 3 argues that only with the emergence of the novel as the art form par excellence of the middle class was the break with patronage complete, and Tamil publishing fully a market venture. With this background, the emergence of the fuzzy categories of authors, publishers, and printers is traced in the chapter that follows. Chapter 5 then reconstructs the world of popular publishing and suggests that, despite some interaction with the elite, this was a more or less distinct and autonomous domain which the middle class could not hegemonize. The penultimate chapter studies the role of the colonial state in relation to book publishing. It is suggested that the state was marginal, if not an epiphenomenon of, the world of Tamil publishing. Its legislative interventions were more knee-jerk reactions to agitational political movements, which in any case were ineffective due to a weak administrative structure. The last chapter studies readers, reading practices, and modes of reading in colonial Tamilnadu. After detailing cultural practices surrounding the book over the period of study, it argues that, while the new (silent) mode of reading did emerge as the cultural marker of the middle class, it could not displace earlier modes of reading. Tamil society presented a picture of plurality, with a differentiated use of cultural materials. The epilogue traces the broad contours of the changing face of Tamil publishing from the time of Independence to the present and speculates on the future of the book. The appendices provide data on Tamil book production, the most comprehensive to date; printing costs in colonial Tamilnadu, and excerpts from the cashbook of a printing press. The bibliography at the end is necessarily select. For a book of this kind every published artefact is a source. It being impossible to list every such item, the bibliography lists works that I have found particularly useful, or to which I owe some debt. Stand-alone citations in the notes have not been consolidated in the bibliography.

# 1

# The Age of Patronage

> The state of society in India resembles that of the early literary periods in our own county; when standard works could only be produced through the patronage of the great; and then only reached the few.—**Rev. James Johnston**[1]

This chapter studies the material basis of literary production in Tamilnadu in the second half of the nineteenth century. It shows the persistence of certain forms of patronage which had sustained literary production in early colonial Tamilnadu (pre-1850) even as the technology of print was being harnessed for literary production. The emphasis is on the class composition of this patronage and the changes in its character on account of changing socio-economic conditions. I touch upon the nature of literary production, as well as the cultural importance and authority that literary production and patronage carried. I also trace the decline of patronage in Tamil book publishing. This delineation is based on an analysis of three important aspects of patronage publishing: the *arangettram* (premiere), the *sirappu payiram* (the prefatory poem), and the title page.

## Poets, Patrons, and Forms of Patronage

Through the centuries, going as far back as the pre-Christian era, elite literary production had in Tamil society been essentially sustained

[1] Rev. James Johnston, 'The Cultivation and Diffusion of Literature in India' (1889), in no. 598, Educational (hereafter Edl), 22 August 1890. (Documents of the Government of Madras cited are housed in the Tamilnadu Archives, Chennai.)

by patronage—by tribal chieftains during the Sangam period (circa first century BCE to CE third century), by feudal lords and royalty in medieval times (fifth century to eighteenth century).[2] The forms of patronage that survived in the second half of the nineteenth century were those that had emerged and ossified during the Nayakkar period (sixteenth to eighteenth centuries). The Nayakkar kings and their successor *palayakkarar*s, who reigned in pre- and early-colonial Tamilnadu, as well as the religious *matams* (mutts, monasteries) and *zamins*—expropriators of the material surplus—were the patrons of art and literature.[3] Given the importance of patronage, the subject matter of many poems was patronage—the poet's elation at receiving bounteous patronage or fulmination at its paucity. This aristocracy of sorts is well known in literature for its patronage of literary production, but the nature of its patronage requires much more research.

## *Poets and Patronage*

The literary career of Meenakshisundaram Pillai (1815–1876) serves as a convenient entry point for studying the age of patronage. A literary historian says of him: 'No single English term or phrase can adequately describe the role that [he] played in nineteenth-century Tamil literary culture.'[4] Hailed as Mahavidwan ('great scholar') and arguably the most celebrated Tamil teacher of his day, Meenakshisundaram Pillai was born in Tiruchirappalli. His early education under his father's

[2] See K. Kailasapathy, *Tamil Heroic Poetry* (Oxford: Clarendon Press, 1968), ch. 2, for an excellent analysis of patronage in the Sangam period. For patronage in the post Sangam period down to the Nayakkar period, see D.D. Shulman, 'Poets and Patrons in Tamil Literature and Literary Legend', in Barbara Miller (ed.), *The Powers of Art* (Delhi: Oxford University Press, 1992).

[3] S. Vaiyapuri Pillai, 'Pathonbatham Noottrandil Tamil Ilakkiyam' (Tamil Literature in the Nineteenth Century), *Ilakkiya Chinthanaigal* (Literary Thoughts; Chennai: Tamil Puthakalayam, 1947). For a description and analysis of literary patronage immediately before our period, see Sascha Ebeling, *Colonizing the Realm of Words: The Transformation of Tamil Literature in Nineteenth-Century South India* (Albany: SUNY Press, 2010), ch. 3.

[4] Paula Richman, *Extraordinary Child: Poems from a South Indian Devotional Genre* (Honolulu: University of Hawaii Press, 1997), p. 112.

supervision was followed by tutoring under traditional Tamil teachers. Even in his youth he showed prodigious powers of versification and went on to become one of the prolific poets of his time.[5]

Being a renowned teacher, Meenakshisundaram Pillai led a peripatetic life, accompanied everywhere by devoted young students. His time was divided between teaching and versification, all his material needs being taken care of by his patrons. His literary output consisted for the most part of *thala puranams* (a hagiographical genre focused on a sacred place, or a deity, or a temple) as well as minor forms of highly conventional literary genres (*prabandam* or *chittrilakkiyam*),[6] all of which he composed at the invitation of local patrons. Some of his earlier compositions included *Palasai Pathittrupattu Andadi*,[7] *Thiruppaigneeli Thiribandadi*,[8] *Uraiyur Puranam*,[9] *Vatpokki Kalambagam*,[10] and *Thirumylai Puranam*.[11] By 1860 he had become such a name that he was made the *adheena vidwan* (official scholar) of the Thiruvavaduthurai Adheenam or Mutt, the renowned Saivite monastery.[12] From then on his needs and those of his pupils were largely taken care of by the mutt. Here, apart from teaching his many pupils, Meenakshisundaram Pillai wrote a *kalambagam* (a minor literary form) on Ambalavana Desigar, the senior pontiff (*peria pattam* or *pandara sannithi*) of the mutt, for which he was awarded the title of Mahavidwan.[13] He remained closely identified with the Thiruvavaduthurai

[5] Biographical details on Meenakshisundaram Pillai are drawn from the brilliant biography by his illustrious pupil U.V. Swaminatha Iyer, *Sri Meenakshisundaram Pillaiyavargal Charithiram* (The Biography of Meenakshisundaram Pillai), 2 vols (1938–40, facsimile rpnt. Thanjavur: Tamil University, 1986). Henceforth cited as *SMPC*.

[6] *Chittrilakkiyam* refers to a number of minor literary genres which grammatical works conventionally count as ninety-six. Some of these genres, such as *andadi*, *kovai*, *ula*, and *parani*, were both ancient and popular, while many others, such as *pallu*, *kuravanji*, and *vilasam*, originated later.

[7] *SMPC*, vol. 1, p. 30.

[8] Ibid., p. 40.

[9] Ibid., p. 118.

[10] Ibid., p. 139.

[11] Ibid., pp. 168–9.

[12] Ibid., pp. 198–202.

[13] Ibid., p. 204.

Mutt, and, on his sixtieth birthday in 1875, a year before his death, the conventional celebration of *sashtiyapthapurthi* was held in grand style as a fitting honour.[14]

Apart from patronage by the Thiruvavaduthurai Mutt, Meenakshisundaram Pillai also received an occasional bequest from the Dharumapuram Adheenam, another leading Saivite monastery. On the request of its pontiff, he composed *Sachidananda Malai* and *Thirukkurukkai Puranam*.[15] On the occasion of the latter's premiere he was honoured and rewarded. He was also on a few occasions provided patronage by the Kundrakkudi Thiruvannamalai Adheenam.[16] Many of Meenakshisundaram Pillai's thala puranams were sponsored by local men of influence, especially landlords, *tahsildar*s, traders, and caste headmen. *Kudandai Puranam* was sponsored by the tahsildar of Kumbakonam, Sivagurunatha Pillai,[17] *Mangalambikai Pillaitamil* (1866) by Kanakasabhai Pillai, a textile merchant,[18] and *Kudandai Thiribandadi* (1866) by one Ambalavana Chettiar.[19] *Kandadevi Puranam* (1867)[20] and *Veeravana Puranam* (1868)[21] were commissioned by the Chettiar community, while *Thiruthurithi Puranam* (1867) was sponsored by some Sengundha Mudaliars,[22] and *Thaniyur Puranam* (1868) by Saliyars.[23] The puranams on Attroor, Vilatholi, and Thiruvaloliputtroor were sponsored by the Saiva Vellalars of those localities.[24]

The thala puranam, a genre of mythological history pertaining to a religious centre, was the art form par excellence in this age of patronage. As U.V. Swaminatha Iyer remarks, 'Most of Meenakshisundaram Pillai's works are puranams. People in every Saivite centre of the day wished that at least one puranam or some prabandam be

[14] Ibid., vol. 2, p. 208.
[15] Ibid., vol. 1, pp. 145, 192–3, 229.
[16] Ibid., vol. 2, p. 196.
[17] Ibid., vol. 1, p. 259.
[18] Ibid., p. 276.
[19] Ibid., p. 278.
[20] Ibid., p. 279.
[21] Ibid., p. 308.
[22] Ibid., p. 295.
[23] Ibid., p. 300.
[24] Ibid., p. 215.

composed by him.'[25] The head of the Dharumapuram Mutt went so far as to state that a puranam (for a particular holy centre) was more important than even the *Thevaram* (the compositions of the seventh-century Saiva Nayanmar saints).[26] Such was the prestige of the puranam that the gullible people of Sooraikkudi politely insisted that Meenakshisundaram Pillai write no less than four lines in every verse of his puranam on their town![27]

Given the authority and prestige that thala puranams carried, poets like Meenakshisundaram Pillai had a field day in the age of patronage. As we shall see below, many of these men were much sought after during the second half of the nineteenth century by a range of patrons.

### *The Patrons*

The first category of patrons was the zamindars and native princes. These vestiges of Nayakkar rule, preserved by colonialism as hollow crowns,[28] continued with their earlier, though reduced, patronage of poets and other cultural producers.[29] Courtly largesse was a major form of redistributive politics practised by zamins and native princes, generosity being an essential element of the self-image that these potentates wished to portray.[30] The patrons of literary production in the immediate pre-colonial and early colonial periods do not figure all that prominently in the era of print, save Pudukkottai, Ramanathapuram, and Ettayapuram. Well into the late nineteenth century,

[25] Ibid., vol. 2, p. 280.

[26] Letter of Dharumapuram Mutt's head, in ibid., vol. 1, p. 230.

[27] Ibid., pp. 281–2. Thala puranams were usually written in quatrains.

[28] The phrase is derived from Nicholas Dirks, *The Hollow Crown: The Ethnohistory of a South Indian Little Kingdom* (Cambridge: Cambridge University Press, 1987).

[29] Only the patronage of literary production is explored here. Similar exercises may be carried out in relation to music and the other arts. The patronage of classical music in colonial Tamilnadu is touched upon in Lakshmi Subramanian, *From the Tanjore Court to the Madras Music Academy: A Social History of Music in South India* (Delhi: Oxford University Press, 2006), ch. 1.

[30] Pamela Price, *Kingship and Political Practice in Colonial India* (Cambridge: Cambridge University Press, 1996), pp. 77–80.

especially under the dewanship (1878–86, and later dewan regentship, until 1894) of A. Seshia Sastri, the native state of Pudukkottai conducted an annual function on the occasion of Navaratri, when gifts up to even Rs 100 were given to poets and scholars.[31] A. Seshia Sastri won much respect in the world of Tamil letters for sponsoring C.W. Damodaram Pillai's edition of the Sangam classic *Kalithogai*,[32] and helped in U.V. Swaminatha Iyer's publishing ventures too. The zamin of Ettayapuram, whose zamindar was called a raja, was another important patron, who sustained Subramania Bharati in his early career (more on this in Chapter 2).

Ponnuswami Thevar (1837–1870), a brother of the Raja of Ramanathapuram, was well known as a patron of art and literature.[33] Some of the poets that he patronized were Thillaiyambur Chandrasekara Kavirayar, Mambala Kavirayar, Mahamahopadhyaya Raju Sastrigal, and Vidwan Thyagaraya Chettiar.[34] Ponnuswami Thevar employed a scholar to read out verses to him and discuss them.[35] He provided the funds for many of Arumuga Navalar's editions, especially those of *Thirukkural Parimelalagarurai*, *Thirukkovaiyarurai*, *Sethu Puranam*, and *Tharukka Sangiragam.*[36] The publication of Chandrasekara Kaviraja Pandithar's pioneering anthology of occasional verses (*thanippadal*) by various Tamil poets, *Thanicheyyut Chintamani* (which incidentally, contains a number of verses in praise of traditional patrons), was also sponsored by Ponnuswami Thevar.[37]

Ponnuswami Thevar's good work was continued by his son Pandithurai Thevar (1867–1911), the zamindar of Palavanatham.

[31] U.V. Swaminatha Iyer, *Ninaivu Manjari* (A Bouquet of Reminiscences), vol. 1 (1940, rpnt. Chennai: U.V. Swaminatha Iyer Library, 1991), pp. 42–5.

[32] C.W. Damodaram Pillai, *Kalithogai* (Chennai: Author, 1887), Preface.

[33] See M. Raghavaiyangar, *Sentamil Valartha Thevargal* (The Thevars who Patronized Tamil; Tiruchi: T.G. Gopaul Pillai, 1951), for a biography of Ponnuswami Thevar and his son Pandithurai Thevar.

[34] Ibid., pp. 39–42.

[35] Ibid., p. 30.

[36] Ibid., p. 47. Also see T. Kailasam Pillai, *Arumuga Navalar Charithiram* (A Biography of Arumuga Navalar; 1916, rpnt. Chidambaram: Sri Arumuga Navalar Saivaprakasa Vidyasalai Arakkattalai, 1985), p. 16.

[37] Raghavaiyangar, *Sentamil Valartha Thevargal*, p. 76.

Among his court poets were Narayana Iyengar, Ettayapuram Veeraswamy Iyengar, and Mu.Ra. Kandasamy Kavirayar.[38] He contributed Rs 500 towards Swaminatha Iyer's edition of the Sangam classic *Purananuru*,[39] and sponsored his edition of the ancient Buddhist epic *Manimekalai*.[40] Pandithurai Thevar also sponsored numerous other works, such as Ramasami Pillai's edition of *Thevaram: Thalamurai*, Sivagnana Munivar's collected works, Sabapathy Navalar's *Sivasamavatha Maruppu*, the works of Sunnagam Kumaraswamy Pulavar of Jaffna, and, shortly before his death, the monumental encyclopaedia of Tamil literature compiled by A. Singaravelu Mudaliar, *Abidhana Chintamani*.[41] Pandithurai Thevar's crowning achievement was the founding of the Madurai Tamil Sangam in 1901, which went a long way towards materially encouraging Tamil works.

Some of the other zamindars who provided patronage to literary production in the second half of the nineteenth century were Hirudalaya Marudappa Thevar of Uttrumalai zamin, who is best remembered for having supported Annamalai Reddiar, composer of the erotic-religious poems in praise of Murugan, the *kavadi chindu*;[42] and Ramalinga Thevar, the zamindar of Siruvayal who patronized U.V. Swaminatha Iyer's edition of *Purananuru*.[43] Namakkal

[38] Ibid., pp. 39–40.

[39] *Purananuru* (Chennai: Author, 1894), Preface. Also see his autobiography, *En Charithiram* (My Story; 1950, rpnt. Chennai: U.V. Swaminatha Iyer Library, 1990), pp. 740–2 (originally serialized in *Ananda Vikatan* between 1940 and 1942).

[40] *Manimekalai* (Chennai: Author, 1898), title page.

[41] Raghavaiyangar, *Sentamil Valartha Thevargal*, p. 80; A. Singaravelu Mudaliar, *Abidhana Chintamani* (1910, facsimile rpnt. New Delhi: Asian Educational Services, 1982), Preface.

[42] *Uttrumalai Thanippadal Thirattu*, n.d. See Aranga Srinivasan, *Kavadi Chindum Kavignan Varalarum* (Kavadi Chindu and the Life of the Poet; Chennai: Sekar Pathippagam, 1984), for a biography of Annamalai Reddiar. Annamalai Reddiar, with just 24 *kavadi chindus*, achieved literary immortality—the poems are still on the lips of devotees, musicians, and connoisseurs alike. For a detailed account of the royal treatment extended to Tamil scholars at the Uttrumalai zamin, see Swaminatha Iyer, *En Charithiram*, ch. 113.

[43] *Purananuru* (Chennai: Author, 1894), Preface.

Ramalingam Pillai, the poet, mentions that the zamindar of Namakkal, Duraiswamy Reddiar, was a Tamil enthusiast who contributed little sums to poets who sought his help.[44] The zamindar of Chokkampatti, and Pethachi Chettiar, zamindar of Andipatti, were also known as patrons of literature. The place of Ettayapuram zamin in the life of Subramania Bharati is discussed in the next chapter. Ettayapuram had a printing press of its own which was employed to publish works patronized by the zamin. This included the monumental four-volume musical treatise in Telugu, *Sangita Sampradaya Pradarsini* (1904) by Subbarama Dikshitar.

Religious mutts or monasteries, especially of the Saivite fold, were also in the forefront of patronage to Tamil scholars. Established in the late seventeenth and early eighteenth centuries, these mutts were 'organized around the concept of a teaching tradition related to a famous teacher who first enunciated the philosophical–religious system of the order.'[45] The mutts were well endowed, and controlled many subordinate mutts and temples. In the late nineteenth century the Thiruvavaduthurai Mutt alone owned over 30,000 acres of prime irrigated land, apart from being in charge of thousands of acres of temple land. They derived enormous economic and religious power from these holdings, though their power was beginning to be undermined by colonial rule. Such mutts had a long tradition of providing education and sponsoring literary production, and they housed dozens of *thambirans* or ascetics and novices.[46] This tradition continued

[44] Namakkal Ramalingam Pillai, *En Kathai* (My Story; 1944, rpnt. Chennai: Palaniappa Bros, 1977), p. 135.

[45] Geoffrey A. Oddie, *Hindu and Christian in South East India* (London: Curzon Press, 1991), p. 98. See esp. ch. 5, 'The Character, Role and Significance of non-Brahman Saivite Maths in Tanjore District'. Also see Ooran Adigal, *Saiva Adheenangal* (Saiva Mutts; Vadalur: Samarasa Sanmarga Araichi Nilayam, 2009).

[46] For a history of the Thiruvavaduthurai Mutt, see *Arasavanathu Aranilayam* (The Righteous Institution in the Peepul Grove; Thiruvavaduthurai: Thiruvavaduthurai Adheenam, 1962). For the Dharumapuram Mutt, see *Tamil Valarkkum Dharumapuram* (Dharumapuram that Fosters Tamil; Dharumapuram: Dharumapuram Adheenam, 1981).

through the second half of the nineteenth century. The historian of nineteenth-century Tamil literature, Mylai Seeni. Venkatasamy, lists the monasteries of Thiruvavaduthurai, Dharumapuram, Thiruppanandal, Kanchi Gnanaprakasar, Madurai Thirugnanasambandar, Kumbakonam, Chidambaram, Thiruvannamalai, Thuraiyur, and Myilam as patrons of literature during this period.[47]

Like Meenakshisundaram Pillai, Arumuga Navalar (1823–1879), the great Saiva revivalist from Jaffna, who almost single-handedly transformed Saiva religion in Sri Lanka and had an enormous influence in the Tamil country as well, was provided patronage by the Thiruvavaduthurai Mutt. In fact, his title Navalar, or 'the skilled orator'—the title by which he is known—was conferred by the mutt,[48] which also sponsored Navalar's editions of *Ilakkana Kothu* and *Tholkappiya Suthira Viruthi*.[49]

U.V. Swaminatha Iyer was only a vidwan at the Thiruvavaduthurai Mutt before he was coaxed by Thyagaraya Chettiar to join the Kumbakonam Government College in 1880.[50] His every publication had the blessings, if not the financial assistance, of the Thiruvavaduthurai Mutt.[51] In fact his first work was published by the Adheenam. His 1892 edition of the classic Tamil epic *Chilappadhikaram* was financed by, among others, the pontiffs of the Thiruvavaduthurai, Thiruvannamalai, and Thiruppanandal mutts.[52] Similarly, C.W. Damodaram Pillai, Swaminatha Iyer's senior contemporary and pioneering editor of long forgotten Tamil classics, was provided patronage by the Thiruvavaduthurai Mutt. The mutt provided Rs 100 for each of his publications, apart from paying for copies purchased.[53] Damodaram Pillai's estimate of the importance of mutt patronage is evident from the fact that, in his periodization of Tamil

[47] *Pathonbatham Noottrandil Tamil Ilakkiyam*, p. 66.
[48] Kailasam Pillai, *Arumuga Navalar Charithiram*, p. 82.
[49] Ibid.
[50] Swaminatha Iyer, *En Charithiram*, pp. 478–84.
[51] Ibid., pp. 450–1.
[52] *Chilappadhikaram* (Chennai: Author, 1892), Preface.
[53] C.W. Damodaram Pillai (ed.), *Ilakkana Vilakkam* (A Treatise on Grammar; Chennai: Author, 1889), Preface. For his biography, see T.A. Rajarathinam

literary history, he categorized his own times the Adheena Kalam (The Age of Mutts).[54]

The third category of traditional patrons comprised landlords and caste leaders, who, as administrators of local temples, sponsored the composition of thala puranams and other forms of minor literature about their locality, thereby deriving much authority and legitimacy in their domain. As we saw earlier, Meenakshisundaram Pillai composed scores of such works and lived off the patronage they provided.

All these traditional patrons were remnants of the feudal upper classes of pre-colonial times. Zamindars, native princes, monasteries, and landlords controlled large tracts of land, and thrived by expropriating the surplus. These social classes, especially the zamindars and monasteries, had begun losing ground in the late nineteenth century, and by the first decades of the twentieth century were being displaced by a new class of wealthy peasants who had reaped rich harvests from the expansion of commercial crops.[55] The monasteries, too, had begun losing absolute control over their lands, and, perhaps as a consequence, were involved in protracted litigation. Moral degeneration seems to have set in, and, as a result, their religious authority had waned. Intrigues were rife within mutts; the poisoning of a particularly long-lived pontiff by the *chinna pattam* (his heir apparent) was not uncommon—it became a recurrent theme of fiction and films in the early part of the twentieth century. (As a result mutts took to employing an *undukatti*, a food-taster, to check on food served to the pontiff!) By the late nineteenth century these social classes could not provide sustenance to cultural production. The decline of traditional patronage becomes apparent from the rise of a new form of financing

---

Pillai, *Ci. Vai. Damodaram Pillai Avargal Charithiram* (A Biography of C.W. Damodaram Pillai; Chennai: Author, 1934).

[54] *Veeracholiyam* (Chennai: Author, 1881), Preface.

[55] C.J. Baker, 'Tamilnad Estates in the Twentieth Century', *The Indian Economic and Social History Review*, 13 (1), January–March 1976. Also see his *An Indian Rural Economy: The Tamilnad Countryside, 1880–1955* (Delhi: Oxford University Press, 1984), pp. 461–3.

publications: a system of subscriptions. This was largely sustained by a new social class made up of professionals and overseas bankers spawned by colonialism.

### Changing Forms of Patronage: The Subscription System

By the last decades of the nineteenth century there were visible signs of the dwindling of traditional forms of patronage. Literary producers were, naturally, adversely affected. Meenakshisundaram Pillai, who functioned in the heyday of traditional patronage, when asked by his leading pupil Thyagaraya Chettiar why his later works, such as *Ambar Puranam*, did not match the high quality of his earlier *Uraiyur Puranam*, attributed the richness of the latter to the ample patronage of earlier times. He added that if given similar patronage, he could write better still.[56]

During the 1880s and 1890s we find literary producers often complaining of a lukewarm response from traditional patrons. Somasundara Nayagar (1846–1901), a Saiva Siddhanta scholar and stormy petrel active in the hair-splitting theological debates of his time, complained in a series of letters to U.V. Swaminatha Iyer about the inadequate response of the Thiruppanandal Mutt to his appeals for patronage: 'What can I do if the Thiruppanandal Swamigal chooses to be so reluctant in my case! There are no limits to my commitments. The promises I made to the pressmen in anticipation of receiving money from the Swamigal have all been broken.'[57] A couple of weeks later Somasundara Nayagar wrote to Swaminatha Iyer, urging him to intervene on his behalf: 'I find it delicate to remind persons of such high standing. But my commitments are so pressing that I cannot keep quiet. That *Acharya Prabhavam* has been held up for the last two months will go to show my uncomfortable situation. Another part of *Kuresavijayabangam* needs to be printed. I had nurtured the

[56] *SMPC*, vol. 1, p. 122.

[57] Somasundara Nayagar to Swaminatha Iyer, 5 September 1884. U.V. Swaminatha Iyer Papers (hereafter U.V.S. Papers), U.V. Swaminatha Iyer Library, Chennai.

fond hope that with the help of [the Thiruvavaduthurai] Swamigal I could complete the printing of all pending books.'[58]

In this context of dwindling support from traditional patrons, writers and poets were forced to look elsewhere for sustenance and their attention turned to the new affluent classes spawned by colonialism. C.W. Damodaram Pillai, who had long sung praises of the mutts and their patronage, had by the mid-1880s lost about Rs 3,500.[59] Consequently he was forced now to sing a different tune: 'My efforts are not geared towards pecuniary gain. I will be content if I can avoid losses. The sums I have lost thus far by publishing books are far from mean. In order that people who involve themselves in such projects not lose money, all those who have passed university examinations and are well placed in high jobs ought to buy a copy each of all the classics published in their mother tongue.'[60] He made similar appeals on other occasions too.[61] The *Swadesamitran* of 8 November 1898, reviewing U.V. Swaminatha Iyer's edition of *Manimekalai*, also called upon English-educated people to subscribe to the cause of Tamil books, especially the classics.[62]

To tap the resources of this class, the system of financing publishing via subscriptions was hit upon. In response to C.W. Damodaram Pillai's appeal in the *Hindu*, a substantial number of subscribers came forward to fund his publication of the classic *Kalithogai*. Apart from residual traditional patrons like the zamindars of Perur and Uttrumalai, and the pontiffs of Thiruvavaduthurai and Thiruppanandal, many of the subscribers were English-educated professionals. They included Poondi Aranganatha Mudaliar, Professor of Mathematics at the Presidency College, Madras; A. Ramachandra Iyer, Judge of the Mysore Chief Court; T. Ganapathy Iyer, Judge of the Kumbakonam Sub-court; Sir Raghavaiyangar, an advocate at Kumbakonam; and S. Seshaiyar, Professor at the Kumbakonam Government College.

[58] Somasundara Nayagar to Swaminatha Iyer, 17 September 1884, U.V.S. Papers. Also see his letter dated 25 October 1899.

[59] *Kalithogai* (Chennai: Author, 1887), Preface.

[60] *Tholkappiyam: Porulathikaram* (Chennai: Author, 1885), Preface.

[61] See, for instance, his preface to *Kalithogai* (Chennai: Author, 1887).

[62] Reprinted in *Kumari Malar*, August 1976.

Many others were magistrates, lawyers, and teachers. G. Subramania Iyer and M. Veeraraghavachari, founders of the *Hindu* and rising stars of the new profession of journalism, also offered to print free of cost any classic not exceeding 30–31 formes that Damodaram Pillai chose to publish.[63]

Similarly, U.V. Swaminatha Iyer's first major publication, the Jain epic *Seevaka Chintamani* (1887), was largely financed by subscriptions. Swaminatha Iyer first released a prospectus calling for subscriptions. The first subscription was taken by the Thiruvavaduthurai Mutt, this initiative being followed by a number of subscribers from the new social classes. As many as 70 subscriptions were collected in Kumbakonam alone, where Swaminatha Iyer taught Tamil in the Government College. Another 20 to 25 subscriptions came in through the efforts of Thyagaraya Chettiar.[64] Poondi Aranganatha Mudaliar, apart from signing up himself, canvassed subscriptions from Pammal Vijayaranga Mudaliar, Savalai Ramasamy Mudaliar, and others who held high positions in the colonial administrative machinery.[65] Salem Ramaswamy Mudaliar, the man who had provoked Swaminatha Iyer into taking up the task of editing ancient manuscripts, was a judge: he too canvassed subscriptions.[66] Sir Ponnambalam Ramanathan and his brother, both highly placed potentates in the government at Colombo, also contributed regularly to Swaminatha Iyer's publishing ventures.[67]

Frequently, subscribers to one publishing venture offered a subscription to subsequent projects as well,[68] indicating the enthusiasm of a new class keen on acquiring further social respectability. In the copious autobiographical writings of U.V. Swaminatha Iyer, we find,

[63] *Kalithogai*, Preface.

[64] Swaminatha Iyer, *En Charithiram*, p. 576.

[65] Ibid., p. 589.

[66] Salem Ramaswamy Mudaliar to U.V. Swaminatha Iyer, 22 October 1887, U.V.S. Papers.

[67] Swaminatha Iyer, *Ninaivu Manjari*, vol. 2 (1942 rpnt. Chennai: U.V. Swaminatha Iyer Library, 1991), p. 110.

[68] See, for instance, the letter of one Arangasami Mudaliar, Cuddalore, to Swaminatha Iyer, 2 August 1892, U.V.S. Papers.

when we reach the last decades of the nineteenth century, references to traditional patrons growing infrequent. Not only his operations, but also his scouting for patronage, now shifts to the city of Madras, the seedbed of the new affluence. He frequently refers to persons like Justice (Sir S. Subramania) Mani Iyer, the advocate V. Krishnaswamy Iyer, and Poondi Aranganatha Mudaliar, all eminent professionals of their times, as his benefactors.

Apart from first-generation English-educated professionals, a new prosperous community which financed publishing with subscriptions was the Nattukkottai Chettiars. By the 1880s, having gained windfall profits by entering the financial markets of South East Asia (which was being opened up for colonial exploitation), the Chettiars took to philanthropy to acquire social prestige commensurate with their affluence.[69] Over a 100 of the 180 or so subscribers to *Sodasa Prabandam* were Chettiars.[70] Scores of subscribers to Dandapani Swamigal's publications were Chettiars too, especially from Colombo.[71] Similarly, Damodaram Pillai received substantial funds from Chettiars in Burma.[72] Upon getting money from one such—a Nattukkottai Chettiar banker of Rangoon—he made bold to state: 'I pray [. . .] that following this example, other Nattukkottai Chettiars too, who have gained renown from their philanthropic activities these days, should assist similar undertakings.'[73] U.V. Swaminatha Iyer too wrote at length on the generosity of the Chettiars.[74]

Thus, by the last two decades of the nineteenth century Tamil book publishing was largely sustained by subscriptions. The Registrar

[69] See Raman Mahadevan, 'Entrepreneurship and Business Communities in Colonial Madras, 1900–1929: Some Preliminary Observations', in Dwijendra Tripathi (ed.), *Business Communities in India: A Historical Perspective* (Delhi: Manohar, 1984).

[70] P. Arumugam Pillai, *Sodasa Prabandam* (Chennai: n.p., 1899), Appendix.

[71] See, for instance, Dandapani Swamigal, *Nangunool Arulatchi* (Chennai: n.p., 1877), List of Subscribers.

[72] See *Kalithogai* (1887); *Choolamani* (1889); *Tholkappiyam –Chollathikaram* (1892).

[73] Ibid., Preface.

[74] *Nallurai Kovai*, vol. 1 (Edifying Essays; 1937, rpnt. Chennai: U.V. Swaminatha Iyer Library, 1991), pp. 16–17.

of Books noted a burgeoning volume of publications and commented in 1893 on 'new editions, with commentaries, of standard Indian epics and legends which, as serial publications, are appearing in parts with the aid of subscriptions.'[75]

The earlier traditional forms of patronage and the new system of subscriptions were not exclusive; the overlap was in fact considerable. Damodaram Pillai's *Kalithogai* was subscribed to by the zamindars of Perur and Uttrumalai and the pontiffs of Thiruvavaduthurai and Thiruppanandal mutts, as well as by the nouveau riche. Likewise, Swaminatha Iyer's *Seevaka Chintamani* subscription list was opened by none other than the pontiff of Thiruvavaduthurai Mutt. Essentially, the problem was that the new class of professionals was small in number. It had jumped into the fray to fill the void created by the demise of traditional patrons. Consequently, the age of traditional patronage was on its way out and the contribution of the new professional class lay in making the breakthrough for the middle classes to take over publishing.

## The Decline of Patronage

The decline and fall of this period can be traced by looking at three characteristic aspects of patronage-publishing: the arangettram, the sirappu payiram, and the title page.

The arangettram (premiere; literally, 'climbing the podium') was a highly ritualized cultural event which was carried over from the pre-print era to the latter half of the nineteenth century. It corresponded to the debut performance of a musician or dancer, being the occasion on which a literary text was premiered and made available for 'public' consumption. The event was usually fixed for an auspicious day, the news of it being passed on to the local people and potentates in neighbouring localities. Organized by the patron of the work, the premiere was the occasion when he derived social prestige and cultural

[75] Review and Analysis of Books (1892), G.O. nos 184–5, Edl, 10 March 1893. (All G.O. references pertain to the Government Orders of the Government of Madras, housed in the Tamilnadu Archives, Chennai.) Also see the Review and Analysis for 1897, G.O. nos 182–3, Edl, 18 March 1898.

authority by publicizing his patronage. Consequently, it was often a very pompous affair. In the pre-modern period such premieres were held in royal courts. But in the mid-nineteenth century the premiere of the literary text was usually held in a public place, often the local temple, thereby giving religious sanction and authority to the event and the text. Meenakshisundaram Pillai's *Uraiyur Puranam* (1860) was premiered in the Uraiyur temple,[76] his *Seekali Kovai* (1861) at the Valampuri Mantapam in the southern *piragaram* (corridor) of the Brahmapureeswarar temple,[77] and his *Mannippadikkarai Puranam* (1864) in the *sannidhi* (sanctorum) of the concerned temple.[78] Dandapani Swamigal's *Thillai Ithalagalandadi* was premiered in the thousand-pillared *mantapam* of the Chidambaram temple.[79]

The mantapam (the hall) would be festooned in the traditional manner with bunches of mango shoots and split coconut leaves and the premiere would begin at an appropriate *muhurtam* (auspicious time). The palm-leaf manuscript would then be placed before the presiding deity of the temple and worship offered. The text would then be placed in the hands of the author, who, after accepting the *prasadam* (usually, sacred ash and flower garlands) would proceed with the premiere. Often the text would be read out by a *kattrucholli*—a novice being trained by the author in the craft of verse-making.[80] This act of reading was called *kaiyedu padithal* or *kaiyedu vasithal*. It was a practice common in religious discourses, where the task of the novice was not only to read from the manuscript but also when required to act as a prompt, provide cues, and fill the silence when the speaker was out of breath.[81] During the reading the author would

[76] *SMPC*, vol. 1, pp. 131–2.

[77] Ibid., pp. 172—3.

[78] Ibid., p. 236.

[79] Dandapani Swamigal, *Guruparathathuva Nool* (Siravanapuram: Gaumara Madalayam, 1966), p. 268.

[80] The meaning of *kattrucholli* later shifted from an understudy to a person who parroted things mindlessly.

[81] Vallalar Ramalinga Adigal, the precursor of modern Tamil poetry, made his first public appearance at the age of 9 as one performing the task of *kaiyedu padithal* for his elder brother.

elaborate on the meaning of his verses and explain the literary and mythological allusions to the devout audience. These sessions, scheduled usually for late afternoons, could continue for a number of days, depending on the length of the composition, its terseness, and the ability and inclination of the author, the intensity of the inclination being often in proportion to the value of the patronage.[82]

Fig. 2: Representation of an *arangettram*. The ritual premiere of Kachiyappa Swamigal's *Vinayaka Puranam* at the Prasanna Vinayakar temple, Chennai (from *Vinayaka-manmiya-saram*, 1877).

[82] The description of the arangettram is largely based on the premiere of *Thirupperunthurai Puranam* in *SMPC*, vol. 2, pp. 175–6.

During the course of the premiere the audience could raise questions and seek clarifications. For instance, Kanchipuram Sabapathy Mudaliar raised a bona fide question regarding the use of a dialect word when Dandapani Swamigal premiered *Guhan Pillaitamil* in Madras. Dandapani Swamigal observes in his verse autobiography that he had never in his life encountered such a learned or intimidating audience.[83]

Not infrequently, the premiere turned into an occasion for the venting of jealousies, the showing off of scholarship, and the raising of sectarian disputes. Instances of such confusion created during premieres are recorded by U.V. Swaminatha Iyer in his biography of Meenakshisundaram Pillai. Various people jealous of his high standing tried to cause a commotion during the premiere of *Uraiyur Kanthimathi Pillaitamil*,[84] while a Vaishnavite scholar raised sectarian questions during the premiere of *Kudandai Puranam* (1865).[85] Since the premiere was an occasion for the accrual of social prestige to the patron who had commissioned the composition, the patron took great care to make such occasions a grand and unqualified success. Often he made arrangements to forestall unauthorized questions being asked by—in his view, undesirable—people out to spoil his show.[86] Depending on the wealth and predisposition of the patron, such a premiere could even continue, with short breaks for well up to a year: this happened with *Nagai Karona Puranam* (1869).[87]

As reciprocation for the receipt of patronage, the author would often refer flatteringly to the patron's largesse both in the text and in its exposition to the audience. Everyone seems to have been acutely aware of the prestige that the premiere conferred on the patron. Jealous rivals spreading rumours to scuttle premieres were common, as happened in the case of Sivagurunatha Pillai, the tahsildar of Kumbakonam, who commissioned *Kudandai Puranam*.[88] Given the cultural

[83] Dandapani Swamigal, *Guruparathathuva Nool*, pp. 232–7.
[84] *SMPC*, vol. 1, p. 137.
[85] Ibid., p. 274.
[86] See, for instance, ibid., p. 137.
[87] Ibid., p. 319.
[88] Ibid., p. 259.

importance of the event, patrons were also liable to take offence at the drop of a hat. For instance, during the course of the premiere of *Thirupperunthurai Puranam* Meenakshisundaram Pillai delayed the beginning of a particular day's discourse because he was waiting for a favourite student to turn up. Subramania Desigar, the sponsor of the puranam and administrator of the local temple, had already arrived and was offended by the delay, and so refused to preside over the premiere in the subsequent days.[89]

The valedictory day of the premiere was celebrated to match the festivity of the inauguration. It usually attracted huge crowds, even from neighbouring localities. The text could be taken in a procession on an elephant, as happened in the case of Meenakshisundaram Pillai's *Kudandai Puranam*,[90] and Karuthamuthu Pillai's *Thiruvidaimarudur Thalapuranam*;[91] or in a palanquin, as in the case of *Thirupperunthurai Puranam*.[92] It was on this occasion that the author received, apart from ritual and ceremonial gifts like silk towels, etc., remuneration both in cash and kind. Meenakshisundaram Pillai got Rs 2,000 for *Thirupperunthurai Puranam*,[93] and a similar sum for *Kudandai Puranam* collected by the patrons at Kumbakonam, apart from an exquisitely designed palanquin.[94] For *Seekali Kovai* he received purses ranging from Rs 50 to Rs 300 from a number of patrons.[95]

In the heyday of patronage, the idea of publishing the manuscript was mooted only at the end of the premiere. After Meenakshisundaram Pillai had premiered *Mayura Puranam* (1868), many emphasized the need to print it. It seems almost part of the ritual for the authority of the composition to be seen to have derived from the successful conclusion of its premiere, the printing being more or less an

[89] Ibid., vol. 2, pp. 176–7.

[90] Ibid., vol. 1, pp. 274–5.

[91] Ka. Andiyappa Pillai, *A. Karuthamuthu Pillai-avarkal Charithiram* (A Biography of Karuthamuthu Pillai; Tirunelveli: Aryaprakasini Press, 1897), pp. 4–5.

[92] *SMPC*, vol. 2, p. 192.

[93] Ibid.

[94] Ibid., vol. 1, pp. 274–5.

[95] Ibid., p. 177.

afterthought. Print was seen thereby as an effective way of multiplying an already sanctified text.

However, with the gradual advance of print culture and technology, and the erosion of patronage with all its cultural deadweight, the institution of the arangettram began to crumble. Even by 1869, when the premiere of Meenakshisundaram Pillai's *Nagai Karona Puranam*, with all its attendant paraphernalia, was still in progress, the manuscript was being printed in Madras under the supervision of his student T. Subbaraya Chettiar. By the time the palm-leaf manuscript was taken in ceremonial procession through the streets of Nagapattinam, the printed volumes were already available.[96] The arangettram was thus becoming something of a hollow crowning, a ritual emptied of its earlier cultural significance.

The premiere of Poondi Aranganatha Mudaliar's *Kachi Kalambagam* in 1889 further highlights the diminishing importance of the event, if not its hollowness, in the changed context. The function was held in the Thondai Mandala Thuluva Vellalar High School, Madras, and not in the precincts of a temple. The hall was filled by 'Tamil and English scholars, High Court judges and advocates and other gentlemen',[97] and not the crowd of earlier days. The text had already been printed and distributed to an audience which flipped through its pages as the premiere progressed. 'As the discourse progressed, everyone in the audience followed the verse on the printed page. At the end of a page, the entire audience would turn it over; though the paper was thin, the rustling of the paper could be heard, indicating the considerable size of the audience.'[98] This matter-of-fact description scarcely conceals the irony of the whole situation. This was a far cry from the days of Meenakshisundaram Pillai when the audience had no text at hand and no option but to listen.

[96] Ibid., p. 321.

[97] *Vallai Sanmugasundara Mudaliar Ninaivu Malar* (Commemorative Souvenir of Vallai Sanmugasundara Mudaliar; Chennai: n.p., 1943), p. 10. Also see Swaminatha Iyer, *Nallurai Kovai*, vol. 1, p. 103.

[98] Ibid., p. 104.

The sirappu payiram or *sattrukkavi*, a poem prefatory to the text, was usually composed by one of the author's teachers, colleagues, or students. Its function was to introduce the text and, by extension, confer authority upon it. In some ways it can be seen to have functioned like the 'exordium' of Latin rhetoric and the 'invocation' of Renaissance epic poems, both of which were prefatory devices to predispose an audience to regard the ensuing matter with the seriousness that was its due. In Tamilnadu this broadly analogous practice fell more closely within the domain of sanctification, with the vogue becoming evident in early medieval times as well as codified in *Nannool*, the twelfth-century grammatical text. The sirappu payiram, set in verse, usually elaborated in flattering terms on the standing, lineage, tutelage, and scholarly abilities of the author, as well as the importance of his text and subject matter. References to the patron who had commissioned the work were quite common. It was a highly conventional form which seems not infrequently to have been put in the hands of less-gifted practitioners, cliché ridden, fitting a template. In a traditional society where education and knowledge were the preserve of a restricted social stratum, authority naturally derived from the recommendations of those already in possession of the requisite qualifications.

Meenakshisundaram Pillai, as could be expected from his literary standing, was inundated with requests for prefatory poems. Even Arumuga Navalar had to seek such prefatory poems from Meenakshisundaram Pillai for *Thirukkovaiyarurai* and *Thirukkural Parimelalagarurai* in order to get Ponnuswamy Thevar's patronage.[99] During his long literary career Meenakshisundaram Pillai probably composed scores of such prefatory poems for a variety of poets and scholars. Acquiring a sirappu payiram was a matter of contacts and nearness to the culturally powerful. U.V. Swaminatha Iyer noted that anyone who managed to get a prefatory poem from the Tamil scholar Sabapathy Mudaliar also got one from Meenakshisundaram Pillai, using the former's good offices.[100] The fact that Meenakshisundaram Pillai wrote many sirappu payirams did not exempt his own works from the requirement that they adorn *all* worthy compositions. His

[99] *SMPC*, vol. 1, p. 227.
[100] Ibid., p. 69.

*Akilandanayaki Pillaitamil* includes fifteen poems composed by contemporary Tamil scholars, including by the widely respected Malavai Mahalingaiyar and Uraiyur Muthuveera Upathiyayar.[101]

Similarly, U.V. Swaminatha Iyer had to respond to frequent requests for sirappu payirams. On one occasion Ambalavana Desigar, the pontiff of the Thiruvavaduthurai Mutt, virtually ordered him to write for Sabapathy Navalar's *Dravida Pirakasikai* (1899).[102] Likewise one Sabapathy Pillai of Coimbatore requested him to contribute a preface to *Avinasi Karunambikai Satakam.*[103] C.W. Damodaram Pillai also acquired and published prefatory poems for his editions of the Sangam classics and other texts.[104] *Suta Samhitai,* which appeared under Valloor Devarasa Mudaliar's name, had prefatory poems by 28 scholars; Vedanayakam Pillai's *Nidinool* had no less than 60![105] Dandapani Swamigal's *Thillai Thiruvayiram* had a more modest 11.[106] In fact, rarely did a printed book of the nineteenth century lack a sirappu payiram.[107]

Often, the prefatory poems were written even without the main text having been read by the poet, with the author indicating the lines on which he wanted the sirappu payiram to be written.[108] Swaminatha Iyer claims that in this matter Meenakshisundaram Pillai was more discerning:

> The sirappu payirams of Meenakshisundaram Pillai were in keeping with the standing of the authors for whom they were composed. A consequence of his prefatory poems was that the authors gained much prestige. Therefore, many tried in myriad ways to get him to write them

[101] Ibid., p. 67.

[102] Ambalavana Desigar to Swaminatha Iyer, Kadaga Ravi 21, Vigari (Tamil Calendar, 1899), U.V.S. Papers.

[103] Sabapathy Pillai to Swaminatha Iyer, 3 May 1891, U.V.S. Papers. Also see the letter by Mu.Ra. Arunachala Kavirayar, 9 November 1906, asking for a *payiram* to Palvanna Mudaliar's *Siddhanta Ratnavali.*

[104] See, for instance, *Veeracholiyam* (Chennai: Author, 1881).

[105] (Chennai: n.p., 1860, 2nd edn).

[106] (Chennai: n.p., Sarvathari [Tamil calendar, 1888]).

[107] Venkatasamy, *Pathonbatham Noottrandil Tamil Ilakkiyam*, p. 351.

[108] See Pinnathoor Narayanasamy Iyer to Swaminatha Iyer, 13 March 1907, U.V.S. Papers.

> prefatory poems. He would write these in [the verse forms of] *agaval*, *viruthham*, and *tharavu kochagam*. If the work was a very good one he would write an *agaval* [a lengthy verse form] or many *viruthams*. Or else he would write a short verse or two indicating in plain terms that such and such a book was written by such and such a person. It was in his time that sirappu payirams were much in vogue.[109]

This is a succinct view of the importance and authority attached to the sirappu payiram.

If the experience of Gopalakrishna Bharati is any indication, the sirappu payiram could not be taken for granted. Gopalakrishna Bharati had to move heaven and earth to get Meenakshisundaram Pillai to write one for his *Nandanar Charithira Kirtanai*, a composition on Nandanar, the low-caste devotee of Siva. The great man had initially refused the request on the grounds that the poems in Gopalakrishna Bharati's work were written in a demotic which included popular metres and colloquial words. Ironically, it is *Nandan Charithira Kirtanai* which continues not only to be read but also sung at musical concerts, whereas scores of other works to which Meenakshisundaram Pillai gave his stamp of approval have fallen into oblivion.[110]

As this context of limited circulation and literary privilege dwindled, and Tamil publishing sought to enter a wider social sphere peopled by the emerging middle classes, sirappu payirams became redundant and anachronistic. As a historian of nineteenth-century Tamil literature puts it, 'The practice of printing *sattrukkavis* was in vogue until the beginning of the twentieth century. Later, it disappeared completely.'[111] Subramania Bharati, the first modern Tamil poet, whose entry into the world of letters coincides with the end of the age of patronage, provides an illustration of this cultural fact. Bharati never sought a sirappu payiram for any of his books and himself wrote but two *payirams*, both in the early part of his career.[112] And his protégé

[109] *SMPC*, vol. 2, pp. 282–3.

[110] Ibid., vol. 1, pp. 193–5. Subramania Bharati was heavily influenced by *Nandan Charithira Kirtanai*.

[111] Venkatasamy, *Pathonbatham Noottrandil Tamil Ilakkiyam*, p. 351.

[112] *Bharati Padalgal: Aaivu Pathippu* (Poems of Bharati: A Critical Edition; Thanjavur: Tamil University, 1989), pp. 10–11, 108–9.

Bharatidasan ridiculed the poets of the pre-Bharati era for their supplicatory chase of prefatory poems.[113]

By the last decades of the nineteenth century, the practice of writing 'modern' prefaces in prose had begun to emerge, ousting the era of payirams. C.W. Damodaram Pillai and U.V. Swaminatha Iyer were among the first to espouse the new practice.[114] In his autobiography Swaminatha Iyer says of his *Seevaka Chintamani* (1887): 'In those days, most printed Tamil books had no preface. Because I felt it would be of use to readers, I planned to write a preface which could form part of the book. Then I thought out the various things that needed to be said in the preface.'[115]

Compared to the arangettram and the sirappu payiram, the title page was a later phenomenon, a product of the technology of print. The title pages of nineteenth-century Tamil imprints were crammed with a range of information on the text, the author, the patron, the printer, etc., which could baffle modern readers.[116] U.V. Swaminatha Iyer's *Seevaka Chintamani* is a good example.

**The text of Seevaka Chintamani**
**by Thirutthakka Thevar**
**with the commentary of**
**Maduraiaciriyar Bharatvasi Nacchinarkkiniyar**

**These**
**as per the wishes of**
**M.R.Ry. Salem Ramaswamy Mudaliar avargal**
**were examined by**

113 *Kuyil*, December 1946.

114 The brilliant editorial prefaces of C.W. Damodaram Pillai have been compiled and brought out as a handy volume. See *Damodaram* (Jaffna: Jaffna Cooperative Tamil Books, 1971).

115 Swaminatha Iyer, *En Charithiram*, p. 608.

116 As the Librarian in Charge of the Maraimalai Adigal Library, Chennai, during 1987–90, I often found even postgraduate Tamil students fumble with nineteenth-century title pages, unable to write proper bibliographic entries.

**Ve. Swaminathaiyer**
**of**
**Uthamathanapuram**

**the student of**
**Subramaniya Desiga Murthigal**
**of Thiruvavaduthurai Atheenam of the**
**Thirukkailaya tradition**
**and**
**Meenakshisundaram Pillai**
**the Mahavidwan of the above adheenam**
**and**
**Tamil teacher at the Kumbakonam**
**Government College**

**Printed at Madras**
**at the Dravidarathnakara Achukkudam**
**of T. Govinda Acharya**
**Price Rs. 8**
**1887**
**Copyright Registered**

While the prominence given to the printer's name could be explained in terms of colonial administrative stipulations—a most stringent surveillance had been imposed on all purveyors of printing technology—the other copious details indicate what mattered in the age of patronage: the title had to be elaborate and self-explanatory; the name of the patron had to be given precedence; and the authority of the author derived less from his position in a government college than from his having been the pupil of traditional scholars.

With changes in the material basis of literary production, the title page too changed; many of the earlier details began to be omitted. As patrons ceased to exist, and the authority of the author derived no more from his tutelage under traditional scholars, the title page drew a blank on these counts. With the elevation in stature of the author as a distinct professional and intellectual, his was the only name that mattered and so it acquired a new prominence on the title page. Parallel

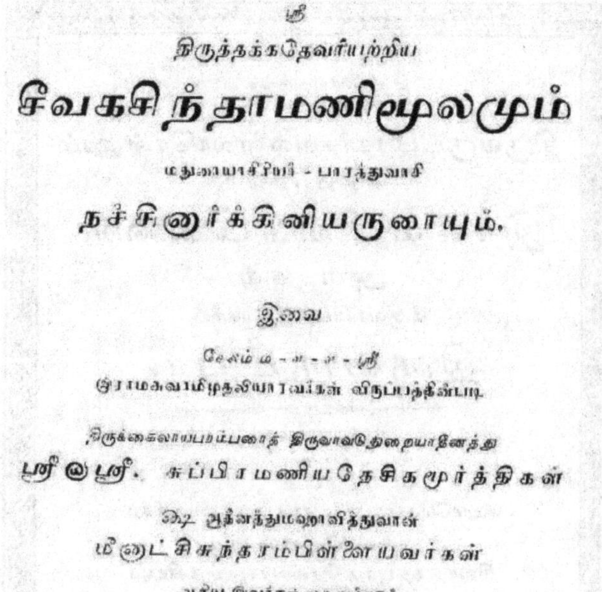
ஸ்ரீ
திருத்தக்கதேவரியற்றிய
சீவகசிந்தாமணிமூலமும்
மதுரையாசிரியர் - பாரத்துவாசி
நச்சினார்க்கினியருரையும்.

இவை
சேலம் ம - ள - ள - ஸ்ரீ
இராமசுவாமிமுதலியாரவர்கள் விருப்பத்தின்படி

திருக்கைலாயபரம்பரைத் திருவாவடுதுறையாதீனத்து
ஸ்ரீ-ல-ஸ்ரீ. சுப்பிரமணியதேசிகமூர்த்திகள்
ஷை ஆதீனத்துமஹாவித்துவான்
மீனாட்சிசுந்தரம்பிள்ளையவர்கள்
ஆகிய இவர்கள் மாணாக்கரும்
கும்பகோணம் கவர்ன்மெண்டு காலேஜ் தமிழ்ப்பண்டிதருமாகிய
உத்தமதானபுரம்
வே. சாமிநாதையரால்
பரிசோதித்து

சென்னை:
த. கோவிந்த ஆசாரியரது
ஜீவரத்நாகர அச்சுக்கூடத்திற் பதிப்பிக்கப்பட்டன.
விலை - ரூபா ௮.
1887.
[Copyright Registered.]

Fig. 3: Title page of U.V. Swaminatha Iyer's pathbreaking edition of *Seevaka Chintamani* (1887). Note the copious information on the title page.

to the author's rise was the emergence of the institution of the publisher/publishing house, coinciding with the diminishing importance of the printer (see Chapter 4). These changes in the organization of

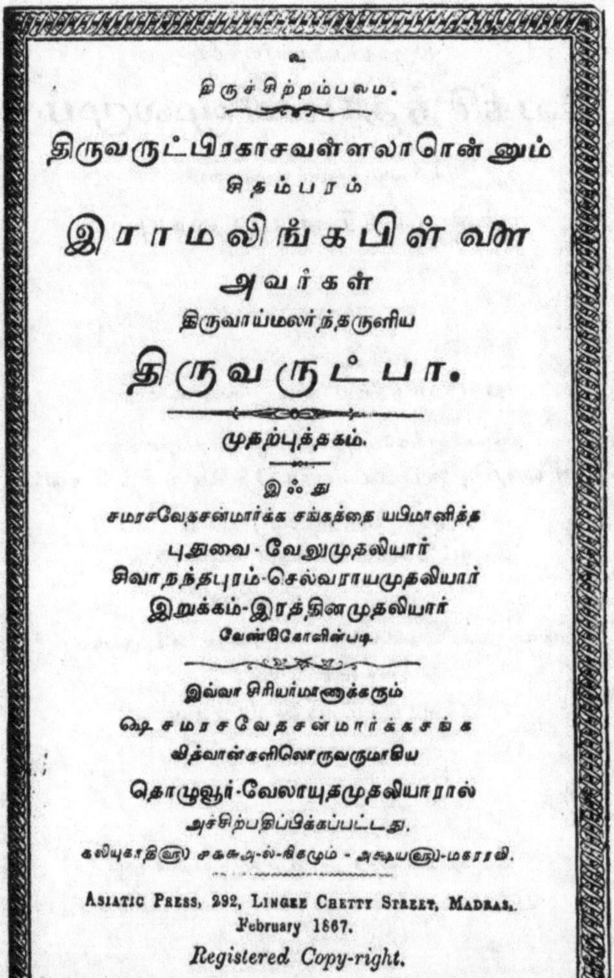

உ

திருச்சிற்றம்பலம.

திருவருட்பிரகாசவள்ளலாரென்னும்

சிதம்பரம்

இராமலிங்கபிள்ளை

அவர்கள்

திருவாய்மலர்ந்தருளிய

திருவருட்பா.

முதற்புத்தகம்.

இஃது

சமரசவேதசன்மார்க்க சங்கத்தை யபிமானித்த

புதுவை - வேலுமுதலியார்

சிவாநந்தபுரம்-செல்வராயமுதலியார்

இறுக்கம்-இரத்தினமுதலியார்

வேண்டுகோளின்படி

இவ்வாசிரியர்மாணாக்கரும்

ஷை சமரசவேதசன்மார்க்கசங்க

வித்வான்களிலொருவருமாகிய

தொழுவூர்-வேலாயுதமுதலியாரால்

அச்சிற்பதிப்பிக்கப்பட்டது.

கலியுகாதி௪௯௬௮ சகசு௭௱௮௯-ல்-நிகழும் - அக்ஷய௵-மகரரவி.

ASIATIC PRESS, 292, LINGEE CHETTY STREET, MADRAS.

February 1867.

*Registered Copy-right.*

Fig. 4: Title page of Ramalinga Adigal's *Thiruvarutpa* (1867). The publication of this book triggered a tract war that raged for decades in Tamilnadu and Sri Lanka.

the book-publishing trade are reflected in the title page of twentieth-century Tamil books. The publisher's name finds a place here, whereas the printer is relegated to the imprint (or copyright) page, in line with statutory requirement. The major historian of printing and publishing in India, B.S. Kesavan, misses the point on title pages because he overlooks the changing material basis of literary production which these nineteenth-century title pages manifest:

> [The title page] used to be crowded with information and hardly could we isolate the author's name at a glance. A change is now noticeable and simple title pages are in vogue. We have reached a stage when the title page contains minimum information necessary for a reader to know about the document. It is interesting that the earlier title pages even mentioned the names of those who financed the book, as also the names of the father and grandfather of the author, and also gave the names of the different eras for the date at the same time (Kollam, Saka and Salivahana).[117]

The pre-colonial and early colonial classes which provided patronage to literary production were losing out in the context of the social transformation effected by colonialism in its early industrial-capitalist phase. The first generation of Western-educated professionals attempted to fill the breach. The subscription system of publishing was a product of this social formation. Yet this revised form of patronage did not survive either, for it did not match the changing worldview of the emerging middle classes. U.V. Swaminatha Iyer stopped collecting subscriptions for his edition of the Sangam classic *Pathupattu* when he heard the complaint that subscriptions were a ploy to earn money.[118] In keeping with changed times, he chose to sell the book as a finished product, in other words as a commodity.

In this context of economic and social change, art forms altered. The predominant literary genres of the age of patronage were thala

[117] B.S. Kesavan, *History of Printing and Publishing in India*, vol. 1 (New Delhi: National Book Trust, 1985), p. 81. R. Muthukumaraswamy, the noted librarian and Tamil bibliographer, shows more cultural sensitivity, when, after a broad and informative survey of Tamil title pages, he sees aesthetic considerations behind the transformation. 'Tamil Noolgalil Thalaippu Pakkam' (The Title Page in Tamil Books), *Tamil Vattam*, 2nd anniversary number, Chennai, 1969.

[118] Swaminatha Iyer, *En Charithiram*, p. 659.

puranams and related minor literary genres. With the widening public sphere and the tentative beginnings of a larger reading public, literary production had to change. '[C]ommon monotonous compositions, pilgrims' songs and verses in praise of deities, saints and religious apostles and reformers, native princes and chiefs and patrons of authorship',[119] these were not fare for the middle classes that were beginning to dominate the emerging public sphere.

No wonder the system of patronage and its literary products came in for criticism from middle-class intellectuals. One V. Meenakshisundaram, writing in the *Viveka Chintamani*, an organ of the 'Diffusion of Knowledge Agency', though gently lamenting the decline of patronage, was quick to add that it was preferable to provide patronage to books suited to present times.[120] T. Lakshmana Pillai made similar observations in an article on 'developing the Tamil language'.[121] Comparisons were made to the wide range of books published in England and the state of indigenous publishing deplored. Both writers laid stress on the need to spread education and emphasized that for the growth of the language patronage by the public was essential in the age of print. This was to set the agenda for the Tamil publishing world.

The system of patronage made one last-ditch effort. Pandithurai Thevar, a leading patron of earlier times, sought to give institutional form to traditional patronage by founding the Madurai Tamil Sangam in 1901, which received financial support from the likes of Pethachi Chettiar, the zamindar of Andippatti: a sign of the difficult times individual patrons had fallen into. The Sangam published or patronized a number of Tamil classics but became more or less defunct after Pandithurai Thevar's death in 1911.[122]

By the end of the nineteenth century the age of patronage was effectively over. The year 1905 is emblematic of the decisive break

[119] Review and Analysis of Books (1899), G.O. nos 114–15, Edl, 10 March 1900.

[120] *Viveka Chintamani*, 8 (11), March 1900.

[121] Ibid., 1 (4), August 1892.

[122] Raghavaiyangar, *Sentamil Valartha Thevargal*, pp. 89–91.

that Tamil publishing made with traditional forms of patronage. In that year U.V. Swaminatha Iyer, who had spent three decades in the world of publishing with the support of traditional patrons and the first generation of English-educated professionals, petitioned the Government of Madras to say that the pecuniary support 'that I have received [thus far] has been by no means adequate'; he requested its support for his work.[123]

[123] G.O. nos 600–1, Edl, 6 September 1905. The government sanctioned Rs 1000 for his past work and Rs 500 for the following two years.

## 2

# From Patronage to the Public

We saw in the previous chapter that during the late nineteenth century patronage was the basis of Tamil book publishing. Also that in the changing socio-economic conditions traditional patrons of the pre- and early-colonial social classes were no longer able to sustain literary production. The disintegration of patronage-publishing was accompanied by a criticism of that system by middle-class intellectuals. A call was made to produce 'useful knowledge', or literatures suited to contemporary times, and publish it for the consumption of the public—which essentially meant the middle classes.

But a period of transition intervened between the complete disintegration of patronage on the one hand and sustenance by the public on the other, the latter being dependent on the development of economy and society along capitalist lines. The actual social transformation effected by colonialism was, however, stunted, and therefore the transition was extremely traumatic for cultural producers, who were caught in a double bind: they could neither turn to patrons nor sustain themselves through the market.[1]

It is this dilemma to which I now turn. I will flesh out two cases in detail in order to do justice to the intensity and poignancy of the dilemma of cultural producers during the period. First, I look at C. Subramania Bharati (1882–1921), widely acknowledged as the first and greatest of modern Tamil poets, who wrote on contemporaneous matters and attempted to communicate to the populace in

[1] Asok Sen, *Iswar Chandra Vidyasagar and His Elusive Milestones* (Calcutta: Riddhi, 1977). I have drawn much from Asok Sen for insights into the dilemmas of middle-class intellectuals in a colonial context.

order to mobilize them for the nationalist project. Next I look at M.V. Ramanujachari, who single-handedly edited and published a monumental Tamil translation of the Mahabharatam. These case studies are followed by a deliberation on some of the problems in the transitional phase of Tamil publishing.

## Subramania Bharati

> Poetry, working for the cause of the nation,
> and never to be idle even for a moment
> is my occupation.[2]

So wrote Subramania Bharati in 1918. I shall, however, devote myself to looking only at the first of his avowed professions.

Bharati's working life began around 1902 as a court poet in the zamindari of Ettayapuram. When he died in 1921 he was a sub-editor at *Swadesamitran*, the Tamil daily.[3] Excepting a short period of a hundred days, when he worked as a Tamil teacher, Bharati spent his entire adult life as an author, poet, and journalist. As a journalist he was, apart from being a sub-editor at a daily, the editor of another daily as well as two weeklies and two monthlies. During his life he published twenty books, of which only four saw second impressions.[4]

[2] *Bharati Padalgal: Aaivu Pathippu*, p. 505. I have relied on this chronological edition with numerous appendices for references.

[3] There is no definitive biography of Bharati. R.A. Padmanabhan, *Chitrabharati* (Nagercoil: Kalachuvadu Pathippagam, 2006, 3rd edn), is a valuable work with a wealth of photographs, facsimiles, and documents. While I cite this volume for some biographical details, much of the information given in this section is based on my own reading of Bharati's works and other primary materials on his life. Also see Seeni. Viswanathan, *Mahakavi Bharati Varalaru* (A Biography of Mahakavi Bharati; Chennai: Author, 1996).

[4] Seeni. Viswanathan, *Bharati Noolgal: Pathippu Varalaru* (The Writings of Bharati: A Publishing History; Chennai: Author, 1989) is a near-exhaustive narrative of his publishing ventures. In addition to this, Seeni. Viswanathan has published two annotated bibliographies of works by and on Bharati: *Mahakavi Bharati Noorpeyar Kovai* (Mahakavi Bharati: A Bibliography; Chennai: Vanavil Prasuram, 1981) and *Bharati Noolgal Vivarak Kovai* (Bharati: A Bibliography; Chennai: Balaji Puthaka Nilayam, 1987).

Each impression ran to less than a thousand copies. The price of his publications ranged from zero—his first work was distributed free of cost—to Re 1, that being the price of his last book, which was on the history of the Congress (basically a work of translation). His books of poems, on which his reputation and fame largely rest, were sold for a couple of annas each. Most of his early works were self-published; his later books were published by an admirer of his. Yet, towards the end of his life, he put forth a grand prospectus for a fantastic publishing scheme wherein forty of his books would be issued in impressions of 10,000 copies each, priced at half a rupee per copy. Needless to say, Bharati's plans failed. He died a broken man, in utter penury.

Bharati was born in the zamin of Ettayapuram in 1882. Ettayapuram was then the second most populous of the zamindaris in Madras Presidency and the third largest in terms of acreage and income. As we saw earlier, Ettayapuram was a major patron of arts and letters in the early colonial period. Bharati's father was an official in the estate and was known for his enterprise. In fact he promoted a cotton ginning factory in the area—in the aftermath of the cotton boom in southern Tamilnadu, in the context of the American Civil War. Evidently this project was foiled by the machinations of European business interests. Bharati himself writes of it with much bitterness in his verse autobiography.

Even as a young boy he seemed a born versifier and 'Bharati' (the Hindu goddess of learning) was an honorary title conferred upon him at the age of around 11, when he displayed his prodigious talents to a scholarly audience.[5] Traditional recognition was one thing, formal education entirely another. The first extant piece of Bharati's writing is a verse epistle addressed to the Raja of Ettayapuram, seeking monetary help to continue his education.[6] This uncharacteristically pedantic epistle was written in 1897 when Bharati was barely 15. It is not known whether the raja provided help.

[5] Somasundara Bharati, 'Sri Subramania Bharati Charithira Churukkam' (A Short Biography of Bharati), *Bharati Padalgal: Aaivu Pathippu*, App. 2, p. 1069. Somasundara Bharati also received the title of Bharati on the same occasion.

[6] Ibid., pp. 1–3.

Bharati did his schooling at Tirunelveli Hindu College for three years and thereafter moved to Varanasi, where he stayed at his aunt's home, eventually passing the intermediate examinations of Allahabad University. He returned to Ettayapuram around 1902 in order to be a companion and court poet to the raja. His work consisted of hobnobbing with the raja, gossiping, and discussing bawdy and erotic literature. Essentially, this was what patronage of the arts entailed in late colonial Tamilnadu. But Bharati was not cut out to be a sycophant: a rich oral tradition exists on his distaste for this sort of a job.[7] After nearly two years he quit the Ettayapuram estate, a biting poem criticizing the goings-on at court being his parting shot.[8] The oral lore is supplemented by first-hand information from Bharati about his short stint as court poet. In 1913 he wrote an incomplete but hilarious work titled *Chinna Sankaran Kathai* (The Story of L'll Sankaran). This is a transparently autobiographical story about L'll Sankaran who composes verses from an early age and is inducted into the court of the 'Maharaja Rajabhoopathi Maharaja Rajashri Rajamarthanda Sanda Prasanda Anda Bhakiranda Goundathi Gounda Goundanoorathipa Ramaswamy Gounder of Goundanur'—Goundanur, however, being only as big as a five-minute horse ride. (As it turns out, even the horse is not a horse but only a goat, the 'valorous' raja being terribly scared of horses.) Bharati parodies various eulogical verses sung in praise of the raja and generally mocks the goings-on at court. The satire is brilliant and the impression that we are left with is of soreness at the sycophancy rampant in the Ettayapuram zamin, and the anachronistic existence of a 'feudal' court.[9]

Bharati then came to Madurai. Here, for the short period of a hundred days, he taught Tamil at the Sethupathi School in place of the great Tamil scholar Arasan Sanmuganar. It is not clear how he came to be noticed by G. Subramania Iyer, the doyen of Tamil

[7] Padmanabhan, *Chitrabharati*, p. 19. Also R.A. Padmanabhan (ed.), *Bharati Puthaiyal Perumthirattu* (A Mammoth Treasury of Bharati; Chennai: Vanathi Pathippagam, 1982), pp. 5–8.

[8] Ibid., pp. 5–8.

[9] *Bharatiar Kathaigal* (Stories of Bharati; Chennai: Bharati Prachuralayam, 1957), pp. 362–93.

journalism and co-founder of the *Hindu* and *Swadesamitran*. He joined as sub-editor of *Swadesamitran* in November 1904, and then on there was no looking back—writing was to be his only occupation. Apart from the numerous translations (mostly of agency reports) which he made as part of his vocation, he contributed occasional songs. Just nine months after joining *Swadesamitran* he was made editor of *Chakravartini*, 'a Tamil monthly devoted mainly to the elevation of Indian ladies', as the journal described itself in English on its masthead. When, with the Swadeshi Movement, the Indian nationalist movement first took on the semblance of a mass movement, Bharati became very actively involved in politics on the side of the extremist faction of the Congress led by Tilak. He found it difficult to toe the essentially moderate but at times ambivalent extremism of *Swadesamitran*. He left it and joined *India*, a weekly founded by the Mandayam family, as its de facto editor. Meanwhile, swadeshi meetings at the Madras beach and other places had become a daily affair. Bharati's nationalist songs were recited at these meetings and subsequently published in *Swadesamitran* and *India*.

Bharati's first publication appeared in late 1907: three of his poems were bunched into a four-page booklet financed by V. Krishnaswamy Iyer, the leading moderate nationalist leader of Madras. Bharati being known for his extremist leanings, the story goes that the editor-publisher G.A. Natesan took Bharati to V. Krishnaswamy Iyer and made him sing his poems without revealing his identity. Krishnaswamy Iyer was so moved by the songs that he offered to underwrite the entire cost of publication, and ensured its free distribution.[10]

It was a great irony that a poet whose consistent aim was to reach the masses had his first book published through a patron, and the contradiction flared up within a couple of years. After the brutal repression of the Swadeshi Movement, by which time the extremists and the moderates had parted beyond conciliation, Krishnaswamy Iyer was offered a judgeship of the Madras High Court and he willingly accepted. Bharati's ire was aroused. In his daily, *Vijaya*, he wrote an

[10] Seeni. Viswanathan, *Bharati Noolgal: Pathippu Varalaru*, pp. 62–8; Padmanabhan, *Chitrabharati*, pp. 38–41.

editorial directly hostile to Krishnaswamy Iyer, condemning him for betraying the Congress and ending on a personal note:

> It is in keeping with normally understood etiquette and morals not to disclose private conversations. But in unusual circumstances unusual acts may need to be performed. About a year and a half ago, at your Mylapore residence, when you were conversing with a patriot [Bharati himself], do you remember having said in a very moving way, 'We too thirst for freedom like you. We have the same devotion as you for our country. Only our ways are different. But our goal is the same. We should not engender enmity on this count.' Is this the same thirst for freedom which has now made you accept the High Court judgeship? Tomorrow, if the same patriot makes a speech in the cause of freedom in Madras, won't the police then produce him before you? Will you then 'mix mercy and justice' and sentence him to eight years' rigorous imprisonment? 'Our goal is the same!' Is there any doubt? O, fie! O, Krishnaswamy Iyer, what words you've uttered! 'Our goal is the same!' Would you repeat these words now? Oh! Krishnaswamy Iyer, what a life you've led![11]

For the writer now—at least for one with Bharati's ideological leanings—it was becoming impossible to live on patronage. He was now writing for a different and larger audience to whom he felt he was morally answerable. Patronage entailed sycophancy and this was incompatible with a large public as audience.

In early 1908 Bharati published three books. *Swadesa Geethangal* (Nationalist Songs) was fairly well received. Mu. Raghavaiyangar, a great traditional scholar, wrote a rave review of it in *Sentamil*, the monthly organ of the Madurai Tamil Sangam.[12] This was followed by a Tamil translation of Tilak's *Tenets of the New Party*, and a booklet on the Madras extremists' trip to the Surat Congress. Meanwhile by March 1908 the Swadeshi Movement had in Tamilnadu reached its peak. A series of repressive measures by the Government of Madras

[11] A.R. Venkatachalapathy (ed.), *Bharati: 'Vijaya' Katturaikal* (Bharati's Writings from *Vijaya*; Nagercoil: Kalachuvadu Pathippagam, 2004), pp. 52–3.

[12] *Bharati Padalgal: Aaivu Pathippu*, App. 2, pp. 1024–5.

left the movement badly broken and demoralized. Bharati sought refuge in Pondicherry, then a French enclave, to escape arrest for his writings in *India*. After a brief period of a month, *India* was resumed in Pondicherry and, by all accounts, was even fierier.[13] A year later, in 1909, he became editor of a Tamil daily, *Vijaya*. With the petering out of the Swadeshi Movement, Bharati began to edit *Karmayogi*, a Tamil monthly devoted to, as it described itself, 'Arya dharmam, arts of India, industry, poetry, science and [only lastly] political affairs, etc.' from January 1910. With the Indian Press Act 1910 the Government of Madras banned the entry of *India* and *Vijaya* into British India.[14] The two periodicals, entirely dependent on subscribers in the Tamil districts of the Madras Presidency, had to be closed down. Bharati was thus left without periodicals to write in. As he remarked in a long open letter to Ramsay MacDonald, the British Labour Party leader, complaining against 'Police Rule in India', in 1914, 'After I came to Pondicherry, I was living as an independent journalist not attached to any particular paper but receiving money from various newspapers for signed articles.'[15]

Over this time (1909–10), Bharati published four books: two of poetry and two of fiction. Of these, *Kanavu*, his autobiography in verse, and *Ariloru Pangu*, a social reform novelette, were proscribed.[16] The first part of his poetic masterpiece *Panchali Sabhatham* was published in 1912. It was followed the next year by *Puthiya Athichudi*, and in 1914 by *Matha Manivachagam* and *The Fox with the Golden Tail*, the last a satire exposing Annie Besant and the Theosophical Movement, which he described in its preface as 'the most colossal spiritual fraud of the ages'.

With these books a phase of sorts comes to an end in the publishing career of Bharati. But for *Matha Manivachagam*, which was published in South Africa, all his books thus far were published by Bharati himself. From this point, his close associates and admirers began to

[13] S.G. Ramanujulu Naidu, *Amirtaguna Bodhini*, 3 (36), 13 March 1929, pp. 636–7.

[14] G.O. no. 424, Judicial (hereafter Judl), 18 March 1910.

[15] A.R. Venkatachalapathy (ed.), *Bharati Karuvoolam* (The Bharati Treasury; Nagercoil: Kalachuvadu Pathippagam, 2008), p. 56.

[16] G.O. no. 1588, Judl, 11 October 1911.

publish him. In this sense, the artisanal stage in Bharati's career as a published writer comes to an end, and he now moves into a post-artisanal stage.[17] With this a change in Bharati's understanding of book publishing is observable.

He had continued to rely on patronage at the start of the artisanal stage. In the preface to his autobiographical poem *Kanavu* (1910), he says, 'That the printing of this book is not good is not my fault. It is the fault of the rich men of our country',[18] squarely blaming shoddy production standards of his books on lack of patronage. And the dedication of *Panchali Sabhatham* (1912) runs: 'To those gifted poets who are going to write epics which will give undying life and light to the Tamil language, and to those patrons who are going to aid them in the appropriate fashion, this book is dedicated.'[19] Counterposing this lingering faith in patronage there appears an important shift in his perception of the audience. In the preface to *Kanavu* he remarks: 'This little book of verse is written in a novel way. Some of the poems may give pleasure. There may also be a lot of chaff. Its nature lies in the first person: that is, the hero narrates his story himself; that's the style [adopted] . . . I am publishing this little book to see if this new way is acceptable to the *learned men* in Tamil. If these *learned men* test it and okay it, I will publish more of this sort.'[20] Read alongside the preface to *Panchali Sabhatham*, published two years later, the shift seems dramatic: 'Simple words; a simple style; an easily grasped rhythm; a lilt liked by common people—anyone who writes an epic with these qualities today will actually give new life to our mother

[17] For concepts regarding artists and their relation to the market, I have drawn on Raymond Williams, *Culture* (London: Fontana, 1983), ch. 2, 'Institutions'. Williams speaks of several post-patronage stages. In the artisanal stage, an independent producer offers his own work for direct sale. Though he is wholly dependent on the immediate market, his work remains under his own direction but within the terms of the market. This is followed by a post-artisanal stage wherein the producer sells his work not directly but through a distributory middleman. Later, a productive intermediary directly buys the work from the producer and then sells the book as a commodity in the market.

[18] *Bharati Padalgal: Aaivu Pathippu*, App. 2, p. 1036.

[19] Ibid., p. 1038.

[20] Ibid., pp. 1036–7. Emphasis added.

tongue. *Not only must it be easily comprehensible to all Tamil people familiar with book reading, even if only for a couple of years*, it must not fall short of artistic requirements either.'[21] From putting his faith on the 'learned men' of an earlier generation, Bharati is now casting his lot with the emerging class of neo-literate readers. Thus, during this period Bharati's attitude towards patronage and the public was marked by ambivalence, a characteristic feature of the transition period.

After *The Fox with the Golden Tail* (1914), there was a lull in Bharati's publishing activities until his friend, Parali Su. Nellaiyappa Pillai took over in 1917. This interregnum coincides with some articles that Bharati wrote on book publishing in general. They are insightful essays revealing the course that book publishing had taken in Tamilnadu. His views on patronage had by then undergone a clear change. In 1916 he wrote:

> The world over, the custom of practising various arts with the support of kings and lords has long gone. We must now begin relying on the folk. From now on support and succour for the arts will come from the common people. It is the duty of artists to instil good taste in them. It will yield them good returns. A lord may at best give [artists] Rs 100 a month. But if people get together and contribute a quarter of a rupee each, they will get a thousand rupees a month. We must make the people our masters.
>
> The country is king. If you instil this king with some knowledge, the arts will never suffer.[22]

From 1917 Parali Su. Nellaiyappa Pillai took on publishing Bharati's works. *Kannan Pattu*, *Nattu Pattu*, *Pappa Pattu*, and *Murasu* were all published in a single year and reprinted in 1919. Letters written by Bharati to Nellaiyappa Pillai, some of which survive,[23] make it clear that, in institutional terms, the latter was a productive intermediary in a post-artisanal stage. Their relationship was never, however, just

[21] Ibid., pp. 1038–9. Emphasis added.

[22] *Swadesamitran*, 19 December 1916, in *Bharati Noolgal: Katturaigal*, vol. 3 (Chennai: Bharati Prachuralayam, n.d.), p. 116.

[23] R.A. Padmanabhan (ed.), *Bharatiyin Kadithangal* (Bharati's Correspondence; Nagercoil: Kalachuvadu Pathippagam, 2005; 2nd edn) letters dated 19 July 1915; 21 December 1918, pp. 53–5, 67–9.

the common business deal. There was between them no talk of copyright or royalty, and Nellaiyappa Pillai's moving publisher's notes show he was performing what he thought was his duty to the Indian nation and the Tamil people.[24]

By 1918 Bharati was tired of his self-imposed exile in Pondicherry. Ten years in a cramped little town made him claustrophobic. Constant surveillance and underhand methods used by the police to capture him aggravated his discomfort. But with the beginning of World War I the surveillance eased a little and, after the armistice was signed, Bharati ventured into British India in November 1918. He was immediately arrested at Cuddalore. Deputy Inspector General of Police Hannington met him at the jail. Bharati was released upon giving a written undertaking that he would abstain from politics for a certain period, during which time all his writings would need the prior approval of the Deputy Inspector General of Police before their publication.[25]

After his release Bharati moved to Kadayam, the native village of his wife Chellamma. Clearly, he had no money and nowhere else to go, else he would not have moved in with his parents-in-law. Within a week of his release from prison he wrote to Nellaiyappa Pillai in connection with publishing matters. His urgency can be sensed in a letter dated 21 December 1918 urging Nellaiyappa Pillai to act fast; evidently Bharati was eager to pursue his work and occupy himself.

> I arrived at Kadayam safely. The very day after my arrival I received letters from many people asking for *Pappa Pattu*, *Murasu*, *Nattu Pattu*, and *Kannan Pattu*.
>
> I do not have copies of the above. If you have them, please send all you can manage. I don't yet know how far the effort to print both parts of *Panchali Sabhatham* has progressed [. . .] If *Pappa Pattu* etc. are not in stock with you, they need to be printed immediately.
>
> I want to talk to you in person about matters related to this. I request you to come over as soon as you see this letter . . . I've many more manuscripts to be published.
>
> Please come over immediately.[26]

[24] See *Bharati Padalgal: Aaivu Pathippu*, App. 2, pp. 1048–9.
[25] G.O. no. 13, Public (hereafter Pub.), 15 January 1919.
[26] Padmanabhan (ed.), *Bharatiyin Kadithangal*, pp. 67–9.

We do not know if Nellaiyappa Pillai did as asked and go to Kadayam, but he did reprint all four books over the ensuing year. Bharati had written prolifically during his exile, with over a score of manuscripts awaiting publication. Nellaiyappa Pillai's means were moderate. On the other hand Bharati had no means at all and a family to support.

Egged on by his family and relatives, he wrote a verse epistle on 2 May 1919 to none other than the Raja of Ettayapuram, from whose employ he had walked out fifteen years earlier.

> O, king,
> when you were to be crowned,
> the blame was that
> there was no king in the Tamil land
> well versed in the Tamil language
> . . .
> And the blame
> that there was no king of poets
> to give fame to Tamil
> and bring it world renown—
> was it not wiped off by me?
> . . .
> I bring my wondrous poetry
> to your court.
> May you listen to it,
> and bid the sound of victory drums,
> and confer on me
> shawls, purses, palanquins, and retinue,
> and long may you live![27]

Apparently there was no reply to Bharati. He followed it up with another verse epistle the very next day. The pride stark in the first epistle is toned down in the second.

> In the old Tamil country
> where Pari once lived,
> now you reign.

[27] *Bharati Padalgal: Aaivu Pathippu*, pp. 516–18.

If poets come to see you,
seeking something
would you not meet them immediately?
O, king Venkatesa Reddi
your fame is up to the skies,
while my song is as good as the best song
and my verse is as good as the best verse.
And if poets
with fame and lofty ideas come
would you not rush to confer
a million gifts on them.[28]

Silence was the reply again. Bharati grew desperate and three months later wrote another letter, this time in prose. He was stooping low. The bang of the first epistle is barely a whimper now.

> Your lordship is well aware that *Vamsamani Deepikai*, the royal genealogy of Ettayapuram written by Kavi Kesari Sri Swami Dikshitar, is in a colloquial style with a number of shortcomings. I shall correct it and set it in good, sweet, and clear Tamil. If that is done, it can be arranged to get it prescribed in Government schools [. . .]
>
> Moreover, given my reputation, and the manner in which I propose to write it, it will make an exemplary work of prose which will survive forever in Tamilnadu.
>
> The book can be printed in the royal printing press itself. The very day after your lordship's orders are received, the printing can begin. Whatever needs to be printed for the day, I will write the night before. Through this, the royal family will gain eternal fame and the Tamil language will gain a glorious work of history.
>
> I request that orders be issued in this regard at the earliest. The copyright will, of course, vest in the royal court.[29]

The whole business of these three letters is tragic. Here was a man who had vowed to 'sustain the world with the power of my song'[30] cringing before a petty zamindar whom he had not only rebuffed fifteen years earlier but also severely satirized.

[28] Ibid., pp. 519–20.
[29] Padmanabhan (ed.), *Bharatiyin Kadithangal*, pp. 77–8.
[30] *Bharati Padalgal: Aaivu Pathippu*, p. 566.

The zamindar's stony silence to Bharati's overtures stopped the poet dead in his tracks. A little later, Bharati made one last ditch effort, this time to seek the patronage of a Nattukkottai Chettiar merchant and banker, Vai.Su. Shanmugam Chettiar. A letter dated 15 November 1919 says:

> Please give the Bhagavat Gita [Bharati's translation] for printing quickly. If you so wish I will write a lengthy commentary. And also a long foreword.
>
> Let the book not be priced at less than a rupee. Thick paper, clear print, bold types, lots of space—these are to be indispensable qualities not only for the Gita but all other books we are to publish.
>
> We should try to print our books in the same manner in which the works of English poets are printed in England. If the printer says that a rupee a copy will not suffice for a production of this quality, I don't mind an increase in the price.[31]

But nothing came of his plans; for reasons unknown not a single book was published by Shanmugam Chettiar.

Finally, towards the end of his life, Bharati made his grandiose plan to publish everything, the accumulated labour of his exile. In June 1920 he issued a prospectus of his plans in English and appealed for loans and donations. A few months later he released an even more detailed prospectus in Tamil.[32] The scheme was this: Bharati wanted to publish his books in forty volumes and print a first run of 10,000 copies each. He was sure his books would be 'sold as easily and quickly as kerosene or boxes of matches'.[33]

> Most of the works which I have now selected for publication are prose-stories, sensational and, at the same time, classical; very easy, lucid, clear, luminous, and all but too popular in style and diction and, at the same

[31] Padmanabhan (ed.), *Bharatiyin Kadithangal*, pp. 80–1.

[32] The two prospectuses are reproduced in ibid., pp. 83–4, 90–4. For the facsimiles, see Padmanabhan, *Chitrabharati*, pp. 154–9. Padmanabhan has used the copy of the prospectus sent to Srinivasa Varadan of Madurai. The copy sent by Bharati to Gooty P. Kesava Pillai is in the P. Kesava Pillai Papers, Nehru Memorial Museum and Library, New Delhi.

[33] Padmanabhan (ed.), *Bharatiyin Kadithangal*, p. 92.

time, chaste, pure, correct, epic, and time defying. This fact and (2) the ever-growing increase of Tamil reading men, women, and children in the Tamil world overseas; (3) the historic necessity of my works for the uplift of the Tamil land which, again, is a sheer necessity of the inevitable, imminent, and heaven ordained Revival of the East; (4) the novel and American like improvement which I propose to make in the printing, binding, and get up of my editions—which, added [to] by beautiful and suitable pictures illustrating the interesting events occurring in the stories, will make them a tremendous attraction to our public and such a wondrous surprise; (5) the comparatively low price of my books: for I am going to sell my prose-works uniformly at 8 annas a copy and my poems at, so far as possible, 4 annas a copy; and (6) my high reputation and unrivalled popularity in the Tamil reading world due to my past publications—all these are bound most evidently to make my sales a prodigious success.[34]

Bharati estimated that the plans would require Rs 20,000 as production costs and Rs 10,000 towards advertising expenses. At half a rupee a copy the turnover would be Rs 200,000. With such returns, Bharati offered to pay 24 per cent annual interest on the loans contracted.

Evidently, Bharati sent copies of this prospectus to all his friends and acquaintances. He followed this up with personal letters. In a letter to Thangaperumal Pillai, a leading merchant of Erode, he wrote in English:

> the publication of my work is a matter of great national urgency. Erode has rich merchants. Utilize the Appeal, kindly, and let me have for the above mentioned work as much money as can be collected before the ensuing month as loans or otherwise from among friends, acquaintances, and also from others through them.
>
> As this is also patriotic work—otherwise I would have some scruples troubling you on this score—kindly start operations immediately & very earnestly.[35]

[34] Ibid., pp. 83–4.
[35] Ibid., p. 96.

Bharati's plan was a non-starter. There is no evidence to show even a single person offering funds. Patrons and public alike seem to have spurned him. By the end of 1920 he had eaten humble pie and, notwithstanding his earlier stints as an editor at a daily and four periodicals, rejoined *Swadesamitran* as sub-editor. Bharati had come, it could be said, full circle and was frustratingly back to square one, dying in September 1921 a broken and disillusioned man. Notices of his death bore no relation to his importance in Tamil life and society.[36] It was not until the 1940s that the high cultural place he now occupies was secured—after a series of ideological struggles.

Towards the end of Bharati's masterpiece, *Kuyil*, the koel is transformed into a beautiful damsel. As the poet hugs her and showers her with kisses, his dream is suddenly shattered. He awakes with a start and all that he sees around him are old books, a pen, some dated newspapers, and a tattered mat. The dream could be said to represent the shattering of Bharati's publishing plans.

## M.V. Ramanujachari and the Tamil Mahabharatam

Manalur Veerasami Ayyangar Ramanujachari (1866–1940) was born in Manalur in the erstwhile Thanjavur district. He studied at Varanasi and Thanjavur under the tutelage of respected Saiva scholars. Beginning his career as a clerk in the Chief Auditor's office at Tiruchy, he was later a Tamil pandit at a school in Srirangam and a village munsif in his native village. He also served as Tamil pandit at the Native High School, Kumbakonam, over 1893–1911. In 1911 he became Head Tamil Pandit at Government College, Kumbakonam, where he finally retired in 1921.[37]

At Kumbakonam Ramanujachari was fortunate to have U.V. Swaminatha Iyer's acquaintance—the two would often discuss a considerable variety of literary matters. It was during one such discussion that the idea of translating the Mahabharatam came up as a

[36] For obituary notices and reports of memorial meetings, see Padmanabhan, *Chitrabharati*, pp. 181–4.

[37] *The Who's Who in Madras, 1934* (Cochin: Pearl Press, [1935]).

possibility. Given his preoccupation with editing Tamil classics from palm-leaf manuscripts, Swaminatha Iyer predictably enough declined to venture into such a large project. Swaminatha Iyer shifted to Madras in 1903 to teach at the Presidency College, leaving the seed firmly sown in Ramanujachari's mind and heart.[38]

By about 1907, egged on by colleagues and friends, Ramanujachari had embarked on the mammoth task of editing and publishing the Tamil Mahabharatam. When the first fascicule was published in August 1908, he had not foreseen that the whole project would take up 9,000 or so pages, over a quarter of a century, and about Rs 150,000, pushing him in the process to the brink of bankruptcy.

Ramanujachari planned to publish the Mahabharatam in fascicules of about 200 pages each at two-month intervals, for which he hoped to acquire subscriptions. U.V. Swaminatha Iyer sent in the first contribution of Rs 30, while Professor K. Sundararama Iyer donated Rs 200, apart from committing himself to Rs 10 for every future fascicule.[39]

Considering that even reading the Mahabharatam was quite a task, little needs to be added on the magnitude of translating it, given the complicated nature of the text with its various recensions and versions. Rather than entrusting the task of the translation to a single scholar, Ramanujachari employed a team of Sanskrit scholars for both translation and verification. One Ramachandracharya was the first to be commissioned; he translated the Nalopakhyanam by himself. His pace being far from adequate for Ramanujachari's needs,

[38] This section is based on the absorbing 56-page preface written by M.V. Ramanujachari on the completion of the project, *Sri Mahabharatham: Vana Parvam*, part 2 (Chennai: Author, 1932). Additional information has been drawn from governmental records. Unless otherwise indicated, the source is Ramanujachari's preface. For a fuller treatment in Tamil, see my 'Bharatam Thanta Bhagiratar' (The Bhagiratha Who Gave the Mahabharatam) *Kalachuvadu* 73, January 2006.

[39] Curiously, his biography, competently written by his own son, makes no mention of this impressive benefaction: K.S. Ramaswami Sastri, *Professor K. Sundararama Aiyar: His Life & Works* (Srirangam: Sri Vani Vilas Press, [1944]).

A. Venkatacharya and T.E. Srinivasacharya were contracted to continue with the translation. Later in the day renowned scholars like T.V. Srinivasacharya, Mahamahopadhyaya Ganapathy Sastri, and Kadalangudi Natesa Sastri translated parts of the Mahabharatam. Ramanujachari also provided paid assistants to help the translators with their work.

By then he had advertised the forthcoming publication and was overwhelmed with queries about the exact recension and version being translated. It turned out that Ramanujachari had until then given little thought to the matter. Realizing that it was a serious issue, on the resolution of which continuation of the project depended, he began serious consultations. These revealed that, during the great famine of 1876–8 a philanthropist of Karichankal in Chingelpat district had attempted to commission a Tamil translation. Ramanujachari acquired palm-leaf manuscripts of this translation but found it unsuitable. Considering that Pratap Chandra Roy's version was based on the northern recension, it is not surprising that Ramanujachari did not favour it. V.S. Sukthankar's edition for the Bhandarkar Oriental Research Institute was of course unavailable to Ramanujachari—it lay in the future. Ultimately, after much careful deliberation, Ramanujachari decided upon the southern recension edited by T.R. Krishnacharya of Madhava Vilas Book Depot, Kumbakonam. Meanwhile, substantial portions—Virata Parvam, Udyoga Parvam, and most parts of Adi Parvam—had already been translated from a different version. Despite the time, labour, and money spent, Ramanujachari discarded these translations.

He was also confronted by other hurdles. Discouragement topped the list. Many of his friends and relatives discouraged him by pointing out the sheer scale of the undertaking. They included Vai.Mu. Sadagoparamanujachari, who had made a fortune by publishing annotated university textbooks; and R. Raghunatharayar. Ramanujachari's uncle, Mudumbai Srinivasa Iyengar, and his sister, too, advised him to desist. Mu. Raghavaiyangar, the renowned Tamil scholar, wrote at the behest of Pandithurai Thevar to say that the Madurai Tamil Sangam was already on the verge of publishing a Tamil Mahabharatam based on Pratap Chandra Roy's English version. This was a double shock: first, competition from a rival publication, and second, the fact that getting the help of Pandithurai Thevar, the greatest patron of Tamil letters of the time, was now precluded. V. Krishnaswamy Iyer, the moderate Congress leader, chipped in with tales of many abortive attempts to translate the Mahabharatam. Such discouragement put Ramanujachari on the horns of a dilemma. If this was such a laudable project, as everyone conceded, why should he not forge ahead?

So Ramanujachari decided to seek out an oracle. He approached a renowned astrologer. The prediction was even more discouraging. The astrologer foresaw with certainty a darshan of Vishnu—a euphemism for death—before the completion of the project. Ramanujachari did not breathe a word about the astrological forecast to anyone, quietly putting it away in an envelope sealed with lac. He was to break the seal and read it aloud in the midst of friends only after twenty years, when the whole project had reached fruition.

The world of Tamil letters had its share of bickering and animosity, too. One of Ramanujachari's translators betrayed him at the instigation of a rival and published his part of the translation on his own. Naturally, this meant that bit of the translation could not be continued, thereby delaying Ramanujachari's project. Yet Ramanujachari persisted.

The task of translation was enormously time consuming. When Ramanujachari entrusted the translation of a particular parvam to a scholar, he also asked the translator to revise the translation after comparing it with the original before submitting it to him. This manuscript would then be given to other scholars for comparison, comments, suggested revisions, and queries. The original translators had then to make final revisions. The manuscript was then given to another scholar to ensure the translation read true to the original. Despite these inputs from other scholars, the translation was published in the name of the original translator.

In 1914 Ramanujachari released a prospectus about his venture; an appeal was published in the *Hindu* and endorsed in an editorial. He reminded the public that the Mahabharatam was five times as long as the Ramayanam. 'Those who know assert that there is no other work of greater length in any other language which has so largely served to inspire the later literature.'

> Incurring on this work, during several years and with an immense amount of personal labour and endeavour, by engaging the services of eminent pandits and maintaining an establishment of several helping hands I have had to undergo trials and troubles of several sorts. The magnitude of the undertaking and the exertions and sacrifices entailed by it need not be dwelt here and all men of discriminating power can fully understand them. If I have so far been enabled to persevere and continue the task, it is due to the grace of the Supreme and to the substantial help rendered me by some of my patriotic and high-minded fellow-countrymen.[40]

However, Ramanujachari's desperate plea for 500 more subscribers yielded only two responses: from H.Le. Fann and Sir Ponnambalam Ramanathan, the distinguished philanthropist of Sri Lanka. Notwithstanding the setback he soldiered on and, by June 1915, Moksha Dharmam of the Shanti Parvam had been completed. World War I had broken out by then, and the costs of paper and other printing materials had risen out of control: 'paper that had cost two and a half annas, had now to be bought at over a rupee'—when it was available at all. Ramanujachari was compelled to suspend printing until the end of the war in late 1918.

Initially, the project had received as many as 800 subscriptions. Drawing hope from this none-too-bad response, Ramanujachari had by 1915 published over 3,000 pages.[41] Tabulated, it looked like this:

| | |
|---|---|
| Adi Parvam | 942 pages |
| Sabha Parvam | 356 pages |
| Virata Parvam | 334 pages |
| Santi Parvam | |
| Part I | 603 pages |
| Part II | 815 pages |

[40] 'The Tamil Translation of the Mahabaratham: An Appeal', *The Hindu*, 16 January 1914.
[41] G.O. no. 393, Edl, 14 April 1915.

To meet the rising costs he petitioned the Government of Madras, seeking their assistance. Glowing testimonials from a range of eminent persons were submitted to support the petition. Initially, the government sanctioned the purchase of 40 copies at the rate of Rs 25 a set.[42] Disappointed by the government's order, Ramanujachari submitted detailed accounts of his vast undertaking a year later, as shown in Table 2.1.

Table 2.1
Statement of Expenditure of M.V. Ramanujachari's Tamil Mahabharatam

| | Up to April 1915 (in rupees) | Future Estimates (in rupees) |
|---|---|---|
| Remuneration to Pandits for translation | 4,000 | – |
| 4 Scribes for 7 years @ Rs 40 per month | 3,360 | – |
| 1 Proof-reader for 7 years @ Rs 20 p.m. | 1,680 | 960 |
| 2 Clerks for 6 years @ Rs 35 p.m. | 2,520 | 1,680 |
| 1 Travelling agent for 6 years @ Rs 40 p.m. | 2,880 | 1,960 |
| Paper and printing for 20 parts | 10,500 | 10,000 |
| Pandit (for comparison and revision) @ Rs 25 p.m. | 2,100 | 1,500 |
| Office rent and contingencies | 1,260 | 800 |
| Advertisements | 1,600 | 4,000 |
| Total | 29,900 | 20,860 |
| For printing more copies to complete sets | – | 5,000 |
| | 29,900 | 25,860 |
| Grand total 29,900 + 25,860 | | 55,560 |

*Source*: G.O. no. 835, Edl, 3 August 1915

Receipts until then were Rs 12,600 (by subscriptions for 20 parts) plus Rs 3,200 (by way of donations). As against this, the assets were Rs 3,000 (in the form of the unsold 1,000 sets—which really meant no assets at all) and Rs 12,000 on account of the balance of subscriptions. Consequently, his liabilities totalled a staggering Rs 39,960,

[42] G.O. no. 543, Edl, 12 May 1914.

exclusive of loans and commission on sale. Apparently, the government was not adequately impressed with these accounting details and sanctioned the purchase of an additional 35 sets, thereby enhancing their order to 75 sets in all.[43]

By 1921, when he retired on a pension from his position at the Kumbakonam College, Ramanujachari had published 27 fascicules. He settled down with his family at Madras that October, hoping to find more subscribers in the city and thereby ensure continuity of the publishing venture. He was sorely disappointed; in the year and a half that he spent at Madras, only four more fascicules (nos 28–31) could be published. Additionally, he was compelled to reprint some earlier fascicules to make complete sets of the incomplete ones—otherwise there were few takers for the volumes, an obvious contingency he seems not to have foreseen. Unable to meet the costs of urban living and the lukewarm response to his work, Ramanujachari returned to his native village, Manalur, in May 1923.

It was then that he received some encouragement from V.T. Krishnamachari, Dewan of Vizianagaram, and Sir M.Ct. Muthiah Chettiar and A.M.M. Murugappa Chettiar, the Chettiar philanthropists. In the five years that he spent at Manalur, Ramanujachari had published only five more fascicules (nos 32–36). He was also feeling frustrated by the need to keep reprinting earlier fascicules to maintain the full availability of complete sets, essential for marketability.

By March 1928 Ramanujachari had once again returned to Madras, where he stayed till September 1929. During this time he published four more fascicules and received further subscriptions from a number of professionals, especially advocates. A second prospectus was released, and the response was thoroughly disappointing: only one person, an excise inspector, who was in fact a close friend of Ramanujachari, provided a contribution.

On his return to Manalur Ramanujachari published three more fascicules but felt intellectually isolated in the small village. He opted to reside at Kumbakonam, where he published the final two fascicules (nos 44 and 45). His Tamil translation of Mahabharatam had not

[43] Ibid.

been published in the sequential order of the original text, and self-contained portions had been put through the press as soon as that portion of the translation was ready. Consequently the last part to see the press was Vana Parvam, which is the third of the eighteen books that constitute the Mahabharatam.

When it was completed in February 1932 the whole project had taken up over 9,000 printed pages (demy octavo), and over Rs 135,000 had been spent in cash. By this time Ramanujachari had lost no less than Rs 15,000 of his own money. Subscriptions, which had initially hovered in the range of 800, dipped to under 250 by the time of completion. Certain subscribers, who had patiently received 43 fascicules over 25 years through Value Payable Post, inexplicably refused the penultimate fascicule when it reached their doorstep. How many more might refuse the last fascicule, Ramanujachari wondered.

In the end, Ramanujachari was close to being a financial wreck. He had ploughed money from his wife's ancestral property into the venture. His son had left a decent job in Longman, Green & Co., the British-owned publishing firm, to assist his ailing father in the task of publishing. Despite this financially unhappy state, Ramanujachari was a happy man: 'That so much has been done despite unending troubles is due to the Lord's grace. When compared with other similar ventures in terms of the time taken, facilities available and work completed, the achievement of our Mahabharatam is no doubt praiseworthy.'[44]

Never a man to rest on his laurels, Ramanujachari now felt the need for a comprehensive index and compendium which would be an invaluable aid to users of the volume of 9,000 or so pages. He calculated that the production of such an index would take about two years. By this time, though, he was a much chastened man who had no wish to add to his already considerable debts. He ended the already lengthy introduction to the Vana Parvam (Part 2) with an emphatic statement that he would not embark on the work unless it was fully sponsored.

[44] *Sri Mahabharatam: Vana Parvam*, part 1 (Chennai: Author), Preface, p. 7.

Ramanujachari's mammoth undertaking may not seem the typical publishing venture in Tamil. But what appeared idealistic in the transitional period between the age of patronage and the age of the market turned out to be a commercial success after his death. By the 1950s his son, M.R. Rajagopalan, had reprinted all the volumes more than once. Even during World War II, when paper was again scarce, he spared no efforts to acquire it in the black market: by then there was little doubt about the Tamil Mahabharatam's commercial viability.[45]

### The Dilemmas of Transition

The instances of Subramania Bharati and M.V. Ramanujachari highlight many of the dilemmas facing literary producers during the first decades of the twentieth century. By then they had developed a keen sense of ground realities in the publishing arena. They were certain that the age of patrons was over and that all hope of future succour lay in the hands of the middle classes. Bharati was in any case also ideologically opposed to this reliance on traditional forms of patronage. As he observed in 1916, 'If one sings banal songs of empty praise on zamindars and lords one gets some remuneration',[46] but as the he-crow says to his spouse in one of Bharati's fables, 'I belong to the Republican party; I cannot accept royal gifts.'[47]

Intellectuals began now to look up to the middle classes for sustenance. Bharati identified 'the Tamil reading middle classes' who supported periodicals such as *India* and *Swadesamitran* as 'merchants, landlords, elementary school teachers, petty traders, lawyers, clerks, etc., as well as a large section of Tamil reading ladies',[48] and repeatedly called on the 'English educated Tamil people—especially lawyers and school teachers' to support Tamil authors.[49]

[45] See M.R. Rajagopalan to U.V.S. Kalyanasundara Iyer, 13 August 1941, U.V.S. Papers.

[46] *Bharati Noolgal: Katturaigal*, vol. 3, pp. 101–2.

[47] Padmanabhan (ed.), *Bharati Puthaiyal Perumthirattu*, pp. 97–8.

[48] 'Political Evolution in Madras Presidency', incomplete manuscript drafted *circa* 1919, ibid., p. 553.

[49] *Bharati Noolgal: Katturaigal*, vol. 3, pp. 101–2.

It was to these classes that Bharati had addressed his grandiose plan of 1920.

Over this period of transition the Tamil middle class had not come of age, so to speak. It was in its nascent form, without possessing the clear consciousness of a class for itself. Consequently, it did not heed the call of intellectuals who had emerged from within, people who were seeking to give this rising class a sense of homogeneity and an awareness of its social function. No wonder therefore that the efforts of middle-class intellectuals failed, and many of them, in desperate attempts foredoomed to failure, had to supplicate traditional patrons. Bharati is only one such instance, perhaps the most prominent. Ramanujachari, too, was let down by his middle-class subscribers and had to turn to patrons, who, apart from a large number of professionals, included zamindars, monasteries, and Chettiar bankers.

V.V.S. Aiyar, the revolutionary nationalist and literary figure, observed in 1919: 'In older times, kings bestowed large amounts on writers and kept them away from worrying about trifles, thereby helping them to cultivate their skills. Nowadays, it is the common people interested in learning who occupy the position of kings.'[50] But the common people failed V.V.S. Aiyar too. In the mid 1910s Aiyar had launched the Kamba Nilayam in Pondicherry to publish quality books. He released a prospectus calling for a modest sum of Rs 3,000. The response was, as usual, tepid: he could not find even 500 people to buy his publications.[51] Likewise, the attempt of A. Singaravelu Mudaliar to publish in fascicules his *Abidhana Chintamani* (an encyclopaedia of Tamil literature running into over a thousand pages) fell flat. It was not until the intervention of Pandithurai Thevar, the eminent patron, that the volume saw the light of day in 1910.[52] And there is finally the instance of V. Swaminatha Sarma,

[50] Preface to Bharati's *Kannan Pattu, Bharati Padalgal: Aaivu Pathippu*, p. 1047.

[51] Letter of V.V.S. Aiyar to an anonymous friend, 17 October 1920, reproduced in V. Swaminatha Sarma, *Nan Kanda Nalvar* (The Four Personalities I Knew; Pudukkottai: Prapanjajothi Prachuralayam, 1974), pp. 146–50.

[52] *Abidhana Chintamani* (1910, facsimile rpnt. New Delhi: Asian Educational Services), Preface.

who had to get Rs 200 from S. Srinivasa Iyengar, an advocate and a leading Congressman, to publish a topical book on the Jallianwallabagh massacre.[53]

Their frustration at having to seek patronage and subscriptions was compounded by the realization that even the existing market among the middle classes was not being properly tapped. Once again it was left to Bharati to observe, with characteristic insight:

> Because entrepreneurs who will take up publishing as a business have not yet emerged, there is still some difficulty [for Tamil authors] . . . Surprisingly, our entrepreneurs have not taken sufficient interest in [book publishing]. Books are, of course, being published now. And a vast number of people do indeed buy and read them. If the book trade were systematically carried out, people would have better books to choose from [. . .] There is no doubt at all that good profits will accrue from book publishing if it is pursued with enterprise.[54]

Besides the time lag that is often bound to exist between material conditions and institutional structures, the transitional phase in Tamilnadu also coincided with World War I. Book publishing was badly hit by the war. Authors and editors, who doubled up as publishers during this period, complained bitterly of rising costs. M.V. Ramanujachari, as we saw, had had to suspend publication of the Mahabharatam during the war. Maraimalai Adigal observed that 'the cost of paper is shooting up every day. A ream of paper that could be bought for Rs 2–13–0 earlier now costs Rs 7–8–0.'[55] The editor of *Vivekodhayam* planned to stock paper for a year to enable continued publication of his journal.[56] In one of its book reviews it observed that the book under review was a good bargain for Rs 1–8–0 considering the cost of paper![57] Subramania Siva had to suspend the

[53] Swaminatha Sarma, *Nan Kanda Nalvar*, pp. 41–2.

[54] *Bharati Noolgal: Katturaigal*, vol. 3, pp. 85–6.

[55] Maraimalai Adigal to V. Thiruvarangam Pillai, 19 June 1916, Maraimalai Adigal Papers, Maraimalai Adigal Library.

[56] *Vivekodhayam*, December 1917.

[57] Ibid., August 1916.

publication of a Tamil translation of Adi Sankara's *Viveka Chudamani* after only five fascicules because of the unavailability of paper.[58]

It was only after the war that the transitional phase between patronage and the public ended in Tamil publishing. By then the middle class had emerged more or less fully, and now even entertained hegemonic aspirations. The novel, the bourgeois art form par excellence, gave the necessary breakthrough to distance publishing from patronage and cement the writer's links with the middle class.

It is to the rise of the Tamil novel that we turn next.

[58] *Jnanabhanu,* March 1916.

# 3

# Towards the Market: Domesticating the Novel

In this age, when printing machines have become legion and the business in paper has expanded, novels have started to proliferate like termites [. . .] Tamil people who know not the true novel are gobbling up this trash like fowl eating termites.—***Panchamirtam* 1 (7), October 1924**

The novel, like the bourgeoisie, always seems to be rising.—**Robert Darnton, 'History of Reading'**

Tamil publishing, after half a century of being sustained by patronage, began to move towards the market in the first decades of the twentieth century. The publishing quandaries of Subramania Bharati and M.V. Ramanujachari suggested that the transition from patronage to the public was traumatic for writers. It was only with the rise to pre-eminence of the novel that Tamil publishing switched decisively in favour of the public for its sustenance.

## The Scourge of the Novel

The novel was one of the most conspicuous cultural fruits of the colonial encounter. If the new Indian elite was 'crushed by poetry', the novel seemed to have given them wings. This elite first encountered the novel, in its Victorian English form, in their curriculum but pursued reading it outside the walls of schools and colleges. Virtually no autobiography or memoir of the times is without reference to novels and novel-reading. One cultural historian refers to the 'curious amalgam' of 'prescribed novels and Victorian pulp' that animated readers and writers of the times.[1] A huge volume of imported novels flooded the Indian book market from the late nineteenth century. One observer writes of how Reynolds' novels were piled as high as a man in Moore Market, Madras.[2] Research based on trade and publishing data has tried to quantify this phenomenon. British firms such as Macmillan, Murray, and Kegan Paul were in the forefront of this business of publishing and distributing novels.[3] Contemporary periodicals regularly carried advertisements placed by booksellers such as Higginbothams for these novels. Apart from such imports, some enterprising Indian firms published cheap reprints, especially of Reynolds' novels. There is no mistaking the enormous appeal such novels had for the newly educated. Soon, in an act of cultural translation, this fiction was imitated, adapted, copied, plagiarized, and translated. This was an all-India phenomenon but one that in Tamil had its own specific slant. The earliest instance of such a 'translation' is attested to in 1899.[4]

A flood of novels deluged Tamil society in the early decades of the twentieth century and was widely commented upon. One novelist said, in the preface to one of his novels, that 'The author [. . .] is not unconscious of the fact that there is already a glut in the market of novels of which a few are good, some indifferent, and many decidedly bad.'[5] Such prefatory comments were noticed contemporaneously: 'In the preface to many of the novels published in those times we can

[1] Meenakshi Mukherjee, *The Perishable Empire: Essays in Indian Writing in English* (New Delhi: Oxford University Press, 2000), p. 4.

[2] N. Subrahmanian, *En Valkai Varalaru: Iruveru Ulagathu Iyarkkai* (My Life; Udumalaippettai: Ennes Publications, 1993), p. 209.

[3] Priya Joshi, *In Another Country: Colonialism, Culture, and the English Novel in India* (New York: Columbia University Press, 2002), pt 1, 'Consuming Fiction'.

[4] *Umaru Pasha Yuddha Charithiram*, based on Reynolds' three-part novel *Omar, a Tale of the War* (1855–6), was translated by a respected Muslim poet-scholar Gulam Kadir Navalar and published in four parts between 1899 and 1904. This has recently been recovered and republished: Murali Aroopan (ed.), *Umaru Pasha Yuddha Charithiram* (Chennai: Kalthachan Pathippagam, 2001).

[5] M.A. Nellaiyappar, *Vidyanandar* (Chennai: n.p., 1911), Preface in English.

find the comment that Tamil novels were coming out in great numbers!'[6] Such was the surfeit of novels that accounts of the period often likened it to the proliferation of termites. The volume of advertisements in contemporary journals is only the most obvious indicator of the extent of this phenomenon. Periodicals like *Ananda Bodhini*, *Amirtaguna Bodhini*, *Viveka Bodhini*, and *Lakshmi* abound in these advertisements. Scores of novels are listed in them and their very titles suggest their content: *Venkala Chilai allathu Kanniyin Mutham* (The Bronze Statue, or, the Virgin's Kiss); *Kanakangi allathu Kalugumalai Kallan* (Kanakangi, or, the Dacoit of Kalugumalai); *Ponnuswamy Thevar Kolai* (The Murder of Ponnuswamy Thevar); *Ratnapuri Rahasyam* (The Mystery of Ratnapuri); *Pachai Mothirathin Marmam* (The Mystery of the Emerald Ring), etc. Most of these novels flaunted the subtitle 'a detective story': a signpost for the new reader. The advertisements also emphasized the suspense, thrills, and titillation in store. The advertisements are replete with terms such as 'terrific', 'rapturous', 'magnificent', 'fantastic', 'heart-warming', 'romantic', etc. One advertisement even promised narration at 'the speed of electricity' with infinite twists and turns! Fantasy and melodrama were the dominant elements in these novels.

Every periodical worth the name published novels in serial form during this period. *Ananda Bodhini* and *Vivekodhayam*, even as early as their first editorials, stated that novels would be published in serial form in their issues.[7] *Ananda Bodhini*'s sister publication, *Manamohini*, published only novels.[8] *Naveenagam*, *Naveenam* (both terms were neologisms for 'novel' based on the semantic of novelty), and *Novel* were monthlies and, as the titles make clear, devoted to serializing novels.[9] It is said that Vaduvur Duraiswamy Iyengar ran a journal *Manoranjani* during 1919–27 especially for the purpose of serializing his novels, as did Vai.Mu. Kothainayaki Ammal with her *Jaganmohini*.

[6] Ka.Naa. Su[bramanyam], 'Tamil Novelgal', *Chandrodhayam*, 11 (5), 30 September 1946.

[7] *Ananda Bodhini*, 1 (1), July 1915, editorial; *Vivekodhayam*, 1 (1), April 1916, editorial.

[8] See advertisement in *Ananda Bodhini*, April 1934.

[9] See advertisement in *Lakshmi*, August 1924.

J.R. Rangaraju (1875–1959), Arani Kuppuswamy Mudaliar (1867–1925), and Vaduvur Duraiswamy Iyengar (1880–1942) were acknowledged masters of this variety of fiction: 'Arani' and 'Vaduvur' eventually became shorthand for popular fiction and were often used in the plural. These writers were later joined by Vai.Mu. Kothainayaki Ammal (1901–1960) who wrote maudlin stories, and S.S. Arunagirinathar (1895–1974). Their novels were extremely popular and went into numerous reprints. For instance, J.R. Rangaraju's *Rajambal* saw 23 impressions by 1928, and as a contemporaneous journal observed, it achieved this 'without advertisements, high discounts or [remaindering at] half rates at the Srirangam fair.'[10] By about the same time, Rangaraju's *Chandrakanta* had seen 13 impressions, *Mohanasundaram* 12, *Anantakrishnan* 10, and *Rajendran* 9.[11]

There is further evidence attesting to the popularity of these novels. A number of Rangaraju's novels were staged. Stalwarts of the Tamil theatre such as M. Kandaswamy Mudaliar and Avvai T.K. Shanmugam adapted his novels for their plays. While Pammal Sambanda Mudaliar was paid only Rs 10 per staging, Rangaraju was paid as much as Rs 30.[12] Rangaraju's *Rajambal* was also made into a film. *Menaka* (1935), reputed to be the first Tamil social, was based on Vaduvur's novel of the same name. *Digambara Samiyar*, also based on his novel, was a big hit in the early 1950s. As many as five of Vai.Mu. Kothainayaki Ammal's novels were made into films.

It is said that when S.M. Natesa Sastri first published his detective novel *Dhanavan* in 1894, there were few takers. But then, as *Amirtaguna Bodhini* remarked in 1932, 'That time had passed. Now it's detective novels that command demand.'[13]

While the remarkable growth of the Tamil novel is too obvious to be missed, we do not have sufficient data to quantify this phenomenon.

[10] Review of *Rajambal* in *Amirtaguna Bodhini*, 15 August 1928.

[11] See advertisement in J.R. Rangaraju, *Mohanasundaram* (12th impression, Chennai: Author, 1927).

[12] Avvai T.K. Shanmugam, *Enathu Nataka Valkai* (My Life on the Stage; 1972, rpnt. Chennai: Vanathi Pathippagam, 1986), pp. 134–5, 174, 184–5, 328–9.

[13] *Amirtaguna Bodhini*, 16 July 1932.

The annual Review and Analysis of Books registered, prepared by the Registrar of Books, unfortunately do not give a language-wise split. However, Table 3.1 has been constructed from the *Classified Catalogue of Books Registered at the Office of the Registrar of Books*. A caveat is in order here as the colonial administrative machinery to police the book was notoriously weak (see Chapter 6), and the figures pertain only to the books actually registered. There is no way of ascertaining the number of books which escaped the attention of the Registrar of Books. Further, 'Fiction', the head under which novels were classified, included a wide range of moral tales and fables, such as the stories of Alauddin, Alibaba, Panchatantra, and Vikramaditya, apart from straight reprints.

Table 3.1
Tamil Fictional Works, 1890–1925

| Years | No. of Fictional Works |
|---|---|
| 1890–1900 | 39 |
| 1901–1910 | 201 |
| 1911–1915 | 350 |
| 1916–1920 | 244 |
| 1921–1925 | 255 |

*Source*: *Classified Catalogue of Books Registered at the Office of the Registrar of Books*, Government of Madras, vols I–V, Madras, 1961–71

As the table shows, while only 39 and 201 fictional works were published in the last decade of the nineteenth and the first decade of the twentieth centuries respectively, there was a quantum leap in the subsequent quinquennial periods. Even the Registrar of Books, not the most perceptive of observers, was forced to comment on 'the large increase under Fiction (in the vernacular languages).'[14] In fact, novels were so popular that the District Magistrate of Tiruchy, surveying the sorts of reading material available to people in the Swadeshi period,

[14] Review and Analysis of Books (1913), G.O. nos 558–9, Edl (Confidential) (hereafter Confdl), 14 May 1914.

found no less than 114 Tamil novels in a reading room in the small-time town of Lalgudi.[15]

This growth was indeed phenomenal by the standards of Tamil publishing in the age of patronage and during the transition, when writers struggled hard not only to find patronage to meet expenses but also to interest a sufficient number of readers and buyers in their books (Chapters 1 and 2).

More important, the novel was becoming the art form par excellence of a growing middle class, and it was due in large measure to this middle class that Tamil publishing broke decisively from patronage and made inroads into the market, in the process making the Tamil book a commodity.[16] But the Tamil middle class, much like the English working class,[17] was not born at an appointed time: it was present at its own making. The Tamil middle class attempted to gain a consciousness of a class for itself through, inter alia, a series of ideological struggles against the novel in its popular manifestation. It was through these debates that the novel was indigenized or 'domesticated' in Tamil literary culture.[18] Therefore it is crucial to elaborate on and understand these struggles, especially because the middle class had hegemonic aspirations. In these debates a whole range of issues, from the content and printrun of books to the social composition of readers and their reading practices, not to speak of the construction of a canon of modern classics, came in for deliberation by middle-class intellectuals.

[15] G.O. no. 363, Edl (Confdl), 10 June 1911.

[16] See K. Kailasapathy's brilliant study of the rise of the Tamil novel, *Tamil Novel Ilakkiyam* (Novel Literature in Tamil; 1968, rpnt. Chennai: New Century Book House, 1987), esp. pp. 25–37, 203–5. He argues that the birth of the Tamil novel is directly linked to the emergence of the middle class. Drawing attention to the middle-class background of the novelists, he demonstrates how the novels reflect the travails of their class. For Kailasapathy, the emergence of the short story in the early 1930s is explained by the maturing of the Tamil middle class.

[17] E.P. Thompson, *The Making of the English Working Class* (New York: Vintage, 1968), Preface.

[18] I draw the evocative term 'domestication' from Amitav Ghosh, 'The Indian Story', *Civil Lines I*, 1994, p. 44.

This was largely to determine the course of mainstream Tamil publishing during the century. So we must turn to debates surrounding the novel to gain a better understanding of the emerging Tamil publishing world.

## The Critique of Popular Fiction

The spate of novels that deluged Tamil society did not go unnoticed. It was widely commented upon by a number of perceptive middle-class intellectuals.[19] The following formula, delineated by a writer in *Suthanthira Sangu* on how to write a popular novel, aptly sums up the nature of popular novels as the critics saw them.

1. The title should pertain to a woman. There should be some novelty in the name. *Miss Leela Kamini*, *Fashionable Vallibhai*—titles should be of this sort.
2. Don't worry about the story. You can adapt the novels of Reynolds or Le Quex. There should be at least a dozen lovers, half a dozen whores, ten dozen thieves, and a few detectives.
3. For a start there should be a murder. At frequent intervals there should be interesting twists and turns. There should also be a conflagration at some point. These are the characteristics of the modern novel.
4. There is money only if there is titillation. Beware, if you write like Madhaviah or Rajam Aiyar, your book won't sell.[20]

The intellectuals who critiqued the popular novels differed on many points but they all agreed on the above characterization of these novels.

Saivite intellectuals and champions of the Tamil 'renaissance' were among the first to raise their voice against the rise of the novel. Thiru.Vi. Kalyanasundara Mudaliar (Thiru.Vi.Ka.) claimed to have never read novels in his life after Reverend G.G. Fox, the principal of Wesleyan College where he studied, warned him of their dubious

[19] For the full text of the various critiques of the novel discussed in this section, see A.R. Venkatachalapathy, *Novelum Vasippum: Oru Varalattru Parvai* (Novels and Reading: A Historical Perspective; Nagercoil: Kalachuvadu Pathippagam, 2002), appendices.

[20] *Suthanthira Sangu*, 8 July 1933.

moral effects. In any case, it is hardly surprising that Thiru.Vi.Ka., with his near-puritan beliefs, despised novels. His criticism of novels was that they were too concerned with the exterior of human life and did not penetrate deep into the hearts of men. 'Can [novels] open the inner recesses of the heart? Can they nurture morality? Profundity of thought is required for the flowering of the inner heart and the attainment of morality. Can these lowly novels induce profound thinking?' So he dubbed all novels trash.[21] When it came to women reading novels he was even more strident in his criticism (an issue we will consider in detail later).

Maraimalai Adigal, champion of the Pure Tamil Movement which was launched to free the Tamil language from the influence of Sanskrit, held similar views, though he too tried his hand at novel-writing. In the English preface to one of his novels he wrote: 'In most of the Tamil novels that I have come across, I find neither plot nor character delineation, neither a true representation of life nor a chaste and felicitous diction of language. The story chiefly turns only upon love passion—love in its most degraded type and grossly earthy form [. . .] [I]n all the Tamil novels published [over the last] decade or two the diction is rendered unwholesome by the introduction of unassimilated foreign words [. . .] and by the unhappy combination of words and phrases [. . ..]'[22]

*Kumaran*, the journal run by S. Murugappa—a staunch Saivite in the 1920s who later moved over to the Self-Respect Movement under 'Periyar' E.V. Ramasamy—was also carping in its criticism of popular fiction: 'but for a few exceptions, most of the novels that get published are plain trash. They are full of murder, theft, detection, whoring, and anarchism. But for these the novels would never have been written.'[23] And when *Kalaimagal* wrote, 'These stories that are written

[21] Thiru.Vi. Kalyanasundara Mudaliar, *Valkai Kurippukkal* (Autobiographical Notes; 1944, rpnt. Chennai: Saiva Siddhanta Works Publishing Society, 1982), pp. 106–7.

[22] Maraimalai Adigal, *Kumudavalli, Naganattarasi* (Pallavaram: Author, 1921), p. vii.

[23] *Kumaran* 2 (6), September 1923. For more of *Kumaran*'s views, see 3 (3), June 1924; 2 (1), April 1923; 2 (10), January 1924; 6 (4), January 1928.

as novels, oh! They make their readers lustful and drown them in the ocean of immorality',[24] it was only expressing the views of the Tamil scholarly world. M.S. Purnalingam Pillai, one of the most respected scholars of the period, in his history of Tamil literature written in English, said much the same: 'Arni Kuppuswamy Mudaliar has flooded the market with his novels which are adaptations of Reynolds [. . .] What was pure and instructive at first became lax and lewd, and though the plots are well knit, they cannot be placed in the hands of boys and virgins with safety [. . .] In most cases the present-day novelist cares less for style than for producing an impression or tickling his readers.'[25]

The nationalist and conservative critique was launched by Subramania Siva, a firebrand speaker who was one of the earliest to be sentenced during the Swadeshi Movement. In his literary monthly *Jnanabhanu* he attacked novels for their corrupting influence, and more generally the debasing effect of Western values on Indian culture.[26] This Hindu nationalist critique was extended by V.V.S. Aiyar. In a pioneering article titled 'Marumalarchi' (Renaissance), published first in the 1918 annual supplement of *Swadesamitran*, he wrote: 'when it became clear that "novels" sell well, many petty-minded people started adapting hundreds of obscene stories written by Reynolds, which are despised in the English world', and argued that even an epidemic of plague and rheumatic fever was less harmful than these degenerate novels.[27] *Sri Ramakrishna Vijayam*, the monthly organ of the Sri Ramakrishna Mission, urged people to read puranas rather than be corrupted by novels.[28] Subramania Bharati, too, shared these views and felt many Tamil writers made money by adapting substandard

[24] *Kalaimagal*, 2 (2), February 1914.

[25] M.S. Purnalingam Pillai, *Tamil Literature* (Munnirpallam: Bibliotheca, 1929), p. 368.

[26] *Jnanabhanu*, 3 (1), April 1915; 3 (4), July 1915; 2 (2), May 1914.

[27] *Va. Ve. Su. Aiyar Katturaikal* (Essays of V.V.S. Aiyar; Tirunelveli: S.N. Somayajulu, 1981), p. 28. V.V.S. Aiyar expressed similar views in *Kumaran*, 2 (1), April 1923. J. Vijayaraghavan in his article on Tamil novels in *Vasantham* 4 (1), April 1945 quotes from V.V.S. Aiyar's articles in *Desabhaktan* and his preface to *Valmiki Vijayam* which contain a similar critique of the novel.

[28] An article by one Ramapriyan reproduced in *Navasakti*, 16 February 1927.

English novels.[29] As late as the 1950s C. Rajagopalachari, contrasting novels with puranas, described their function as 'the killing of time' (*kala haranam*).[30] *Suthanthira Sangu*, quoted earlier, which too operated within the nationalist discourse, criticized popular fiction on similar lines. Satirizing the imaginary author (a thinly veiled reference to Vaduvur Duraiswamy Iyengar) of *Miss Thalukku Sundari* (Miss Seductive Damsel), who had written 27 novels, averaging 3 volumes per novel, it sarcastically asked: 'What novels! What sublime portrayals! Would they not weigh three stone! If all 27 books were fed to a cooking stove, seven or eight people might not only get hot water for their bath but also be able to cook their meals. If one gave a set of these books to a chemist, might he not use it a whole year to pack drugs? Or else if all 27 novels were dumped, wouldn't they fill a whole dustbin of the Kumbakonam municipality?'[31]

Intellectuals who valorized literary aspects of the novel genre joined this chorus of criticism. The views expressed by the journal *Lakshmi* in its review of A. Madhaviah's *Muthu Meenakshi* and *Kusikar Kutti Kathaigal* embody the force of opinion within this segment of critique:

> In this age, when printing machines have become legion and the business in paper has expanded, novels have started to proliferate like termites [. . .] As every pen pusher has taken to novel writing in Tamilnadu, the harm caused by contemporary novels is not little. That those who cannot even get their 'r's right have taken to writing can only be attributed to bad times for the Tamil language. One or two playboys, a couple of shameless damsels, a detective Govindan or Gopalan, one Agavali zamindar—the Tamil novel is complete. Contemporary Tamil novels spread the habits, customs, and attitudes of foreign countries and send the Tamil people tumbling into an abyss of immorality. Tamil people who know not the true novel are gobbling up this trash like fowl eating termites.[32]

[29] *Bharati Noolgal: Katturaigal*, vol. 3 (Chennai: Bharati Prachuralayam, n.d.), pp. 85–6.

[30] C. Rajagopalachari, *Mahabharatam* (1955, rpnt. Chennai: Vanathi Pathippagam, 2000), p. 133.

[31] *Suthanthira Sangu* 8 July 1933. Also see the issue dated 4 February 1933, the article entitled 'Novel Kuppaithotti' (The Dustbin for Novels).

[32] Reproduced in *Panchamirtam*, 1 (7), October 1924. There are two 'r's'

Madhaviah shared these views and wrote on identical lines in his review of J.R. Rangaraju's *Vijayaraghavan.*[33] Further, in his journal *Panchamirtam* he published an article on novels written by one A. Rangaswami Iyengar. This likened novels to garbage and called for a thorough purge.[34] P. Kothandaraman of the Aurobindo Ashram expressed identical views in the renowned nationalist-novelist K.S. Venkataramani's *Bharatamani*.[35] Writers of the famed *Manikkodi* camp too critiqued popular fiction on such lines. Pudumaippithan's 'Thirukkural Seitha Thirukkoothu' is evidently a parody of such whodunit stories.[36] In his articles, too, Pudumaippithan makes mocking references to detective stories.[37] Ku.Pa. Rajagopalan, reviewing the Tamil translation of Tagore's *Kumudhini*, remarked that detective novels were corrupting literary tastes.[38] Interestingly, such criticism was not confined to Tamilnadu. It found echoes in the Tamil-speaking areas of Sri Lanka as well.[39]

Thus, all middle-class intellectuals shared a contempt for the new cultural form and their critique revolved around the same themes. First, all the novels were seen as vapid translations of degenerate English novels. The early Victorian popular novelist G.W.M. Reynolds (1814–1879) is ubiquitous in this context. Considering how widely Reynolds was read in the early twentieth century, it is curious that every memoir is apologetically prefaced with words to the effect that no one except the memoirist is likely to have heard of the novelist. Meenakshi

---

in the Tamil alphabet: the hard and the medium. Getting them right is a sign of good education. Govindan is the detective–hero in the novels of J.R. Rangaraju.

[33] *Panchamirtam*, 2 (6), September 1925.

[34] Ibid., 2 (6), September 1925.

[35] *Bharatamani*, 3 (4), 22 October 1939.

[36] A.R. Venkatachalapathy (ed.), *Pudumaippithan Kathaikal* (Stories of Pudumaippithan; Nagercoil: Kalachuvadu Pathippagam, 2000), pp. 69–76.

[37] A.R. Venkatachalapathy (ed.), *Pudumaippithan Katturaikal* (Essays of Pudumaippithan; Nagercoil: Kalachuvadu Pathippagam, 2002).

[38] *Manikkodi*, 4 (8), 15 December 1936.

[39] Naa. Subramaniam, *Eelathu Tamil Novel Ilakkiyam* (Tamil Novel Literature in Eelam; Jaffna: Muthamizh Veliyeedu Kazhagam, 1978), pp. 23–5.

Mukherjee's prescient suggestion that Reynolds was a household name across India has been substantiated by research across the regions.[40] If the reminiscences of Regi Siriwardena, the gifted Sri Lankan writer and translator, are any proof, Reynolds' appeal was spread across the colonies.[41] So striking is the absence of other popular names (such as Charles Garvice, William Le Quex, and Edward Bulwer-Lytton) in latter-day recollections—as against contemporaneous accounts—that one may be forgiven for harbouring the suspicion that 'Reynolds' serves as a metaphor for the whole class of popular fiction.

It was alleged that many of these adaptations were clandestine. Often the same novel was adapted by more than one writer without this being openly stated, and consequently readers were taken for a ride.[42] Perhaps the most caustic comment in this regard was made by T. Chelvakesavaraya Mudaliar in his English preface to the Tamil translation of William Le Quex's *Whoso Findeth a Wife*: 'Many of the so-called Tamil adaptations of English novels are misleading, and most of them appear uncouth in Tamil like the English people of the Salvation Army in Hindu dress.'[43]

The novels were seen as the work of uneducated hacks with mercenary intent. For *Lakshmi*, these novelists could not even get their 'r's right. As a remedial measure it exhorted learned men not to look

[40] Meenakshi Mukherjee, *Realism and Reality: The Novel and Society in India* (Delhi: Oxford University Press, 1985), p. 6. Also see Priya Joshi, *Another Country*; Francesca Orsini, 'Detective Novels: A Commercial Genre in Nineteenth-Century North India', in Stuart Blackburn and Vasudha Dalmia (eds), *India's Literary History: Essays on the Nineteenth Century* (Delhi: Permanent Black, 2004).

[41] Regi Siriwardena, *Working Underground: The LSSP in Wartime: A Memoir of Happenings and Personalities* (Colombo: International Centre for Ethnic Studies, 1999), pp. 3–4.

[42] *Amirtaguna Bodhini*, 16 July 1932; *Katha Mohana Ranjitham* 1915, reproduced in *Kumari Malar*, 31 (4), July 1974. Ka.Naa. Subramanyam says that J.R. Rangaraju was convicted for plagiarism for *Varadarajan* and that this ultimately spelt the end of his writing career: *Ilakkiya Chathanaiyalargal* (Literary Achievers; Chidambaram: Manivasagar Noolagam, 1985), pp. 188–9. I have not been able to find any evidence of this.

[43] *Ellal allathu Nalla Manaiviye Nalla Porul* (Chennai: n.p., 1914), Preface.

down upon novel writing and take it up themselves.[44] It was contended that the Western values expressed in the novels were baneful and injurious to Indian/Tamil society and culture. The common fear was that Western ideals were materialistic, and these were seen to corrupt the spiritual life of India's people. What was worse, novels were seen to titillate base sexual passion. Again and again the point made was that novels were full of obscenity, adultery, and debauchery. So widespread was this complaint that readers took to frequently reading such novels in secret. And, as always, the supposedly pernicious effects of such novels on women were simply dreaded.

Common to all this criticism was contempt for the novel. This contempt is nowhere more explicit than in a resolution passed at the Thondamandalam High School, by a group of respectable men, when the Government of Madras sought to prosecute the publishers of the Tamil classics *Kavadi Chindu* and *Virali Vidu Thoothu* on grounds of obscenity. They argued that these works 'were written only to benefit the learned, the devoted, and so very limited circles of men, whose minds these [obscene] passages of rare occurrence could not poison. The general public of the present day do not or are not likely to read such works [. . .] If the Police wish to protect the minds of the common people, the right books that they have to direct their efforts against are the low-priced Tamil novels coming daily out of the press.'[45]

### Women and Popular Fiction

Novels being published in ever-increasing numbers, more and more women were drawn to them.[46] In the debates discussed earlier, women are often mentioned as readers. *Suthanthira Sangu* remarked that women enjoyed heavenly bliss while reading novels.[47] *Panchamirtam*

[44] A. Subramania Bharati in his preface to Vai.Mu. Kothainayaki Ammal, *Shanbaga Vijayam* (Chennai: Jaganmohini, 1927), pp. 4–5, 7.

[45] Clipping from the *Hindu*, 31 July 1912 in G.O. no. 289, Judl (Confdl), 11 February 1913. This point is reiterated by A. Subramania Bharati, Preface, p. 4.

[46] S. Chandrasekhar, *A Report on South Indian Reading Habits* (Chennai: Southern Languages Book Trust, [1960]), p. 12, observes that 'Tamil women read more than other women.'

[47] *Suthanthira Sangu*, 8 July 1933.

said women were addicted to novels next only to jewels.[48] The most stinging comment was made by A. Subramania Bharati (not the poet), who said novels were being mostly read by women who had no work and by menstruating women who had nothing worthwhile to do while in ritual seclusion.[49] V.V.S. Aiyar went to the extent of squarely blaming women for the proliferation of pulp fiction.[50]

Given the centrality of what is termed 'the women's question' in the political agenda of colonial intellectuals, it is hardly surprising that this issue was taken up in right earnest. Colonial intellectuals, in their struggle against colonialism, had worked out a dichotomy: material/spiritual and outer/inner, which could be extended to man/woman and world/home. While the West was seen to be superior in the material sphere, India could hold its own in the spiritual sphere. Thus only a selective appropriation of Western achievements, namely, science and technology, needed to be made, even as Indian spiritual values had to be clung to. The spiritual purity of home (and woman) was to be the terrain where no quarter could be yielded to the West.[51]

Given this understanding of the women's question, would (male) intellectuals permit pulp fiction to hold 'their' women in its corrupting tentacles? The point is made most dramatically in Thiru.Vi. Ka.'s exemplary text on Tamil womanhood:

> Young women should not be permitted to hear stories of revelry, pseudo novels, and other such stuff; nor should they even touch such books. Parents should take special care in this regard. These pseudo novels are corrupting the woman's world. Women should realize that pseudo novels will ruin their lives, like poison. I know many women, who, reading these pseudo novels and pseudo plays, have ruined their peaceful lives and later rued it. Dear children, don't ever read these novels; don't even touch them. Your life will be ruined. You will suffer disease and ailments. Why did the good Lord make you—to wither away at a tender age? To

[48] *Panchamirtam*, 2 (6), September 1925.

[49] A. Subramania Bharati, Preface, p. 4.

[50] Quoted in *Vasantham*, 4 (1), April 1945.

[51] This passage draws on Partha Chatterjee, 'The Nationalist Resolution of the Women's Question', in Kumkum Sangari and Sudesh Vaid (eds), *Recasting Women: Essays in Colonial History* (New Delhi: Kali for Women, 1988).

suffer disease? To be despised by your brothers, relatives, and those around you? No. No. 'You must become mothers; you must lead happy lives': this is the divine purpose. You who were born to fulfil this sublime goal, should you ruin your life by going crazy after despicable novels? Don't read these pseudo novels. Parents and teachers must take care to keep these pseudo novels away from the sight of young women.[52]

The subconscious male fear of a woman's sexuality unshackled is transparent. Novels were a potent threat to traditional male control of the woman. The hysteric male hostility to novels that might titillate women and cause them to rebel against their traditional bondage to hegemonic ideas of docility and domestic virtue must be understood in this light.[53] The noted writer and translator Saraswathi Ramnath recollects in an interview that, during her girlhood in the mid-1930s, girls were not generally permitted to read novels and that novels were often put away in the loft, out of reach of children.[54] Kumudhini (1905–86), another writer, also observed in the mid-1930s that she never read novels. In a humorous essay by the renowned writer Va.Ra., the mother-in-law and sister-in-law, stereotypical tormentors, rebuke a new bride: 'If you cannot do household chores, go to your father's home! Or else ask him to send money to hire a cook. Did you think you'd stretch your legs out and read novels here?'[55] And in this dialogue from the novel *Chandrasekari*, Gunavathy, a novelist, meets the heroine Chandrasekari and asks her if she has ever read her novels. Upon getting a reply in the negative she asks:

*Gunavathy*: Reading novels has beneficial effects—why not read them?

*Chandrasekari*: Had I known reading novels is good, I'd have read them. Or if I'd known it's harmless, I might have yet read them.

*Guna*: So you seem to believe reading novels is harmful, right?

[52] *Pennin Perumai allathu Valkai Thunai* (The Glory of Women or Life's Support; Chennai: Sadhu Achukkudam, 1927), pp. 97–8.
[53] See the editorial on women and novels in *Ananda Bodhini*, 2 (6), December 1916.
[54] *Subamangala*, March 1992.
[55] Va.Ra., *Valkai Vinodangal* (Oddities of Life; 1947, rpnt. Chennai: Alliance & Co., 1990), p. 90.

> *Chandra*: I have neither a good opinion of novels nor bad. My uncle happened one day to instruct me against reading novels. Ever since I haven't.[56]

All this is testimony to successful policing by middle-class patriarchs,[57] and of avuncular men keeping little women in check. Perhaps they were successful to a considerable degree, but women's appetite for reading had been whetted and there was an ever-growing demand for stories that women could 'safely' read. It was at this juncture that Vai.Mu. Kothainayaki Ammal entered the scene. Born in a Brahmin middle-class family with scholarly antecedents, she started writing novels around 1924, about a decade after the beginnings of popular fiction. Her sentimental stories, woven around middle-class family life, were an instant success. The social consequences of her fiction were liberating, at least in the sense of opening up a new arena: now women could read without fear for these novels held little subversive potential. Between 1924 and the 1950s she wrote no less than 115 novels. The monthly *Jaganmohini*, in which she published all her novels in serial form, sold as many as 10,000 copies a month.[58] By 1940 women constituted an important segment of Tamil readers. So prevalent had the reading habit become among women that women—said a columnist in *Ananda Vikatan* humorously—were of two types: those who read novels and those who did not.[59]

[56] Quoted in P.G. Sundararajan and S. Sivapathasundaram, *Tamil Novel: Noorandu Varalarum Valarchiyum* (The Tamil Novel: A Century of Growth and Development; Chennai: Christian Literature Society, 1977), p. 132.

[57] *Kalaimagal*, vol. 7, May 1935, p. 441.

[58] Biographical details on Kothainayaki Ammal are drawn from the biography by Aranga Srinivasan, *Eluthulaga Nayaki* (The Heroine of the World of Letters; Chennai: Sekar Pathippagam, 1988). For additional information, see R. Prema, *Vai.Mu. Kothainayaki Ammal* (New Delhi: Sahitya Akademi, 2001).

[59] *Ananda Vikatan*, 15 (34), 25 August 1940. For corresponding moments of liberation in colonial Maharashtra and Bengal, which come about when women first become readers and writers, see, respectively, Meera Kosambi's several essays in her *Crossing Thresholds: Feminist Essays in Social History* (Ranikhet: Permanent Black, 2007), and idem, *Feminist Vision or 'Treason Against Men'? Kashibai Kanitkar and the Engendering of Marathi Literature* (Ranikhet: Permanent Black, 2008); and Tanika Sarkar, 'A Book of Her Own, A Life of

Thus a significant aspect of Tamil publishing in the inter-war period was the large presence of women as readers. As *Kalaimagal* of Pondicherry observed, women who had earlier been reading chapbooks and 'big letter' editions were now reading novels.[60]

## Responding to Criticism

The volley of criticism that the novel had to face for a decade or two from around the time of World War I is clear enough. How this critique was confronted by those directly involved in the production of popular fiction will bring into focus the question of the hegemonic hold that the middle class was struggling to acquire in Tamil society.

*Ananda Bodhini* was one of the first to respond to critiques of the novel. This was the journal which published all of Arani Kuppuswamy Mudaliar's numerous novels, both in serial form and later as separate books. It enjoyed immense success, claiming a 5,000-strong subscription list within a year of its inception in 1916.[61] When a correspondent from a village in Rasipuram taluk of Salem district wrote to its editor about a lecture delivered in a local club on the undesirability of reading novels, the editor responded to say that only when both good and evil were made evident could readers understand the need to keep off evil. He cited a Tamil proverb to the effect that only a person who has been out in the sun will understand the importance of shade.[62] *Ananda Bodhini*'s response to criticism continued on the same lines throughout its career. It conceded that there were indeed corrupting novels. But that, equally, there were others which could lead people on the right path.[63]

Arani Kuppuswamy Mudaliar used the same logic to defend

---

Her Own: The Autobiography of a Nineteenth-Century Woman', in idem, *Hindu Wife, Hindu Nation: Community, Religion and Cultural Nationalism* (Delhi: Permanent Black, 2001), pp. 95–134.

[60] *Kalaimagal*, January 1916.

[61] *Ananda Bodhini*, 1 (12), June 1916.

[62] Ibid., 5 (2), August 1919.

[63] Ibid., 10 (4), December 1924.

himself.[64] 'Dear readers, just like my other novels, this one contains no repulsive aspects nor words not fit to be read by chaste women. Some say that stories which speak of evil deeds and evil people should never be read. This is an erroneous view. Only if we get to know the actions of evil people and the price they pay for it later will we resolve to keep clear of such evil—out of fear and repulsion.' Panaiyappa Chettiar, another novelist, defended himself with the same plea in his 1929 preface to *Kanthimathi*.[65] In brief, the self-defence by popular novelists was set within the discourse of middle-class intellectuals. They did not attempt to challenge the terms of the debate and question the moral pontification. Other novelists too conformed to this discourse by remaining silent and continuing to write as usual. All the endings of their novels paid lip service to morality, with culprits punished and nobility rewarded.

The relationship between popular novelists and their critics reveals other complexities, for writers and their critics were in a dialectical relationship, constantly interacting with each other. The novel as art form was becoming so predominant in the inter-war period that the critics themselves had to write novels to offer counter-models.[66] A. Subramania Bharati and Subramania Siva wrote novels, though their attempts fell flat. When the Tamil scholar K.R. Govindaraja Mudaliar wrote novels, they were neither worse nor better than most popular novels.[67] (Only he got his 'r's right!) Maraimalai Adigal, too, only ended up adapting in chaste, high-flown Tamil a Reynolds novel.

[64] *Karkottai* (1919, rpnt. Chennai: Ananda Bodhini, 1955), Preface. Arani Kuppuswamy Mudaliar used the same argument on other occasions too. See the preface to his *Krishnaveni allathu Athisaya Marma Churangam*, quoted in R. Mohan (ed.), *Novel Valarchi* (The Development of the Novel; Chennai: Manivasagar Pathippagam, 1989), p. 187; also *Madana Bushanam allathu Iranthaval Pilaithathu* (rpnt. Chennai: Ananda Bodhini, 1952), Preface.

[65] Quoted in Ve. Seethalakshmi, *Tamil Novelgal: Akaravarisai* (Tamil Novels: An Alphabetical Bibliography; Chennai: International Institute of Tamil Studies, 1985), p. xxvi.

[66] Curiously, this is also roughly the period when the English novel, via theoretician-practitioners such as Henry James, E.M. Forster, and Virginia Woolf, was asserting its right to be recognized as an elevated form of art.

[67] See his *Mathana Manohari* (Chennai, 1924).

This situation perhaps explains why even a radical novel written by Muvaloor Ramamirtam Ammaiyar, critiquing the Devadasi system, had to have a saucy title which translates as 'The Wile Net of the Devadasis, or, a Playboy Turned Wise' (1938).

This contradiction was to be resolved only in the late 1930s.

## Towards Respectability

The Tamil novel's climb from notoriety to respectability is closely linked with the fortunes of *Ananda Vikatan* and its de facto editor, 'Kalki' R. Krishnamurty (1899–1954). S.S. Vasan (the movie mogul of Gemini Studios fame), its publisher and de jure editor, started his career as a mail order businessman and advertising agent. Later he wrote and published a few detective novels and some obscene illustrated books too.[68] But when he acquired a tottering humour magazine, *Ananda Vikatan*, in February 1928, he adopted a new business tactic. Abandoning his earlier ways, he hit upon a successful mix of humour, fiction, and cartoons with a dash of nationalism. Besides, he conducted crossword puzzle contests with fabulous prizes, which gave a boost to *Ananda Vikatan*'s circulation. In this business venture Vasan recruited the services of Kalki towards the end of 1928. Kalki had begun his career as a sub-editor in Thiru.Vi.Ka.'s *Navasakti*.[69] He had later joined C. Rajagopalachari at his Thiruchengode Gandhi Ashram and edited the temperance journal *Vimosanam*. Kalki remained *Ananda Vikantan*'s de facto editor till 1940.

As a young boy Kalki had been an avid reader of detective fiction. Yet he too criticized popular fiction.[70] 'Some time ago I chanced to read a couple of recent Tamil novels. Oh, I cannot express my horror. Before I could get past a few pages, I felt as if I was rolling in the gutter. Well, even when one rolls in the gutter, one can cleanse oneself with soap. But the filth that dirties the mind isn't as easily

[68] See advertisements in *Lakshmi*, 3 (9), April 1926; 3 (10), May 1926.

[69] Sunda, *Ponniyin Puthalvar: Kalkiyin Valkai Varalaru* (Ponni's Son: A Biography of Kalki), pp. 204–5.

[70] See Kalki's preface to the Tamil translation of R.K. Narayan's *Swami and Friends*, *Swamiyum Snehithargalum* (Chennai: Ananda Vikatan, 1939).

cleansed. Only after sleeping for a couple of nights did I feel sufficiently clean. It seemed to me the right punishment to anyone who gives such a book to young men and women is to have his hands chopped off.'[71] For all this, it is certain that Kalki learnt some of the tricks of the trade from the novels he claimed to abhor. Take for instance, his acclaimed *Thyaga Bhoomi* (1939). The story has all the ingredients of popular fiction in ample measure. A cruel stepmother, adultery, a wayward husband, a rags-to-riches story, a lost child, a bank fraud, a sensational court case, and a happy ending. But there was one crucial aspect which gave the novel its respectability—nationalism. The Congress makes its appearance at the most unlikely places. An old conservative Brahmin, Sambu Sastri, all of a sudden dons khadi and leads a procession: jumping into the Congress bandwagon is implicitly equated with renouncing worldly life. In its climax, the wayward and adulterous husband, guilty of defrauding a bank and hardhearted enough to legally press for the restitution of his conjugal rights over an unwilling wife, is condoned by his wife thanks to the Congress because he joins her in picketing and courting arrest. In Kalki's fiction, nationalism is a rootless wonder. Converts to the Congress creed are won over in a jiffy; not for Kalki the tortuous (and, as some would argue, imperfect) process of nationalist mobilization.

Consequently, Kalki's fiction was a resounding success. His biographer writes, 'Three lakhs of Tamils read his *Thyaga Bhoomi* when it was serialized in *Ananda Vikatan* from the new year of 1939. Their eagerness could be seen in the way they jostled with each other to buy *Vikatan* at the stalls. Similar incidents could be seen at railway stations where *Vikatan* consignments landed. Many read it at the railway station either out of sheer eagerness or because there would be many to compete for the copy at their home.'[72] This sounds dangerously close to the earlier demand for popular fiction.

Kalki's political affiliations propped him up too. All through his life he was part of Rajagopalachari's clique. He was an important member of its literary wing too, which was under the magnetic

[71] *Ananda Vikatan*, 10 June 1933.

[72] Sunda, *Ponniyin Puthalvar*, p. 455.

influence of T.K. Chidambaranatha Mudaliar. In their literary world they tried to construct a Tamil tradition which excluded Sangam literature and the medieval scholastic commentaries. *Kambaramayanam* was given a central place and Tamil literary tradition constructed around it. Kalki was accorded pride of place in the pantheon of modern writers alongside Kavimani Desigavinayakam Pillai. When T.K. Chidambaranatha Mudaliar[73] and Professor S. Vaiyapuri Pillai[74] contributed forewords to his books, they had put the stamp of respectability to the Tamil novel. Now—

> we can see women grinding batter [for idlis] with one hand and holding Kalki's book in the other; rocking the cradle with one hand and reading the book in the other. That school boys and girls read *Vikatan* in classrooms is the frequent complaint of teachers. Apart from provision stores, sweetmeat shops, and retailers of mangoes under mango trees, we can see people smoking and reading Kalki in first- and second-class railway compartments. In every nook and cranny of Tamilnadu these stories make people laugh, be startled, and cry. Tamil readership has now reached forty and fifty thousand.[75]

With Kalki the contradiction—which emerged in the Tamil cultural sphere on account of the rise of the novel—was more or less resolved in accord with the preferred goals of the middle class. The 'positive' aspects of popular fiction had been successfully appropriated: thrill, suspense, gripping narrative, pace, unexpected twists, facile prose, sentiment, and melodrama were to be found in good measure in the Kalkian variety of fiction. All these were kept within limits, being deployed in controlled doses to excite and consequently deaden taste and imagination, but never to exceed the boundaries of middle-class

[73] Kalki, *Kanaiyaliyin Kanavu* (1937, rpnt. Chennai: Ananda Vikatan, 1938).
[74] The preface is dated 30 August 1943: Kalki, *Parthipan Kanavu* (Chennai: Bharati Pathippagam, 1952).
[75] T.K. Chidambaranatha Mudaliar's foreword to Kalki, *Kanaiyaliyin Kanavu*, pp. ix–x. Kailasapathy puts across this point more bluntly: 'Using pedestrian themes, in a prose that holds no novelty or creativity, Kalki wrote stories in indifferent Tamil that could be read by the entire family in respectable homes.' Kailasapathy, *Tamil Novel Ilakkiyam*, p. 97.

gentility. To put it metaphorically, women too could now safely read novels held in one hand even as the other ground the batter for *idli* or rocked the baby in the cradle.

It was in the course of debates around the novel that the term '*naaval*' (novel) came to establish itself as the name for the new genre. Until then there had existed a variety of neologisms, such as '*naveenam*', '*naveenagam*', '*pudinam*', etc.—all drawing from the semantics of 'newness' and 'novelty'. That the term '*naaval*' is a homonym and does not require *tarpavam* (Tamilicization) enabled its easy acceptance in Tamil vocabulary.

In another sense, too, the middle class had had their say. This concerned the construction of the canon of works which would constitute the classics of modern Tamil fiction. In the tirades against popular fiction earlier discussed, the self-appointed guardians of culture frequently harked back to the works of Vedanayakam Pillai, Madhaviah, Rajam Aiyar, and Natesa Sastri. By the end of our period their *Prathapa Mudaliar Charithiram*, *Kamalambal Charithiram,* and *Padmavathy Charithiram* had been acclaimed as classics, and their authors pioneering greats. As a corollary, the first three and a half decades of the twentieth century were seen as a Dark Age—until Kalki rode into the scene on *Ananda Vikatan*.[76]

The rise of the novel and its attendant controversies and debates form an interesting part of modern Tamil intellectual history. The course

[76] Kalki's success did not go uncontested. Writers of the *Manikkodi* faction, especially Pudumaippithan, challenged Kalki on artistic grounds, and even accused him of plagiarism. For details, see A.R. Venkatachalapathy (ed.), *Annai Itta Thee* (Nagercoil: Kalachuvadu Pathippagam, 1998). The novels of Arani Kuppuswamy and Vaduvur Duraiswamy Iyengar were reprinted and sold until even the 1950s, though they ceased to be in the limelight. In recent years, however, publisher Alliance & Co. has been reprinting the novels of Vaduvur Duraiswamy Iyengar and Vai.Mu. Kothainayaki. By all accounts these are being consumed with a sense of nostalgia. In a strange inversion, an anthology of present-day pulp fiction has been translated and published in English: *The Blaft Anthology of Tamil Pulp Fiction* (2008). The introduction quotes from *this* research!

of these debates shows the maturing of the Tamil middle class and its self-definition *vis-à-vis* other classes. Given the fact that the middle class entertained hegemonic aspirations and sought to enforce its writ on society at large, especially in the cultural sphere, it had a more direct bearing on the publishing world.

Popular novels were what decisively cut off Tamil publishing from the vestigial conduits of patronage and resolved the dilemmas of the transition to the market. By the 1920s, talk of patronage had effectively ended. Now, in the early inter-war period, attention shifted to the growing number of readers, the widening of the book market, and the proliferation of novels. While these features were welcome to the middle class, it had reservations about the cultural implications of this change. Middle-class intellectuals took up the issue and debated it until the contradiction was resolved with the entry of Kalki and his nationalist novels.

Further, a new mode of reading, i.e. reading in silence, emerged during the inter-war period, and this helped to successfully tackle the new art form, the novel, and ensure its consumption on its own terms (Chapter 7). The emergence of this 'modern' mode of reading, coupled with the fact that it was the cultural practice of a class with hegemonic aspirations, fuelled the expansion of Tamil publishing.

Consequently, through the course of the century mainstream Tamil publishing came into the hands of the middle class. It was now a cultural practice placed squarely in the marketplace. The break with patronage was now absolute. It was only after this rupture that the emergence of the distinct categories/institutions of author, publisher, and printer, which are eminently the products of the market and the book as a commodity, became possible in the world of Tamil book publishing.

# 4

# Authors, Publishers, Printers

Our discussion of Tamil publishing has thus far centred on the material basis of literary production in the second half of the nineteenth century and the early twentieth century. We have seen forms of patronage and their subsequent decline, and the rise of a new genre—the novel—which helped publishing transit away from patronage and into the market. A corollary of this historical change was the somewhat clearer emergence of authors and publishers as identifiable categories, even if their outlines continued fuzzy into the post-transition period. Both these agencies were new, and their emerging shape as separable bodies needs to be closely looked at—as is the role played by printers.

## Authors

In Chapter 1 we saw two sorts of writers: those who wrote thala puranams and other genres of traditional literature, and a new breed of scholar editors who published texts that were originally available only as palm-leaf manuscripts. There were also other varieties of literary producers, mostly teachers, who put together books for educational purposes: 'grammatical primers and glossaries, annotated editions of readers, exercise books, keys and cram books for examinations.'[1] These publications stemmed directly from the new system of education brought in by the British. U.V. Swaminatha Iyer throws light on the nature of this profitable vocation: 'In those days, prescribing text-books was a strange matter. Some part of a text that was only known

[1] Review and Analysis of Books (1892), G.O. nos 184–5, Edl, 10 March 1893.

by name would be prescribed. Somebody would fish out the manuscript from palm leaves and print it as it was. Tamil teachers would teach it in a chaotic fashion making whatever sense, or no sense, of the book.'[2]

Sniffing profits, a number of Tamil teachers and scholars took to this business. Vai.Mu. Sadagoparamanujachari, no mean scholar and literary commentator, was a leading author and publisher in this field. His edition of the medieval grammatical text *Nanool* (an indispensable pedagogical tool) went into numerous editions and is very likely to have sold thousands of copies. Sodasavadhanam Subbaraya Chettiar (a student of Meenakshisundaram Pillai), T.T. Kanakasundaram Pillai, Mu.Ra. Kandasamy Kavirayar, and Pinnathoor Narayanasamy Iyer were some of the more prominent Tamil scholars active in this category. Their textbooks, however, were of a generally poor standard, for as T.T. Kanakasundaram Pillai confessed in a letter to U.V. Swaminatha Iyer about his notes for the matriculation examinations, 'as I wrote this with an urgency to be the first, before others get their Notes out . . . there must be a lot of flaws.'[3]

The sale of such textbooks was largely dependent on 'contacts' within prescribing boards and authorities. U.V. Swaminatha Iyer says that Subbaraya Chettiar would often write to him and Vidwan Thyagaraya Chettiar to recommend his books to their students, especially at the Kumbakonam Government College.[4] The papers of Swaminatha Iyer show that he was inundated with such letters and specimen copies of textbooks.[5]

These publications were generally profitable, involved little labour, and assured a quick turnover. As a result, 'competition among printers and publishers of textbooks for schools [was] generally keen.'[6]

[2] Swaminatha Iyer, *En Charithiram*, p. 519.

[3] Letter to U.V. Swaminatha Iyer, 27 January 1890, U.V.S. Papers.

[4] Swaminatha Iyer, *En Charithiram*, p. 606.

[5] See letters from K.S. Gopalachariyar, 12 February 1898 and 20 January 1906; from G. Rajagopalan, 12 February 1888; from Subbaraya Chettiar, 11 February 1881; from Vai.Mu. Sadagoparamanujachari 19 March 1906; from Pinnathoor Narayanasamy Iyer, January 1906, U.V.S. Papers.

[6] Review and Analysis of Books (1896), G.O. nos 133–4, Edl, 5 March

It is said that even the great Meenakshisundaram Pillai was approached on many occasions with offers to get involved in this business—which he evidently cold-shouldered.[7] C.W. Damodaram Pillai ruefully noted that whereas hack writers of textbooks and their publishers made quick money, scholars such as he lost a fortune trying to publish the classics.[8]

Together with traditional versifiers and scholar-editors these textbook publishers may be termed 'authors', but only in the sense that they performed the rudimentary authorial function of compiling a manuscript. The author as an entirely separate agency producing expressive texts arrived later as the product of a modern sensibility and capitalist society. *Jnanabhanu* was making this distinction clear when it condemned traditional scholars for reprinting old texts without a suitable critical apparatus and appendixes, as against the practice in the West.[9] These 'authors', thus, far from being 'authors' in the modern sense of the word, were not even properly editors. They were neither the 'creators' of an 'original' text with ownership over book titles, nor professionally competent editors establishing and authenticating ancient texts in new formats. Coupled with this absence was the fact that Tamil publishing had not yet stabilized as the commercial activity of specialist book-oriented entrepreneurs or larger investment companies focused on print. Consequently, the two functions, namely, physically producing the text and publishing it (i.e. publicizing, disseminating, accounting for sales, keeping track of its life in the market), were carried on by the same person even during the transitional phase—as in the age of patronage. The patronage phase and ensuing transition show equally a scenario in which the published

---

1897. For a satirical analysis of the same phenomenon in recent times, see Rukun Advani, 'Master English, Native Publisher: A Publishing Perspective on English Studies in India', in Rajeswari Sunder Rajan (ed.), *The Lie of the Land: English Literary Studies in India* (Delhi: Oxford University Press, 1992), pp. 112–29.

[7] *SMPC*, vol. 2, 1940, p. 268.

[8] C.W. Damodaram Pillai, *Kalithogai* (Chennai: Author, 1887).

[9] *Jnanabhanu*, February 1916.

text takes precedence over the 'author'. A number of long and detailed advertisements in contemporary journals merely list the titles of books, seldom identifying their authors.[10] Only when modern expressive texts—the novel, literary criticism, the essay, and the short story—find their feet in the region does the literary producer come to acquire the authority of an author.

In the transitional phase the author was very often a publisher. Subramania Bharati published most of his books, until freed of this function by close friends and admirers—though not even these were publishers publishing works along strict business lines. All through his long and productive career U.V. Swaminatha Iyer published books on his own. Only late in his life did his son S. Kalyanasundara Iyer help him discharge this function. A. Madhaviah, among the early novelists, published his novels, short stories, translations, and essays through the self-owned Author's Press and Publishing House.[11] Maraimalai Adigal and Thiru.Vi.Ka. offer the most elaborate instances of the phenomenon of author-publishers in the late transitional period and its immediate aftermath.

In 1902 Maraimalai Adigal, then a little-known 26-year-old Tamil pandit at the Madras Christian College, established a printing press at a cost of Rs 1,000, mainly to publish his books and a monthly review, *Jnanasagaram*.[12] The press, named after his mentor Somasundara Nayagar, soon folded up. Ten years later, now established and well reputed as an outstanding Tamil and Saiva scholar, he was itching to open another press to streamline his publishing activities. In 1915 he wrote to V. Thiruvarangam Pillai, who was later to promote the Saiva Siddhanta Works Publishing Society Ltd, saying that

[10] See, for instance, advertisements in *Vivekabodhini*, December 1908; September 1916; *Lakshmi*, September 1923, September 1926; *Ananda Bodhini*, January 1917.

[11] See advertisements in his *Panchamirtam*, vol. 1, 1923–4.

[12] See the announcement in *Jnanasagaram*, 1 (6), 1905; also see Maraimalai Adigal's letter to U.V. Swaminatha Iyer, 13 June 1902, U.V.S. Papers, and entries dated 19–21 May 1902, Maraimalai Adigal's Diaries (hereafter *MD*), Maraimalai Adigal Papers, Maraimalai Adigal Library. The diaries were maintained in English from 1898 to 1950.

'a printing office is sorely needed to print all my works promptly for the public use.'[13] For the most part of his active life, Maraimalai Adigal published, and sometimes even physically printed, the bulk of his numerous works.

Thiru.Vi.Ka. also published all his books himself, and they were printed in his own press, the Sadhu Achukkudam, established with contributions from the Madras working class. He was ably assisted by his brother Thiru.Vi. Ulaganatha Mudaliar. Murugavel Puthakasalai, the name by which his 'publishing house' was known, was a separate entity only in name: it published only his books. Likewise, virtually all of V.O. Chidambaram Pillai's books were self-published. He too seems to have toyed with the idea of establishing his own printing press.[14]

But by the 1920s there was a considerable widening of the publishing sphere, and the consequent emergence of a modicum of specialization. The novel had effectively expanded readership and opened up a small but not inconsiderable market. In this context the existence of author–as–publisher began to seem outmoded. Maraimalai Adigal was to grumble: 'By doing singly the works of an author, printer, publisher, proof reader, foreman, clerk, steward, etc., I am left little time for dining, sleeping, resting and exercising.'[15] Despite his colossal reputation, Maraimalai Adigal found the going difficult and shifted his press from Pallavaram to Madras, under the supervision of his trusted manager A. Kanagaroyar.[16] When even its relocation proved difficult, he sold it off some years before his death.[17] Another fed-up author-publisher confessed in a letter to an emerging publishing house: 'I am not able to fix the rate of commission . . . as I am absolutely new to this kind of business. You may take the usual rate of

[13] *MD*, 17 September 1915.

[14] See his letter to T. Vedia Pillai, 28 May 1929, in A.R. Venkatachalapathy (ed.), *Va. Oo. Chi. Kadithangal* (Letters of V.O.C.; Sekar Pathippagam, 1984), pp. 105–7.

[15] *MD*, 5 January 1934.

[16] Maraimalai Adigal's letter to A. Kanagaroyar, 19 April 1933, Maraimalai Adigal Papers. Also *MD*, 8 February 1933.

[17] *MD*, 5 and 7 July 1943.

commission . . .'[18] Now that an alternative option had begun to be visible, authors were finding it easier to voice their frustrations at the difficulties of managing the many specialized functions of publishing alongside their writing. In 1929 *Amirtaguna Bodhini* remarked that authors who published their own books spent the amounts received as income on household expenses, being left consequently with insufficient working capital to continue their publishing.[19]

The 1920s saw the decisive emergence of publishers and publishing houses which functioned as publishers are meant to, taking care of publication, distribution, and so on. The assertion by *Amirtaguna Bodhini* that 'Those who publish others' books are called *prachurakarthar* or publishers', does not seem particularly momentous today, but in 1932 it denoted a phenomenon that was relatively recent.[20]

What were the implications of the emergence of publishers for authors? The investor was now the publisher and the author had to look to the publisher to convert his manuscript into a book and thereby turn it into a commodity for the market. In return for his loss of control over the book, the author was provided monetary compensation. As it turned out, the author was more often than not in a subordinate position *vis-à-vis* his publishers. Even reputed scholars were rendered supplicants when facing publishers who might accept or reject their work, never mind the delicate matter of royalties. N.M. Venkatasami Nattar, a much-respected scholar, wrote somewhat cringingly to his publishers: 'I know that my books do not sell well. I realize that even their meagre sale is the result of your efforts.'[21] And E.M. Subramania Pillai, the author of a *panchangam,* a fast-selling ephemeris, had to keep arguing his case for an enhanced and adequate royalty.[22] In

[18] K.S. Srinivasa Pillai to Saiva Siddhanta Works Publishing Society, Ltd (hereafter Kazhagam), 25 April 1921, Kazhagam Papers, Maraimalai Adigal Library.

[19] *Amirtaguna Bodhini*, 16 August 1929.

[20] Ibid., 16 June 1932. Interestingly, the English word 'publisher' has been used in Tamil transliteration.

[21] Letter to Kazhagam, 16 January 1924, N.M. Venkatasami Nattar Papers, Maraimalai Adigal Library.

[22] Letter to Kazhagam, 14 July 1925, E.M. Subramania Pillai Papers, Maraimalai Adigal Library.

a letter to his publisher he complained that he was being paid only Rs 50 whereas other publishers were offering up to Rs 300, even Rs 400.[23] Yet when his publisher Kazhagam reproduced bits from the panchangam in its Thirukkural Diary, thereby cutting into the sale of his panchangam, E.M. Subramania Pillai could only grumble without risking a demand for compensation.[24] The author was in fact so disadvantaged *vis-à-vis* his publisher that the latter could even implausibly claim that a ready seller like the panchangam was incurring a loss, his specious argument being that substantial amounts had been spent on promotion, marketing, and allowing discounts to booksellers.[25] The Indian publisher then—as frequently now—was taking advantage of the author's relative lack of power and perhaps ignorance of the fact that marketing expenses could not legitimately be debited to royalties.

Apart from the fact that royalties were seldom paid promptly or in full, the royalty percentages were very low. Often, they were calculated as a certain sum per forme per printrun, making a mockery of the author's efforts. N.M. Venkatasami Nattar was offered as little as Rs 8 per forme per printrun for his acclaimed commentary of *Thiruvilaiyadal Puranam.*[26] Interestingly, he had expected only Rs 10—an indication perhaps of authors having acclimatized themselves to the parsimonious ways of publishers.[27] Another letter outlines his position poignantly: 'It is not proper to compare the commentaries of the Keelkanakku works [late classical didactic texts] with other commentaries. Had my intention been to make money by writing just anything, I could have written any number of books. To elaborate on the nature of my undertaking and the labour it demands, and to ask for specific amounts as remuneration, is not in my nature.'[28]

[23] Letter to Kazhagam, 18 September 1939, ibid.

[24] Letter from E.M. Subramania Pillai to Kazhagam, 22 October 1937, ibid.

[25] Draft reply of V. Thiruvarangam Pillai, Secretary of Kazhagam, jotted on the back of E.M. Subramania Pillai's letter dated 22 October 1937, ibid.

[26] N.M. Venkatasami Nattar to Kazhagam, 21 September 1925, N.M. Venkatasami Nattar Papers, Maraimalai Adigal Library.

[27] N.M. Venkatasami Nattar to Kazhagam, 8 August 1926, ibid.

[28] Letter to Kazhagam, 8 August 1926, ibid. For similar letters by Avvai S. Duraisami Pillai to Kazhagam, 3 April 1943, 22 December 1943, 29 March

Authors had often to demand statements of accounts,[29] and publishers rarely obliged promptly.[30] This excerpt from a letter written by V.P. Subramania Mudaliar reveals the exasperation of an author at the indifference of his publisher: 'I've asked you on a number of occasions for a statement of accounts. I waited for a few weeks after sending a letter through G. Subramania Pillai, the vakil from Vannarapettai, but to no avail. Please send the statement at the earliest. If you cannot send it immediately, at least let me know when it may be possible [. . .] Please bear with me for repeatedly troubling you in this regard.'[31] By the 1930s the feeling widely shared was that authors always ended up getting a raw deal in their transactions with publishers.[32]

Authors were in no position to take offence: if they did, it invariably led to the relationship breaking down. This happened, for instance, with the publication of *Thiruvachaga Virivurai*. Maraimalai Adigal the author, and V. Thiruvarangam Pillai the publisher, disagreed over the terms and, as a result, the book was never published in full.[33] And the well meaning efforts of S. Satchidanandam Pillai, who was keen on ensuring the publication of Maraimalai Adigal's erudite commentary in full, seem to have cut no ice with the implacable publisher.[34]

Breach of contract in such instances was little more than a phrase,

---

1944, 4 April 1944, and 7 October 1944, see Avvai Duraisami Pillai Papers, Maraimalai Adigal Library.

[29] See K. Subramania Pillai to Kazhagam, 20 August 1932, K. Subramania Pillai Papers, Maraimalai Adigal Library.

[30] See letters of V.P. Subramania Mudaliar to Kazhagam, 8 December 1920; 30 August 1941; 18 October 1940; 19 October 1939; 9 November 1940; and 18 December 1940, V.P. Subramania Mudaliar Papers, Maraimalai Adigal Library.

[31] Letter to Kazhagam, 9 November 1940, ibid.

[32] *Amirtaguna Bodhini*, 16 June 1932.

[33] *MD*, 20, 23, and 26 February 1920.

[34] Letter to V. Thiruvarangam Pillai, 8 April 1921, S. Satchidanandam Pillai Papers, Maraimalai Adigal Library. The cordial relationship that existed between V. Swaminatha Sarma and his publisher Aru. Chockalingam was indeed rare. For a moving account of the association between the two written by Aru.

as authors and publishers rarely if ever entered into formal agreements. In the course of research for this work, I was able to locate few written contracts in the archives of various publishing houses. Some contracts were located at the Christian Literature Society, which is explained by the nature of its organization and its accountability to the Church.[35] Not even the phenomenally well-preserved South India Saiva Siddhanta Works Publishing Society (Kazhagam) Archive posses-ses contracts signed with authors, indicating that these were usually unwritten agreements.[36] Lacking legal recourse for breach of contract, authors and publishers both suffered, their relations being marked by much acrimony and bad blood in the course of breaking down. In one such instance E.M. Gopalakrishna Kone, a leading publisher from Madurai, abused Tamil scholar–authors, terming them unreliable, dishonest, and treacherous.[37]

---

Chockalingam, see V. Swaminatha Sarma, *Aval Pirivu* (Pudukkottai: Prapanjajothi Prachuralayam, 1957), Appendix.

[35] See, for instance, the contracts signed by the Christian Literature Society with J.T. Rajanayagam, author of *Theory and Project Method in Tamil*, dated 27 June 1930, and with T.A. Rajaruthnam Pillai for *Stories from Indian History in Tamil*, dated 14 October 1924, Christian Literature Society Archive.

[36] In the West, unwritten or verbal agreements for books are extremely uncommon. In India, however, the practice persists in some quarters even now—especially in the Tamil publishing world. As recently as in the early twenty-first century, the publisher Ravi Dayal's agreements with the novelist Amitav Ghosh were gentlemanly word-of-mouth arrangements. It is another matter that Dayal, being an old-world gentleman-publisher, kept to his word unfailingly. According to Ghosh, 'The arrival of his [Dayal's] royalty statements were events to look forward to: meticulously accurate and punctually delivered, they were always written in his own hand, in the beautiful flowing script of another era.' *Indian Express*, 7 June 2006: http://www.indianexpress.com/news/Hawk-eye-for-the-ellipsis,-he-was-the-Grim-Reaper-for-the-split-infinitive%09%09%09%09/5935/). I owe this information to Rukun Advani.

[37] R. Venkatachalam Pillai to V. Subbiah Pillai of Kazhagam, 19 January 1946, R. Venkatachalam Pillai Papers, Maraimalai Adigal Library. E.M. Gopalakrishna Kone's tirade seems to concern the publication of the *Chilappadhikaram* commentary.

Possibly the only class of authors who commanded some respect from publishers were textbook writers. Textbooks sold fairly well and yielded quick profits, in contrast with general books which had small printruns and took years to sell. V.S. Srinivasa Sastri recollects how he was pestered by publishers to write textbooks and notes when he was a teacher.[38] Authors of some textbooks commanded as much as Rs 25 per forme per printrun as remuneration.[39] There were also some who could demand an advance against royalties upon submission of their manuscript.[40] In Pudumaippithan's short story 'Nisamum Ninaippum', Professor Sivaramalingam is issued a cheque of Rs 500 for his yet-to-be-published manuscript (which was likely to be prescribed as a textbook).[41] So the prospect of a particular manuscript being prescribed seems to have been enough to tempt a publisher to take it on. As M.S. Purnalingam Pillai said to Kazhagam: 'I have ready with me in 5 formes D.C. 16 a book in MSS entitled "Islamism and Islamic Poets" in Tamil, which may be approved and prescribed as textbook for Mohammedan schools. It is to be dedicated to Begum Amiruddin, B.A. (Hons.), wife of the District Judge, for which she has given her consent.'[42] Late in his life U.V. Swaminatha Iyer made not insignificant sums of money by granting permission to reprint his essays in textbooks. He charged a fee of Rs 15 an essay per edition.[43]

Given the restricted growth of the book trade in colonial Tamilnadu, and the control over it by publishers, authors of successful textbooks

[38] V.S. Srinivasa Sastri, *Meendum Vazhnthal . . .?* (If I Were to Live Again . . .?; Chennai: Kalaimagal Kariyalayam, 1954), p. 2.

[39] M.S. Purnalingam Pillai to Kazhagam, 21 January 1941, M.S. Purnalingam Pillai Papers, Maraimalai Adigal Library.

[40] M.S. Purnalingam Pillai to Kazhagam, 29 April 1928, ibid.

[41] Venkatachalapathy (ed.), *Pudumaippithan Kathaikal* (Nagercoil: Kalachuvadu Pathippagam, 2000), pp. 603–14.

[42] Letter dated 23 December 1939, M.S. Purnalingam Pillai Papers. D.C. refers to 'Double Crown', the size of paper used for producing the book.

[43] See draft reply of U.V. Swaminatha Iyer to V.S. Swaminathan, a leading educational publisher based in Madurai, dated 9 September 1941, U.V.S. Papers. See also letters from T.G. Gopaul Pillai, Educational Publisher, 2 October 1937, and from P.N. Appuswamy Iyer, on behalf of Oxford University Press, Madras 13 March 1942, ibid.

had less cause to grumble than those who thought they might make it big by writing books for general readers. Only a few popular novelists, such as Vaduvur Duraiswamy Iyengar,[44] J.R. Rangaraju, and Vai.Mu. Kothainayaki Ammal, seem to have had substantial incomes, and could boast of their own houses and printing presses. On the other hand Arani Kuppuswamy Mudaliar, the combined sales of whose novels would have crossed a million, was never rich.[45]

It is in this context that the motif of the ever-poor author emerges, recurring often in accounts of the time and continuing into present-day writings. In an obituary on Ku.Pa. Rajagopalan (1902–1944), the gifted short story writer of the *Manikkodi* group, K.S. Venkataramani, the Gandhian novelist, said: 'In the last 35 years (1909–1944), I keep seeing one unchanging sight. Writers walk on cobblestone roads without any footwear, while the "shepherds" (the owners of "renaissance" publishing houses) who claim to "feed" authors roam about in motor cars with resplendent diamond rings on their fingers.'[46] He goes on to outline Ku.Pa. Rajagopalan's life of penury during which he was reduced to translating Bengali fiction in order to eke out a livelihood. K.S. Venkataramani may have exaggerated the affluence of publishers, but not the plight of most authors. Chandilyan, who later became a bestselling writer of pseudo-historical romances, chanced one day in the early 1930s to meet C.R. Srinivasan, the editor of *Swadesamitran*. When he introduced himself as a writer, C.R. Srinivasan, who could be expected to know the ways of the publishing world, asked, 'How can you make a living out of it?' and offered him a reporter's job in his daily.[47] No wonder, even Kalki, the exceptionally successful author and journalist, warned aspiring writers: 'Brother, listen to me. Take up some other occupation: never pursue this

[44] The money that Vaduvur Duraiswamy Iyengar made through his novels he lost by publishing a bulky volume of amateur anthropology, *Long Missing Links or the Marvellous Discoveries about the Aryans, Jesus Christ and Allah* (Chennai: Oriental Home University, 1931).

[45] See obituary in *Ananda Bodhini*, February 1925.

[46] *Bharatamani*, May 1944.

[47] Chandilyan, *Porattangal* (Struggles; Chennai: Vanathi Pathippagam, 1987), p. 37.

wretched profession of writing. Show me *one* person [in Tamilnadu] who has grown rich writing books and essays. How does it matter to us that Shaw and Chesterton have become millionaires by writing?'[48]

Writing was, in short, not only an unviable occupation but also seen to be one. Authors had often to resort to allied professions like teaching and journalism. This predicament is visible in much of the best works written during the 1930s and 1940s, being underscored in the biographies of several writers. Ku.Pa. Rajagopalan's acclaimed fellow-traveller Pudumaippithan (1906–1948) is a case in point. Despite his phenomenal gifts as a writer (often compared to Bharati), he spent most of his life as a sub-editor in journals and newspapers like *Ooliyan*, *Dinamani*, and *Dinasari*. Later he dabbled in the film world to tide over his difficulties, but failed, and ultimately died of consumption, penniless. The acclaimed biography by his friend Ragunathan begins dramatically with the lines, 'Pudumaippithan's life is the tragic drama of a Tamil author. A warning for living writers.'[49]

In a Pudumaippithan story, 'Oru Nal Kazhindathu', Murugadasar is a poor author who lives in a small tenement in Triplicane, Madras. His dream is to write a novel of epic proportions, but he actually ends up writing advertisement copy for Lipton Tea and Tapasa Energizing Tablets for a European-owned advertising agency. He is always short of money and even borrows sums as little as 8 annas from a friend.[50] In another of his stories, 'Nisamum Ninaippum', a leading short story writer is given short shrift by his publisher, who keeps postponing payments. When a cheque is ultimately issued, it bounces and the author finds himself literally on the streets for his landlord throws him out. The publisher then appears to bail him out by inviting him to stay in his office, but not without the veiled suggestion that he will pay for the roof over his head by reading proof sheets.[51]

[48] *Ananda Vikatan*, 13 March 1931, quoted in Sunda, *Ponniyin Puthalvar*, pp. 192–3.

[49] Ragunathan, *Pudumaippithan* (Chennai: Tamil Puthakalayam, 1951), Preface.

[50] Venkatachalapathy (ed.), *Pudumaippithan Kathaikal*, pp. 375–84.

[51] Ibid., pp. 603–14. For more stories centred on the author, see ibid., 'Karuchithaivu' and 'Kaditham'.

These summaries do not do justice to the nuanced stories of Pudumaippithan which brim with keen observation, wry humour, and biting satire, providing deep insights into the life of Tamil, and by extension human, predicaments.

Even by the end of our period, a career in writing was not by itself financially worthwhile, offering somewhat less than a modest living to Tamil authors foolhardy enough to try it out. Unlike in the West, where, by the nineteenth century the world of letters sustained not only hacks but also professional writers, Tamil society supported neither.

## Publishers

As a distinct agency, the publisher did not emerge in the Tamil world until well into the transitional phase. During the age of patronage, and for a while after, self-publishing authors, as we saw, usually raised funds through patronage and/or subscription, and organized the printing themselves. Given the extremely limited printrun of early books, coupled with the obligation to hand over substantial number of copies to patrons and subscribers, distribution never posed a serious problem.[52] Only with the decline of patronage and the system of subscriptions, and concomitantly with the emergence of the author, the rise of new genres, and the expansion of the economy in the post World War I period, was the need felt for a separate agency to coordinate publishing activities.

Some of the earliest publishers in this newly distinct category were linked with the periodical press. *Viveka Chintamani*, the monthly review, also published tracts and books on 'useful knowledge'. *Swadesamitran*, the leading daily, published a number of books on nationalist

[52] Bharatidasan says derisively that only 200 copies of such books used to be printed. U.V. Swaminatha Iyer printed only 500 copies of his editions. As for distribution, Ponnuswamy Thevar used to distribute free many of the books to which he had provided patronage. See Raghavaiyangar, *Sentamil Valartha Thevargal*, pp. 48–9. Mylai Seeni. Venkatasamy observes that many books during the nineteenth century had printruns of only 200 copies. See *Pathonbatham Noottrandil Tamil Ilakkiyam*, p. 120.

politics and social reform.[53] Thiru.Vi.Ka.'s *Navasakti* was part of an arrangement to publish his books through Murugavel Puthakasalai (the publishing house) and Sadhu Achukkudam (the printing press). A. Madhaviah's literary review *Panchamirtam* and his Author's Press and Publishing House were sister firms.[54]

By the 1920s independent publishing houses unconnected with authors and journals in their ownership or organization began to emerge. Publishing became an exclusive and specialized activity with the appearance of these firms. But given the as-yet-narrow economy under colonial rule and the lack of a fully developed market, many of them functioned mostly within the relatively lucrative area of educational publishing. General, or trade, books were not predominant. As a contemporary observer, P.J. Chester of the Oxford University Press, Madras, remarked, there were 'about 150' publishers registered with the Director of Public Instruction, Madras, while only about 2,000 to 3,000 books were being published annually.[55] An Acting Director of Public Instruction also made a similar observation: 'Many if not most publishing firms established in the Madras Presidency are engaged in the keenest competition to secure the adoption of their books in schools.'[56]

Publishing educational books, which, according to P.J. Chester, amounted to half of the total book production, was an easy and quick way to earn as all that 'seemed to [be] need[ed] was a school master to write, a printer, a few reams of paper and a Textbook Committee'.[57] The sting in the tail is hard to miss—a comment on the rampant corruption in educational publishing. The procedure of prescribing textbooks was (and to this day remains) eminently suited for manipulation and shady deals. Given the easy money involved, 'the most disreputable means' were employed.[58] As even the Director of Public

[53] On *Swadesamitran*'s contribution, see the review of *Congress Mahasabhai Charithiram* in *Amirtaguna Bodhini*, 16 July 1929.

[54] *Panchamirtam*, May 1924 (see advertisements).

[55] *Memoirs of the Madras Library Association, 1944* (Madras: Madras Library Association, 1944), p. 30.

[56] G.O. no. 705, Law (Education; hereafter Edn), 8 April 1935.

[57] *Memoirs of the Madras Library Association, 1944*, p. 32.

[58] G.O. no. 705, Law (Edn), 8 April 1935.

Instruction conceded, 'The conditions in which publishers carry on their business compel them to resort to irregular and shady methods.'[59] The standard procedure adopted was as follows. The Director of Public Instruction had a Central Textbook Committee which periodically selected and approved textbooks submitted to them for school syllabuses. The approved books were periodically notified in the Fort St George Gazette of the Government of Madras, which also contributed to the malaise. With no consolidated lists available, the only practical means to ascertain whether a book was approved or not was the inscription printed on the title page of the book, 'APPROVED BY THE TEXT BOOK COMMITTEE'—a claim difficult to challenge or disprove. Random enquiries resulted in the finding that as many as fifty-one books prescribed in the elementary schools, in one district alone, could not be verified as approved by the committee.

In any case, from these lists of approved textbooks the presidents and chairmen of local bodies prescribed books for use in schools under their control. It was an open secret that books were selected in return for favours rendered to members of the sanctioning local body. The following is an incident from a contemporary fictional account set in a small school:

> *First teacher* (to the Headmaster): You have not told us which textbooks have been prescribed. Students keep asking which books are to be bought. What do we tell them?
>
> *Headmaster*: Why do you want to rake up that vexed issue now?
>
> *Another teacher* (angrily): Why don't you state the truth? The Chairman and the Commissioner have not yet struck a deal with the publisher.
>
> *First teacher*: Oh! Can that be said openly?
>
> *Another teacher*: Why not? Everybody knows of it and the whole affair stinks through to one's nostrils.[60]

[59] Ibid. The following account of corruption in educational publishing is based on the detailed report submitted by Herbert Champion, Acting Director of Public Instruction, in ibid., unless otherwise stated.

[60] Srinivasa Sastri, *Meendum Vazhnthal . . .?*, p. 82. The liberal political figure Srinivasa Sastri (1869–1946) was a distinguished teacher and

In this situation, as the Director of Public Instruction conceded, 'in general, a school book has no chance of being selected on its merits alone.'[61]

In this state of affairs, unscrupulous publishers had a field day. Efforts were made right from the beginning to ensure smooth business. T. Sivasailam Pillai, Deputy Inspector of Schools, who had interests in the Kazhagam, advised its Secretary, V. Thiruvarangam Pillai: 'In the September meeting of the Textbook Committee, [our books] should be approved . . . see to it that the books reach the Committee on time. Ensure that books do not go to members who are not favourably disposed to you. When the books are sent for their opinion to members, *give them your attention*. Write to them. If this is taken care of and approval obtained, we can sell thousands of books every month.'[62]

Every District Board wielded much influence, and its prescription meant sales in the thousands. 'If one Taluk Board prescribes it, it will mean 2,000 to 2,500 copies.'[63] In this state of affairs, contacts were what mattered. The copious correspondence of T. Sivasailam Pillai with Kazhagam bears testimony to this.[64] S. Satchidanandam Pillai, who evinced keen interest in the activities of Kazhagam, advised it

---

headmaster in the early part of his career, at the Hindu High School, Chennai, and could be expected to know of these matters.

[61] G.O. no. 705, Law (Edn), 8 April 1935.

[62] T. Sivasailam Pillai to Kazhagam, 2 August 1928, T. Sivasailam Pillai Papers, Maraimalai Adigal Library. Emphasis added.

[63] T. Sivasailam Pillai to Kazhagam, 10 June 1931, ibid. Also see letter dated 23 October 1929, ibid.

[64] See also S. Satchidanandam Pillai, Deputy Inspector of Schools and Tamil scholar, to Kazhagam, 16 July 1928, S. Satchidanandam Pillai Papers. No wonder this corruption came in for much criticism from all sides. One critic went so far as to say that all writers and publishers of awful textbooks ought to be properly 'flogged with tamarind tree stems', *Kudinool*, 15 October 1938. For Maraimalai Adigal's criticism, see *A Critical Study of 'Mullaippattu'* (Chennai: n.p., 1903), p. iv; for the view of Desigavinayagam Pillai, acclaimed poet and T.K. Chidambaranatha Mudaliar, see M. Arunachalam, *Kumariyum Kasiyum* (Thiruchittrambalam: Gandhi Vidyalayam, 1959), pp. 120–1; also see *Navasakti*, 28 March 1928.

to concentrate on textbook publishing for good profits which could help the cause of Tamil and Saivism.[65] N.M. Venkatasami Nattar, badly in need of money in the summer of 1930, reluctantly asked Kazhagam for money as 'schools are now closed [for the vacation] and cash inflow will be at a low.'[66]

Though these instances indicate the centrality of textbook publishing to the day-to-day functioning of publishing houses, we do not have data to show the scale of educational publishing and its resultant profits. An educational officer's observation that publishers were 'moving about in motor cars with flower garlands in their hands'[67]—no doubt to shower them on the sanctioning authorities—suggests their affluence. E.M. Gopalakrishna Kone offers the most elaborate, if exceptional, case of a successful educational publisher. In 1935 his books were banned from being prescribed when certain malpractices came to light. E.M. Gopalakrishna Kone therefore petitioned the government saying he would lose a turnover of nearly a lakh of rupees, and that about sixty approved textbooks would remain unsold, compounding his difficulties by piling trouble on authors, booksellers, and students. He also claimed to pay an annual income tax of Rs 5,000 and said his annual establishment costs were to the tune of Rs 30,000. In a desperate bid to prove his standing, he listed the positions that he held: member of the senate of the University of Madras, of the Madurai Municipal Council, of the Indian Chamber of Commerce, and of the Madurai Tamil Sangam.[68] He even wielded clout enough to raise a question in the Madras Legislative Council on the ban.[69] E.M. Gopalakrishna Kone, though typifying the broad scenario, was also exceptional inasmuch as he was a leader in the field,[70] and few, if any, could match the scale and weight of his operations.

[65] Letter to Kazhagam, 24 April 1923, S. Satchidanandam Pillai Papers.

[66] Letter to Kazhagam, 6 June 1930, N.M. Venkatasami Nattar Papers.

[67] T. Sivasailam Pillai to Kazhagam, 2 June 1933, T. Sivasailam Pillai Papers.

[68] G.O. no. 705, Law (Edn), 8 April 1935.

[69] Question no. 651, posed by V.T. Arasu, G.O. no. 2089, Edn (Confdl), 1 October 1934.

[70] Maraimalai Adigal refers to him as 'the rich bookseller from Madura', *MD*, 22 November 1945.

In the 1920s, political movements, especially the nationalist, helped widen the market and the publishing trade a little. Reference has already been made to the publications of *Swadesamitran*. G.A. Natesan & Co. were a leading nationalist publisher of the time, but virtually all of their 500-odd titles were in English.[71] S. Ganesan, through his Suthanthira Sangu Prachuralayam, published a number of low-priced Tamil books on Gandhian politics.[72] The son of a retired police head constable, S. Ganesan had started his life as a 'petty bookseller' and 'khaddar hawker' before opening a press in 1925, and doing some excellent work publishing nationalist books.[73] K.S. Venkataramani had a publishing house called Svetharanya Ashramam specializing in books inspired by the Gandhian constructive programme.[74] M.S. Subramania Iyer, under the name Swarajya Berigai, published scores of nationalist books. On the whole, these nationalist publishers succeeded in publishing and distributing their books through a wide, if temporary, network.[75]

The Dravidian Movement, though a late starter, published a number of radical books, including translations of Bertrand Russell, Robert Ingersoll, and Bhagat Singh, apart from the iconoclastic writings of its founder-protagonist 'Periyar' E.V. Ramasamy. Apart from the Kudi Arasu Pathippagam, the movement also promoted the Pagutharivu Noorpathippu Kazhagam to help its rationalistic propaganda.[76] Because these were run on ideological rather than business lines, the

[71] B. Natesan, *In the Service of the Nation, A Golden Jubilee Retrospect* (Madras: G.A. Natesan & Co., 1948). See also *Panchamirtam*, January 1925, on the silver jubilee of G.A. Natesan & Co.; *Souvenir of the Sashtiabdha-Poorthi of Hon. G.A. Natesan* (Madras: 1933).

[72] See the reviews in *Panchamirtam*, June 1924; *Bharati*, June 1931.

[73] History sheet of S. Ganesan prepared by the CID, G.O. no. 316, Judl (Confdl), 26 February 1930; and USS file no. 703, 25 August 1930.

[74] See advertisements in *Bharatamani*, especially 1 January 1939.

[75] For criticism of nationalist book publishing as profiteering, see *Maruppukku Maruppu* (Refuting Refutations; Erode: Kudi Arasu Pathippagam, 1935), especially the essay by Neelavathi. For criticism on the publication of Bharati's works, see *Manikkodi*, 15 October 1937 and 15 November 1937, the columns by Pudumaippithan and P.G. Sunderarajan.

[76] *Kudi Arasu*, 8 January 1933 and 12 February 1933.

books published were very nominally priced and reached a wide public. As Periyar put it: 'All my publications are very, very cheap. (But) there is no systematic sale. Most of them are distributed free. Therefore, it is difficult to conform to set business norms.'[77] By the time the Communist Party ventured into publishing through its Janasakti Prachuram, World War II had begun and colonial rule's deathbed preparations were in the offing.

The publishing ventures of political movements helped broaden the publishing sphere, but publishing in support of an ideology or a movement is not infrequently a transitory phenomenon. As a result, these publishing houses wound up when the political urgency motivating their ventures evaporated. But there were presses of other sorts which continued to contribute to the expansion of publishing activity. The cost price editions of Saivite religious texts, admirably edited and neatly produced by the Saiva Siddhanta Mahasamajam, the apex body of Saivite associations, deserves mention here.[78] So successful was this venture that Saiva Siddhanta Works Publishing Society (Kazhagam) felt jittery—it had until then a virtual monopoly over quality editions of the Saivite texts.[79] Alliance & Co., which had started as a small bookselling firm by V. Kuppuswamy Iyer (1880–1949), grew in size and stature in the 1920s and 1930s by publishing a series of fictional works of the new band of 'renaissance' writers, translations of Bengali fiction, and nationalist literature.[80]

[77] Letter to E.M. Subramania Pillai, dated 30 December 1947, reproduced in E.S. Muthusamy, *Tamil Perumpulavar E.Mu. Subramania Pillai* (Biography of E.M. Subramania Pillai; Chennai: Pari Nilayam, 1984), p. 37.

[78] See *Siddhantam*, June 1945, for a complete list of publications with details of the printrun. Also see the preface to *Sundaramurty Swamigal Thevaram* (Chennai: Saiva Siddhanta Mahasamajam, 1929); write-ups in *Navasakti*, 17 April 1929 and 31 June 1929.

[79] See the statement by the Secretary of the Saiva Siddhanta Mahasamajam, *Siddhantam*, March 1936.

[80] See *Amarajothi Alliance Iyer*, unpublished biography by his grandson V. Srinivasan. Also *Navasakti*, 19 November 1926, G.O. no. 1340, Pub., 14 November 1917. Ka.Naa. Subramanyam provides a pen portrait of Kuppuswamy Iyer in his *Ilakkiya Chathanaiyalargal*, pp. 168–72.

By the mid-1930s a number of such firms had emerged.[81] Interestingly, most of them were sole proprietary firms and lacked even a semblance of corporate organization. An incident narrated by Kalki's biographer puts this point across humorously. One day, in 1927, Kalki arrived home with copies of his first book, *Sarathaiyin Thanthiram,* a collection of short stories. He proudly displayed a copy to his wife, who flipped through it and asked where Saraswati Prachuralayam (Saraswati Publishing House) was located. Kalki quipped, 'our house is the publishing house.'[82]

Given the narrowness of the Tamil book trade, low capital outlays, and limited turnovers, corporate organization would probably have made most publishing ventures unviable on account of unnecessary fixed costs and overheads. An exception to this norm was the South India Saiva Siddhanta Works Publishing Society Ltd, the first of its kind in Tamilnadu. Founded by the brothers Pillai—V. Thiruvarangam and V. Subbiah—the company made a name for itself by publishing Tamil and Saivite classics. Its authorized capital was only Rs 50,000, divided into 5,000 shares of Rs 10 each.[83]

Table 4.1 shows the limited scale of operations of Tamil publishing firms, with stock-in-trade never touching the Rs 50,000 mark and annual profits rarely crossing Rs 5,000.[84] Further, despite being nominally a corporate organization, the company was run on lines that were far from capitalist. The company's members were restricted by its constitution to only Saivites: non-Saivites were barred from holding

[81] In 1933, during the Tamil Anbar Mahanadu, scores of publishers participated for the first time in an elaborate exhibition. See *Tamil Anbar Mahanadu, Tamil Puthaka Katchi Arikkai*, Chennai, 1934.

[82] Sunda, *Ponniyin Puthalvar*, pp. 180–1.

[83] For details about the company, see the biographies of the brothers by Era. Elankumaran, *Thiruvaranganar Varalaru* (Tirunelveli: Saiva Siddhanta Kazhagam, 1982) and *Thamarai Chelvar Va. Subbiah Pillai Varalaru* (Tirunelveli: Saiva Siddhanta Kazhagam, 1981). Also see S.R. Ranganathan and R. Muthukumaraswamy, *Commemoration Bibliography* (Tirunelveli: The South India Saiva Siddhanta Works Publishing Society, 1961).

[84] Similarly, the total stock-in-trade (at market price and not at cost) of Ripon Pusthagasalai, a major bookseller and publisher, in July 1929, was only Rs 92,897–10–4. See their printed Stock Register and Catalogue, July 1929.

Table 4.1
Stock-in-Trade and Profits of South India Saiva Siddhanta Works Publishing Society Ltd., 1920–1939

| Year | Stock-in-trade (at cost price) | Profits | Annual dividend |
|---|---|---|---|
| 1920–21 | NA | (–) 1516-8-1 | – |
| 1921–22 | 4964-10-7 | 696-9-1 | – |
| 1922–23 | 9689-5-6 | 901-13-2 | – |
| 1923–24 | 14,030-1-9 | 1667-1-7 | – |
| 1924–25 | 16,690-15-6 | 1875-7-4 | – |
| 1925–26 | 17,595-2-0 | 1890-9-6 | 5% |
| 1926–27 | 25,484-2-9 | 2675-10-4 | 4½% |
| 1927–28 | 35,063-0-9 | 1951-5-1 | 4% |
| 1928–29 | 37,542-8-11 | 2546-5-1 | 3½% |
| 1929–30 | 36,525-3-0 | 7093-14-1 | nil |
| 1930–31 | 38,144-3-9 | 2358-6-4 | 4% |
| 1931–32 | 39,398-9-8 | 2316-14-9 | - |
| 1932–33 | 39,493-11-3 | 2275-8-1 | - |
| 1933–34 | 40,285-9-9 | 4486-13-3 | 5% |
| 1934–35 | 42,189-5-10 | 3918-7-11 | 4% |
| 1935–36 | 42,391-6-3 | 4029-13-6 | 3 1/8% |
| 1936–37 | 41,057-7-5 | 4560-8-6 | 5% |
| 1937–38 | 37,679-8-8 | 5647-10-1 | 6% |
| 1938–39 | 38,203-8-6 | 5647-14-8 | 4% |

*Source*: Compiled from the annual statements of accounts. Percentage of dividends refers to only half of the actual dividend declared. As per the Memorandum of Association, half of the dividend declared was given to the South India Saiva Siddhanta Sangam, a charitable organization meant for the development of Tamil and Saivism

shares.[85] Sivasailam Pillai, for instance, who evinced keen interest in the growth of the company, often criticized Kazhagam for functioning in 'unbusinesslike ways'.[86] In one of his letters he wrote in frustration: 'Alas!! What a pity!! The Imperial Bank which deals in crores of rupees

[85] Letter from T. Sivasailam Pillai to Kazhagam, 16 April 1929, T. Sivasailam Pillai Papers.

[86] Letters to Kazhagam 2 June 1933; 5 June 1929; 5 March 1929 and 16 February 1929, ibid.

responds positively by return of post and only then does it speak of right procedure for the future [. . .] But your office acts in an unbusiness-like, slow and (please excuse me) not intelligent ways.'[87]

The comparison with a capitalist organization like the Imperial Bank is telling. Towards the late 1930s things had begun to change. Publishers foresaw a widened book market. K.S. Venkataramani dreamed of publishing houses like Penguin and Pelican.[88] The publishers of *Manikkodi* promoted Navayuga Prachuralayam Ltd as a public limited company in 1937, with an authorized capital of Rs 20,000 divided into 2,000 shares. The prospectus expressed the hope that 200-page books priced at 8 annas a copy would sell at least 5,000 copies.[89] The promotion of this company was evidently motivated by the need for corporate organization in the publishing business. As an editorial in *Manikkodi* remarked, 'That corporate organization is a desideratum is a lesson we have learnt from experience.'[90] An earlier write-up in *Manikkodi* referred to the success of one of Rajagopalachari's books:

> Sri Chakravarti Rajagopalachari's *Kannan Kattiya Vazhi* has seen a second printing within a year of its first publication. This gives the lie to those who argue that Tamil publishing cannot be run on business lines. Anyone repeating this contention now can only be termed as unable to see with their eyes. Everything depends on how books are published. If interesting material is offered at an affordable price to Tamil readers, need one worry about successful business?[91]

Navayuga Prachuralayam's publications met with initial success.[92] The daily *Dinamani* also joined the fray with publications during the War.[93] However, all these ventures proved short-lived. As a publisher

[87] Letter to Kazhagam, 2 June 1933, ibid.

[88] *Bharatamani*, 22 October 1939.

[89] See the prospectus of the company in *Manikkodi*, 31 January 1937.

[90] Ibid., 15 October 1937.

[91] Ibid., 25 April 1937.

[92] See editorials in ibid., 15 February 1937 and 5 November 1937.

[93] For a survey of Dinamani publications, see *Bharatamani*, April 1945. For an allegorical criticism, see Ragunathan's 1947 short story 'Jnanamani

in Pudumaippithan's short story remarks, 'The business of publishing is fit only for Kepmaris'[94] (a so-called criminal tribe popularly associated with unscrupulousness; also a word of abuse). Tamil publishing tended never to take off into corporate organization, a situation unchanged between then and now. Even during World War II, when the Tamil book trade expanded and a part of Chettiar capital fleeing from South east Asia moved into book publishing, publishing houses remained under sole proprietors, or at best functioned as partnership firms. It was only after World War I that publishing firms with the exclusive function of publishing books began to emerge in Tamilnadu. They were run by businessmen, as distinct from writer-publishers. But, as we have seen, they remained parasitic upon textbook prescriptions. Consequently, Tamil publishing remained at best a business or trade and never really assumed the dimensions of an industry.

## Printers

With the relaxing of restrictions on Indian ownership in 1835, a number of printing presses owned by Indians came into being. By 1863 there were at least ten 'Native Presses', printing in Tamil, which furnished returns about their publications. According to John Murdoch, there were several more such outfits. Early on they possessed only wooden printing presses, but later many of them acquired iron presses.[95] Some Tamil scholars who owned printing presses in the age of patronage were Ramanuja Kavirayar, Kalathur Vedagiri Mudaliar, Arumuga Navalar, and Sabapathy Navalar. Mylai Seeni. Venkatasamy lists about 75 presses which printed Tamil books during

---

Pathippagam', *Ragunathan Kathaigal* (Madurai: Meenakshi Puthaka Nilayam, 1980).

[94] Venkatachalapathy (ed.), *Pudumaippithan Kathaikal*, p. 610. Also see Mullai. Muthiah, 'Ezhuthalargalum Pirasurakarthargalum' (Writers and Publishers), *Vedikkai Manithar Pudumaippithan* (Chennai: Mullai Veliyeedu, 1956), for an account of the difficulties of publishing as a profitable occupation. Also see Chinna Annamalai, 'Pusthaga Pirasuram' in *Chandrodhayam*, 15 March 1946.

[95] Murdoch, *A Classified Catalogue of Tamil Printed Books*, p. ix.

the nineteenth century.[96] The *Madras State Tamil Bibliography*'s list is more comprehensive, with over 180 presses.[97] These lists attest to increasing printing activity. By 1895 printing presses had become a landmark, and a chapbook of the times points to them. This chapbook, a *valindai chindu*—structured as a poem where a man is showing his wife around the city—points to the beautiful press (Kalarathnakaram Achukkudam) of Pushparatha Chettiar and the Vidyatarangini Achukkudam of Ratna Nayagar.[98]

By the early twentieth century there was a further increase in the number of printing presses operating in Tamilnadu (Table 4.2). The table indicates the fairly wide distribution of printing presses, but the numbers are quite misleading. Not all these presses were involved in printing Tamil books. For instance, a compendium of Southern India published in 1914 provides *inter alia* fairly detailed write-ups on some major printing presses. These printing presses, some of them with as many as 200 employees, were well equipped with machinery and plant, but were only involved in general and fine-art commercial printing. They catered to the needs of colonial establishments such as the Bank of Madras, and the Madras & Southern Mahratta Railway Company, and had nothing to do with the Tamil book publishing business.[99] Handling the printing requirements of large commercial establishments was the only profitable and viable way of running large printing houses. The Tamil publishing world could never hope to sustain such gigantic operations.

A number of smaller printing presses did odd-job work such as printing invitation cards, bill books, etc. The District Magistrate of

[96] Mylai Seeni. Venkatasamy, *Pathonbatham Noottrandil Tamil Ilakkiyam*, pp. 99–105.

[97] *Madras State Tamil Bibliography*, vol. 1, pt 3 (Madras: Government of Madras, 1963).

[98] *Chennai Kandaswamy Vedarpani Mahorchava Valinadai Patham* (Chennai: n.p., 1895).

[99] Somerset Playne, *Southern India: Its History, People, Commerce and Industrial Resources* (1914, facsimile rpnt. New Delhi: Asian Educational Services, 2004). See the entries on Ananda Press, Perumall Chetty & Sons, The Guardian Press, The India Printing Works, and The Law Printing House.

Table 4.2
Printing Presses in Tamilnadu, 1904–1912

| Districts | 1904–5 | 1905–6 | 1906–7 | 1908–9 | 1910 | 1911 | 1912 |
|---|---|---|---|---|---|---|---|
| North Arcot | 10 | 10 | 12 | 16 | 18 | 18 | 20 |
| Madurai | 20 | 2- | 25 | 30 | 24 | 25 | 27 |
| Coimbatore | 11 | 14 | 18 | 18 | 15 | 16 | 17 |
| Madras | 189 | 202 | 209 | 207 | 226 | 242 | 242 |
| Tanjore | 26 | 26 | 31 | 35 | 44 | 43 | 43 |
| South Arcot | 9 | 8 | 10 | 14 | 15 | 13 | 13 |
| Tinnevelly | 16 | 19 | 21 | 23 | 19 | 21 | 23 |
| Nilgiris | 3 | 6 | 6 | 8 | 9 | 9 | 8 |
| Chingleput | 6 | 5 | 6 | 7 | 7 | 7 | 8 |
| Trichi | 11 | 11 | 11 | 12 | 20 | 21 | 21 |
| Ramnad | NA | NA | NA | NA | 15 | 17 | 17 |

*Sources*:
1904–5: G.O. no. 414, Pub., 8 June 1905
1905–6: G.O. no. 465, Pub., 21 June 1906
1906–7: G.O. no. 406, Pub., 29 May 1907
1908–9: G.O. no. 398, Pub., 7 June 1909
1910–12: G.O. no. 1473, Judl (Confdl), 21 June 1913

North Arcot, referring to the 35 presses in his district in 1921, commented: 'All of them are petty ones. They are mostly engaged in doing job work.'[100] Of the presses in Nilgiris district, the District Magistrate said they all 'do only miscellaneous job work'.[101] Apart from presses in Madras city and to some extent in Madurai and Thanjavur, presses in the districts were mainly small and involved in printing stationery and so on. Jayakanthan's poignant short story 'Treadle' (1958) is set in one such press which has only one employee who does all the jobs, including composing, printing on the machine, etc.

The middle level presses were the ones which catered to the needs of Tamil publishing and we have no means of estimating their numbers. In the age of patronage and the subsequent transitional phase, printers functioned as booksellers too, especially as sellers of books

[100] G.O. no. 381, Pub. (Confdl), 17 June 1921.
[101] Ibid.

printed at their own presses.[102] U. Pushparatha Chettiar of the Kalarathnakaram Press was one such. The Madras Ripon Press of Sadhu Rathina Chettiar was another, which indulged in publishing also.[103] As long as printers also combined the functions of printing, publishing, and bookselling, they were open to suspicion. As Subbaraya Chettiar put it, 'if it is a good book, it is customary for printing houses to print some extra copies for themselves, apart from charging actual costs.'[104]

Technologically speaking, the printing presses serving the needs of Tamil publishing functioned with a modest treadle or cylinder machine run on manual power. Maraimalai Adigal's T.M. Press had only a Demy Folio Platen machine.[105] So did the Sivanesan Press.[106] As late as 1957 'Sakti' V. Govindan, the renowned publisher, spoke of manually operated cylinder machines in relation to Tamil publishing.[107] Power presses, not to speak of hot metal technologies such as linotype and monotype, were quite unfamiliar in the world of Tamil publishing.

We get only fragmentary details about how these presses worked, the kind of labour recruited, and their working conditions. Often, only poor people with no other means of employment joined such presses, especially when young. The superintendent of Diocesan Press said: 'The standard of education among workmen is low; most of them are literate only in their own vernaculars; few have sufficient education to take an intelligent interest in what they are doing. There is no apprenticeship system, there are no master craftsmen to teach, and the learner picks up what knowledge he can.'[108] T.M. Rajapather

[102] Murdoch, *A Classified Catalogue of Tamil Printed Books*, p. lxi.

[103] See obituary of Sadhu Rathina Chettiar in *Viveka Chintamani*, December 1900. For an elegy on his death, see V.G. Suriyanarayana Shastri, *Pavalar Virundu* (Madurai: V.S. Swaminathan, 1957), pp. 54–5.

[104] Letter to Meenakshisundaram Pillai, 3 October 1868, U.V.S. Papers.

[105] *MD*, 19 and 20 September 1916. Also see Cashbook of T.M. Press, Maraimalai Adigal Papers. See Appendix 3 for this.

[106] Oo.Ra. Saminathan, assistant editor of *Sivanesan*, to U.V. Swaminatha Iyer, 5 April 1934, U.V.S. Papers.

[107] *Saraswati*, March 1957.

[108] W.H. Warren, *Author and Printer* (Madras: Christian Literature Society,

followed in the footsteps of his father T.V. Manicka Mudaliar and was apprenticed to a press when he was barely 11 because of pressing family commitments.[109] The progressive writer Vindhan who, like Rajapather, lived in the working-class locality of Pulianthope in Madras, also joined a press while in his teens for similar reasons, earning a daily wage of 6 annas.[110] Thiru.Vi.Ka.'s elder brother Ulaganatha Mudaliar was forced to drop out of school and take up a job in a press.[111] Roughly the same happened to M.P. Sivagnanam, who later became a prominent writer and politician, and M.V. Venugopala Pillai, the scholar–editor.[112] A. Subramania Nayagar was a compositor before he made enough money by dealing in German silver articles to run the caste journal *Vanni Kula Mitran*.[113]

We come to know of the experience of printing men only through such exceptional persons who later rose to prominence in other fields. Otherwise, 'A boy may . . . learn to pick up type, impose a frame and put it on the machine; but his setting is full of errors, his imposing results in crooked pages, and on the machine, his type is either sticking through the paper or shows too faintly to read. Except in the very

---

1925), p. 3. Warren, originally from the Cambridge University Press, became superintendent of the Diocesan Press and secretary of the Christian Literature Society in Madras.

[109] T.M. Rajapather, in *Kalki Ponvizha Malar* (Kalki Golden Jubilee Number), 1992.

[110] M. Paramasivam, *Makkal Ezhuthalar Vindhan* (Vindhan, the People's Writer; Chennai: Pookkudai Pathippagam 1983), pp. 4–6.

[111] Thiru.Vi.Ka., *Valkai Kurippugal*, p. 765. For further biographical details, see his sixtieth birthday souvenir, *Thiru. Vi. Ulaganatha Mudaliar Manivizha Malar* (1941); for his obituaries, see *Siddhantam*, July 1945, and *Bharatamani*, July 1945.

[112] M.P. Sivagnanam, *Enathu Porattam* (My Struggles; Chennai: Inba Nilayam, 1974), p. 36; M.V. Venugopala Pillai 'En Valkai Ninaivugal' (My Reminiscences), *Mahavidwan Me. Ve. Venugopala Pillai Manivizha Malar* (M.V. Venugopala Pillai Sixtieth Birthday Souvenir), Chennai, 1956, pp. 6–7.

[113] Report of the Commissioner of Police, G.O. no. 342, Pub. (Confdl), 18 April 1918. Also see A. Subramania Nayagar's preface to *Thirukkaivalam* (Chennai: Vanni Kula Mitran, 1955), p. 8.

rare cases where there is a highly trained foreman able and willing to spare the time for personal interaction, there is no one to show him the correct way to do these things.'[114] Not every press worker was lucky enough to escape the drudgery and poverty of employment in a press. The little boys who joined as apprentices were hardly ever paid during the course of their training: they came from poor families and were in no position to complain. For instance, two of the boys in Maraimalai Adigal's T.M. Press were the sons of his maidservant and gardener.[115] These little apprentices had a tough time working nine hours a day.[116] As Thiru.Vi.Ka., who ran a press himself, wrote: 'Most of the printing shop owners kill their apprentice boys without killing them. They knock the heads of these children [with their knuckles]; slap their cheeks and beat them and kick them. Sometimes they catch hold of their tufts and threaten them with a scowling face and blood-shot eyes. Only the good Lord in Heaven knows the plight of these children.'[117] Adult workers fared little better. In most presses workers had to stand the whole day while composing and printing. This was physically very taxing, especially as the work also needed concentration, attention, and patience.[118] Thiru.Vi.Ka. observed that many of the workmen cursed their parents for pushing them into such a wretched trade at a young age.[119]

Wages were extremely low, in keeping with the general practice in the Tamil book trade. Maraimalai Adigal's pressmen were paid only between Rs 10 and Rs 15 a month. During the 1920s even his manager, Thiru.Vi. Ulaganatha Mudaliar, was paid only Rs 20, and his successor J.S. Kannappar Rs 15 per month.[120] Their living conditions

[114] Warren, *Author and Printer*, p. 4.

[115] *MD*, 1 February 1930 and 9 September 1932. For more references to apprentices, see 19 May 1924; 11 February 1925; 30 September 1925; and 25 January 1928, ibid.

[116] *MD*, 26 April 1924.

[117] *Desabakhtan*, 16 February 1918, reprinted in his *Desabakhtamirtam* (Chennai: British India Achukkudam, 1919), p. 250.

[118] Ibid., pp. 250–1; also the petition of Madras Government Press Workers' Union in G.O. no. 1849, Edn & Pub. Health, 3 August 1938.

[119] Thiru.Vi.Ka., *Desabakhtamirtam*, p. 250.

[120] Cashbook of T.M. Press. See Appendix 3 for extracts from this cashbook.

were hardly any better. Even the Government Press workers, who earned relatively more, lived often as 'subtenants, mostly in slum areas'. They lived huddled in single rooms with poor sanitation. 'Rice water twice a day is prosperity for them.'[121] No wonder press workers kept indifferent health. 'Lead poisoning is the common disease to which compositors and type casters often fall victims.'[122] It was nearly impossible to get rid of the printing ink, especially during the short lunch break, that accumulated in fingernails, leading to lead poisoning. M.P. Sivagnanam is known to have blamed his years as a compositor for a chronic peptic ulcer. A contemporary printers' guide written by the Superintendent of the Government Press, Madras, advised workers to wash their hands properly and never take food in a room where there was lead or lead work.[123] Adequate time and soap to clean their hands was therefore a common demand made by press workers.[124] A medical survey of a large printing press in Madras city found tuberculosis rampant.[125]

Given the poor wages and bad working and living conditions, pressmen often proved inefficient and indifferent. This was reflected in the quality of work produced, especially the proofs. As Maraimalai Adigal remarked, 'The matter composed by my dull-headed pressman was so full of mistakes that I was tired of correcting them.'[126] A contemporary style book put it more elaborately: 'The proofs [. . .] swarm with mistakes for which you can see no reason; [. . .] spelling and punctuation are marvels of misdirected ingenuity [. . .] you spend many weary hours correcting these proofs, and, when they come back to you again, many of your marks have not been attended to, and often fresh errors have been made. Again you correct and

[121] Evidence of C. Basudev, Madras Government Press Labour Union, *Royal Commission on Labour in India*, vol. 7, pt 1, 1931.

[122] C. Basudev, ibid.

[123] W.R. Gates, *The Indian Printer's Guide and Handbook* (Madras: n.p., 1922), p. 61.

[124] See, for instance, G.O. no. 1849, Edn & Pub. Health, 3 August 1938.

[125] 'Tuberculosis: Notes on Institutional Tuberculosis', *Indian Medical Record*, June 1935. I owe this reference to V.R. Muraleedharan.

[126] *MD*, 28 February 1911.

again unsatisfactory proofs are returned to you; till at last, out of sheer weariness the strike order is given.'[127]

Accounts of the period are full of such complaints. At a time when electric lights were uncommon, proofreading was arduous. The ink on proofs impressed on dampened absorbent paper tended to smudge. This was accentuated by worn-out types and the use of fountain pens. V.S. Srinivasa Sastri blamed his prematurely acquired long-sight, at the age of 35, on many years of proofreading by candlelight for G.A. Natesan's publishing company.[128] Thiru.Vi.Ka's failing eyesight and blindness in his old age is popularly attributed to his meticulous proofreading under adverse conditions.

That workers gave unnecessary trouble and absented themselves without leave, especially on occasions when urgent work needed to be done, was the common complaint of press owners. Maraimalai Adigal often grumbled that he had to train novices and tolerate sloppy workers. 'I have had to stand beside the pressman for the last two weeks and teach him press work. He has no education at all and he is unable to grasp anything [. . .]'[129] Maraimalai Adigal's diaries are full of angry remarks born of frustration working with such men.[130] He refers to them as 'wretches' and 'rascals'.[131] Workmen were also proverbially known for stealing type.[132] This is likely to have got them

[127] Warren, *Author and Printer*, p. 3. For an interesting article on the comedy of typographic errors, see K.A.P. Viswanatha Pillai, 'Kavanippeergala', *Sivanesan*, 21 Panguni, Prabava (March 1928); also 'Achup Pey', *Sakti*, March 1946. The best of the oral lore about typographic errors is however unprintable!

[128] V.S. Srinivasa Sastri, in *Souvenir of the Sashtiabdha–Poorthi of the Hon. G.A. Natesan*, p. 2. Srinivasa Sastri prided himself, saying 'My eye had a flair for the detection of wrong spelling and wrong type, and so strong is the bias that I then caught that I cannot now read even a borrowed book without itching to decorate the margin with marks for which every succeeding reader will curse me.'

[129] Letter to V. Thiruvarangam Pillai, 29 December 1919. Also see the letter dated 23 April 1932, Maraimalai Adigal Papers.

[130] See *MD*, 3 May 1917; 25 April 1917; 20 October 1917; 26 December 1917; 5 January 1918; and 18 March 1918, ibid.

[131] *MD*, 23 August 1919 and 5 October 1917.

[132] *MD*, 28 March 1943; also G.O. no. 834, Edn & Pub. Health, 17 April 1939.

little in terms of money. But together with little acts of disobedience, sloppy work, and absence without leave, it can be seen as a form of everyday resistance to their degrading and unremunerative occupation.

The printing men who catered to the Tamil book trade did not gain much even in the wave of unionization that swept the Madras working class in the inter-war period. Only workers in the bigger printing establishments like Hoe & Co. and Dinamani Press were organized and able to make some demands and redress a few of their grievances.[133] Given these conditions, printers were infamous for their unreliability. Apart from certain acclaimed presses like Sadhu Achukkudam, Liberty Achukkudam, and Kabeer Printing Works, most other presses were notorious for not keeping to deadlines, and for shoddy work.

We find in the world of Tamil publishing, the delayed emergence of the categories of authors, publishers, and printers. Only after World War I do these emerge, and even then they are not really distinct and specialized. Authors emerged as a category by the 1920s but they were neither full-fledged professional writers nor hacks who could make a decent living. And then, when publishing houses emerged after World War I, they weren't really better off because publishing houses were small and dependent on textbook prescriptions. Specialized publishing did not exist, publishing houses were not organized and run on corporate lines, and printers had modest technological equipment and poorly paid workers. Tamil publishing never grew to be an industry and struggled even to qualify as a respectable trade.

[133] See *Janasakti*, 22 July 1939; 1 July 1939; *Navasakti*, 30 June 1939. Also see D. Veeraraghavan, 'The Rise and Growth of the Labour Movement in the City of Madras and its Environs, 1918–1939', unpublished PhD thesis, IIT, Madras, 1987.

## 5

# Songsters of the Crossroads

In Kalki's acclaimed novel *Thyaga Bhoomi* (1939) Sambu Sastri, an old Brahmin recluse, is served court summons in a sensational case over the restitution of conjugal rights. When he wonders what it is all about, the surprised *amina* (bailiff) says, 'Yes, sir! This case is much talked about! There is even a quarter anna songbook on it!'[1] The material basis of literary production in Tamilnadu from the mid-nineteenth century to the 1930s has focused thus far on elite publishing. Little has been said about popular publishing. Here I explore this little-known world of 'quarter anna songbooks'.[2]

As Ranajit Guha famously pointed out, the route into uncharted subaltern domains lies considerably through tantalizing bits of information gleaned from elite sources.[3] Pursuing this line of analysis, I try first to document the contempt that the elite classes had for this

[1] Kalki, *Thyaga Bhoomi* (1939, rpnt. Chennai: Vanathi Pathippagam, 1988), p. 325.

[2] For nineteenth-century Bengal, this world of songbooks, ballads, and popular print is brought alive in the first two chapters of Tanika Sarkar's *Hindu Wife, Hindu Nation*, pp. 23–94; Anindita Ghosh, *Power in Print: Popular Publishing and the Politics of Language and Culture in a Colonial Society* (New Delhi: Oxford University Press, 2006). For studies of this domain in Uttar Pradesh over the same period, see Charu Gupta, *Sexuality, Obscenity, Community: Women, Muslims, and the Hindu Public in Colonial India* (Delhi: Permanent Black, 2002), and Francesca Orsini, *Print and Pleasure: Popular Literature and Entertaining Fictions in Colonial North India* (Delhi: Permanent Black, 2010).

[3] Guha's *Elementary Aspects of Peasant Insurgency in Colonial India* (Delhi: Oxford University Press, 1983) as well as his essay 'The Prose of Counter-Insurgency', argue the case for reading elite sources against the grain in order

stream of publishing. Subsequently I look at the term *gujili*, which was commonly used to designate popular publishing. Based on a rich documentation of actual chapbooks and ballads, a reconstruction of this world is then attempted, focusing both on production and diffusion. The final section establishes the interaction between elite and popular publishing. The percolation of nationalism into popular consciousness, the relation of elite poets to popular publishing, and the sanitization and appropriation of popular texts are the other themes thrown up by the material.

## Contempt for Popular Literature

Some of the earliest references to popular literature are to be found in *Viveka Chintamani*, a journal run by the Diffusion of Knowledge Agency founded in 1892 by some English-educated Brahmin intellectuals led by C.V. Swaminatha Iyer. It generally deplored the absence of 'useful knowledge' in the vernacular. Contrasting the once glorious age of the Tamil language, it commented on the fact that contemporary Tamil books were full of chapbooks and ballads, describing them as '*thannane pattukal*' (songs in the 'thannane' rhythm, after the catchy rhythms in which they were set).[4] Their basic complaint was that these songs and ballads instilled lust, vanity, and other despicable qualities in readers. Apart from using the generic term 'thannane pattukal' to refer to these chapbooks, specific mention is made of ballads such as *Kuttrala Kuravanji*, *Mukkudal Pallu*, and *Madanakamarajan Kathai* which were said to be full of lewd descriptions of women.[5]

These are the earliest references, contemptuous or otherwise, available about popular literature. Gradually, the number of such comments increases. The details are embellished and the criticism becomes sharper. In A. Madhaviah's classic novel *Padmavathy Charithiram* (1898) we find Narayanan and Gopu, two schoolgoing young

---

to access peasant consciousness. See Ranajit Guha (ed.), *Subaltern Studies II* (Delhi: Oxford University Press, 1983), pp. 1–42.

[4] *Viveka Chintamani*, 1 (1), May 1892.

[5] Ibid., 1 (8), December 1892.

men, condemning women who read such popular ballads.[6] Subramania Bharati, commenting on a chapbook on the Arbuthnot Bank Crash of 1906—a scandalous European bank crash due to mismanagement, which ruined many native families—said, '[This ballad] unlike other *kummis* [a popular ballad form] is not full of blunders which are repulsive to scholars.'[7] Thus, by the turn of the twentieth century, popular songs and ballads were seen as morally suspect, as well as full of flaws, blunders, and grammatical errors which the well educated could not endure. Thiru Vi. Kalyanasundara Mudaliar, respected scholar and politician, made a most passionate plea against popular publishing, when he complained, 'The writings of some late lamented scholars are grieving in the hands of a few gujili market publishers. To think of it fills one's eyes with tears.'[8] His mentioning gujili, a term which we will consider in detail in the next section, is interesting: it becomes a convenient shorthand to define what was good, 'genteel', and acceptable, and what was not.

*Navasakti*, Thiru.Vi.Ka.'s weekly, lamented that gujili books and popular novels were becoming the order of the day.[9] *Lakshmi* went one step further when, writing a favourable review of V. Swaminatha Sarma's nationalist play based on the Scot nationalist Robert Bruce's life, thought it adequate to describe it as 'not the sort of plays that are heaped up and sold cheap in the gujili'. It went on to describe how well the book was produced, in 'letters clear like pearls, on smooth paper and bound in quality calico, like foreign books',[10]

[6] A. Madhaviah, *Padmavathy Charithiram* (1898, rpnt. Chennai: Vanavil Prasuram, 1978), p. 56. Madhaviah deliberately distorts the names of the ballads to *Kattappa Nayakkan Kummi* and *Moolialankari Pattu*, to caricature them and consequently make them abhorrent. C.N. Annadurai, in a talk delivered in 1948 on 'a library for every home', saw popular books such as these as the repositories of superstition and obscurantism. *Perarignar Annavin Sorpozhivugal*, vol. 1 (The Speeches of Anna; Chennai: Poompuhar Pathippagam, 2005), p. 338.

[7] *India*, 17 November 1906.

[8] Preface to *Pattinathar–Badragiriyar* (1923), reprinted in *Kumari Malar*, 33 (10), January 1977.

[9] Reprinted in *Lakshmi*, 2 (4), November 1924.

[10] *Lakshmi*, 2 (5), December 1924.

implicitly contrasting it with the slipshod production typical of gujili books.

Likewise, when S. Satchidanandam Pillai, Tamil Saivite scholar, in a letter to V. Thiruvarangam Pillai, founder of the Saiva Siddhanta Kazhagam, voiced the general complaint that Kazhagam editions were expensive, the latter replied, 'To those who are used to buying gujili books cheap for generations, it is not easy to buy superior books at a higher price.'[11] Such references to gujili books exist in many other sources.[12] T.K. Chidambaranatha Mudaliar, a connoisseur known for his refined tastes, writes sarcastically about how he bought a copy of *Mukkudal Pallu*:

> How did the book look? [. . .] If one wiped the dust of it, the whole wrapper would peel off. The spine and edges were of calico. An orthodox calico—that is, saffron calico. Actually it was but a plain piece of saffron cloth! Calico is only a euphemism. If you open the cover, you will find a special kind of paper that will put Dacca muslin to shame. So soft. So flimsy. I turned the first page. And it tore away in the middle. But the most fantastic aspect of it all was the manner in which it had been printed. The 'editor' must have given the copy to the compositor boy and said, 'Compose it as you like'. The boy ravaged the vocabulary, grammar, and prosody. Black ink was smeared on the pulp paper, and somehow it became a book. Not a single verse—not a single line—could be seen in its true form. It was easier to solve a hundred crossword puzzles than read this book.[13]

This, in a nutshell, makes clear all the attributes that made gujili books particularly deplorable to the elite.

If this disdain was shared by all sections of elite society, the colonial state did not stint when contributing its own share to it. In the

[11] S. Satchidanandam Pillai to V. Thiruvarangam Pillai, 16 March 1922. Thiruvarangam Pillai's reply of 21 March 1922 has been jotted down on the reverse. S. Satchidanandam Pillai Papers.

[12] See S. Murugappa's comment on *Kambaramayanam* editions in *Kamban Kavithai* (Madras: Navayuga Prachuralayam [1939]), p. 140.

[13] Preface to M. Arunachalam (ed.), *Mukkudal Pallu* (Chennai: Tamil Noolagam, 1949). The preface was originally written as a review of the first edition in *Kalaimagal*, March 1941. The last line refers to the controversial crossword puzzle contests conducted then in *Ananda Vikatan*.

1930s, when the Registrar of Books was burdened with a huge library built up over the years through the mandatory submission of printed books under the Registration of Books Act 1867, he suggested a detailed scheme for the destruction of selected categories of books to make his library less unwieldy. Not surprisingly, popular books were his primary casualty. In his report to the Government of Madras he wrote: 'As a rule the bazaar book, by which I mean publications sold in open places, in markets and on roads, in bad print, bad paper, and bad get-up abounding in printing mistakes and expressed in vulgar language, may well be destroyed. They are a disgrace to any library. Such are, for instance, the ballad songs in Tamil of *Nallatangal*, *Alliyarasani*, *the Song of the Thief*, etc.'[14] Unfortunately for posterity the government accepted this proposal and a substantial part of this rare literature is lost.

### *Gujili*: From Place Name to Metaphor

The earliest reference to gujili is in the paradigmatic Orientalist lexicographical achievement, Rev. Miron Winslow's *A Comprehensive Tamil and English Dictionary* (1862). Winslow defined *kuchili* as 'an evening bazaar in a town'.[15] The authoritative *Tamil Lexicon* (1927) of the University of Madras, evidently drawing from Winslow, defined it in much the same terms: 'Evening bazaar'. It further suggested that the word was derived from Urdu and cited local usage as the authority.[16]

While these dictionaries refer to the gujili bazaar in general terms as an evening market, it was more specifically located in the Park Town area of Madras city, very near the Central Railway Station. The streets surrounding the Kandaswamy Temple or Kanda Kottam were what was called the Gujili Bazaar.[17] The *Tamil Lexicon* is probably

[14] G.O. no. 1349, Pub. (General) (hereafter Gen.), 19 October 1932.

[15] Miron Winslow, *A Comprehensive Tamil and English Dictionary* (1862, facsimile rpnt. New Delhi: Asian Educational Services, 1979), p. 312.

[16] *Tamil Lexicon*, vol. 2, pt 2 (Chennai: University of Madras, 1927), p. 1063.

[17] P.A. Pranatharthihara Sivan, *Vyasa Manjari* (1900), reprinted in *Kumari Malar*, 25 (9), December 1968.

wrong when it suggests an Urdu origin for the word. Between Walltax Road (now V.O.C. Road), adjoining the Central Station, and the Kandaswamy Temple are a number of small lanes wherein lives a sizeable Gujarati population.[18] A celebrated play of the times, *Dambachari Vilasam*, calls this place 'Kuchilikkadai'.[19] We know that the Gujaratis are referred to in Tamil variously as *kuccharar*, *kuchiliyar*, *kuchariyar*, etc.[20]—all Tamilized forms of gujili, the use of the Sanskrit/*grantha* 'j' being obviated by substituting it with 'ch'.

A chapbook of 1895 on the Kandaswamy Temple annual festival provides concrete evidence of the fact that the gujili market derived its name from Gujaratis living in the locality. This chapbook, a *valinadai patham*, a ballad set in the form of a couple going on a journey—usually to a religious centre, wherein the man points out various sights to his spouse—refers to a variety of shops in the vicinity of the Kandaswamy Temple. Some of the shops are specifically referred to as those of the *kucchiliyars*.[21] It seems certain therefore that the gujili market owed its name to the Gujarati residents of the locality.

Gujili market was then well known for a variety of goods and services, especially cheap ones. As a contemporary pilgrim guidebook described it, '*Gujili Bazaar – China Bazaar Street.* In the evenings this street is very crowded and sports a very festive look. Even those who have no wish to spend a paisa will want to buy from the innumerable shops selling textiles, enticing fruits, pictures, gold and silver ornaments, copper, brass and bronze utensils, perfumes, umbrellas, footwear, sticks, sweetmeats, books, and other items.'[22]

[18] See Dilip Kumar, *Moongil Kuruthu* (Chennai: Cre-A, 1985) for two very sensitive stories on Gujarati life in this locality.

[19] Cited in T.M.C. Ragunathan, *Samuthaya Ilakkiyam* (Social Literature; 1964, rpnt. Madurai: Meenakshi Puthaka Nilayam, 1980), pp. 146, 152. *Dambachari Vilasam* was authored by Saidapuram Kasi Viswanatha Mudaliar (1806–71), a Brahmo Samajist.

[20] *Tamil Lexicon*, vol. 2, pt 2; Winslow, *Tamil and English Dictionary* (1862); N. Kathiraivel Pillai, *Tamil Moli Akarathi* (1906).

[21] *Chennai Kandaswamy Vedarpani Mahorchava Valinadai Patham* (Chennai: n.p., 1895).

[22] Mylai Ko. Pattabhirama Mudaliar, *Vishnu Sthala Manjari*, 2nd part

The chapbook referred to earlier also lists similar things that could be purchased at this bazaar: cashew nuts, rice, betel leaves, thread, locks, lanterns, and cane items—hence the name Rattan Bazaar.[23] A compendium on frauds and cheats observed that many unscrupulous mail-order businessmen passed off fountain pens, anklets, bracelets, clocks, etc. bought cheaply at the gujili as quality goods.[24] The gujili bazaar was an important market of those days, especially for inexpensive goods. Maraimalai Adigal often visited this market when he settled down in Madras after being appointed a Tamil teacher in the Madras Christian College. Here he bought plates, vessels, combs, chimneys, paper, silver, etc.[25] Likewise, we discover that T.K. Chidambaranatha Mudaliar had actually gone shopping here for a lantern when he chanced upon a copy of *Mukkudal Pallu*.[26]

But the gujili was no innocuous marketplace: it had its seamier side. Accounts of the period abound in references to the pickpockets and petty thieves active in the bazaar. The pilgrim guidebook cited earlier cautioned pilgrims: 'Instead of gaping at the various sights, people should take care of the purses in their pockets and waists. There are here any number of pickpockets.'[27] Thillai Govindan, the protagonist of A. Madhaviah's eponymous novel, while strolling one evening in the gujili bazaar near a second-hand bookstall, loses a purse containing over Rs 50.[28] T. Chelvakesavaraya Mudaliar, in one of his short stories, writes of how cutpurses proved their mettle in the

(1913), reprinted in A.K. Chettiar (ed.), *Tamilnadu: Payanakkatturaigal* (Tamilnadu: Travelogues; Chennai: R. Ramachandran and A. Veerappan, 1968), p. 17.

[23] *Chennai Kandaswamy Vedarpani Mahorchava Valinadai Patham*.

[24] Raja Gopala Bhoopathi, *Mathimosa Vilakkam* (Chennai: Ananda Bodhini, 1929, 4th edn), p. 131. For an analysis of this book, see my 'Street-Smart in Chennai: The City in Popular Imagination', in *In Those Days There Was No Coffee: Writings in Cultural History* (New Delhi: Yoda Press, 2006).

[25] *MD*, 17 March 1898; 19 January 1899; 5 March 1899.

[26] M. Arunachalam, *Mukkudal Pallu*, Preface, p. 51.

[27] Pattabhiraman Mudaliar, *Vishnu Sthala Manjari*.

[28] A. Madhaviah, *Thillai Govindan* (Madras: Srinivasa Varadachari & Co., 1903), p. 62.

nearby People's Park—an extremely popular amusement centre of the times—when they had no work at the gujili. They were adept at picking currency notes and coins tucked in people's waists, embroidered upper garments, and women's necklaces.[29] So notorious was gujili that it came to be called Thieving Bazaar. It was left to A. Madhaviah to write to his friend J.C. Molony, the Municipal Commissioner, that such a name did no credit either to the police or the public. Consequently, Madhaviah writes, the place was rechristened Gujili Bazaar.[30]

Adding to its notoriety as a hotbed of thieves was its ill repute as the hangout of fraudsters. Some of these would succeed in fobbing off used and poor-quality spectacles, gilded buttons, and scissors as new.[31] Fraudsters who printed a variety of catalogues and sold the goods shown there through Value Payable Post made quick profits because, it was said, they had bought the goods cheap at gujili bazaar.[32] There was a reason why the wares were cheap. *Dambachari Vilasam* says Brahmins who had officiated at funeral rites and obsequies would sell off clothes gifted to them at the gujili bazaar.[33]

Gujili bazaar was also known for its locksmiths. Maraimalai Adigal once had to seek the help of a locksmith here when the key of his almirah broke.[34] Given the nature of their vocation, locksmiths had often to oblige characters less than scrupulous, which perhaps added to the infamy of gujili.

It is also likely that immoral traffic in women took place in the vicinity of the gujili. To this day, streetwalkers are often colloquially referred to as gujili. Whatever be the source of this, 'a fancy mark of mica worn on the forehead by women' came to be called '*gujili pottu*'.[35] This fashionable *pottu* was so closely associated with immoral women that when young girls took to wearing it they were often

[29] T. Chelvakesavaraya Mudaliar, *Abinava Kathaigal* (Modern Stories; Chennai: n.p., 1921), p. 67.

[30] *Panchamirtam*, September 1925.

[31] *Mathimosa Vilakkam*, p. 64.

[32] Ibid., p. 64.

[33] Cited in Ragunathan, *Samuthaya Ilakkiyam*, pp. 146, 152.

[34] *MD*, 23 May 1898.

[35] *Tamil Lexicon*, vol. 2, pt 2, p. 955.

chided or even abused by their elders.[36] The *Tamil Lexicon* defined it as '*thalukku pottu*' (a showy and ostentatious *bindi*), thereby acknowledging its immoral overtones.[37] As one journal, *Vettrikodiyon*, put it, 'Certain persons have made the Guzily Street their resort, and contrive devices to cheat the people. Some offer for sale old clothes and gilt jewels at the corners of streets where there is a great concourse of people; others act in the capacity of brokers and allure ignorant buyers with fair speech to shops where they are fleeced. Cannot these people think of other modes of obtaining a livelihood than by practising upon people and cheating them of their money?'[38] Fittingly, *Mathimosa Vilakkam*, a compendium of frauds, stated: 'It requires no reiteration to say that Gujili Bazaar is the seedbed of all frauds in Chennai.'[39]

It was in this milieu that the book market of the gujili operated. From around the last decades of the nineteenth century to well into the 1960s there were bookshops in the market selling chapbooks, ballads, and a whole range of popular reading material. These were generally characterized by their poor quality of production, catering to the common folk. Kanakalingam, the hero of Vindhan's novel *Palum Pavaiyum* (1951), works in one such bookshop, which mainly deals in panchangams and other such prognostic literature.[40] Part of the larger hegemonic project of the emerging middle class entailed looking down upon this variety of literature, and designating them 'gujili books' after the name of the locality in which they were extensively produced and disseminated. The ignominy associated with the market—cheap goods, unscrupulous locksmiths, pickpockets, cutpurses, petty thieves, and streetwalkers—became the brush with which to tar the books as well. So in several senses the term gujili conjured up in the minds of people, at least in the middle class, a very reprehensible image. A place name became the metaphor for

[36] Interviews with Tha. Kovendhan, 20 June 1992; Sundara Ramaswamy, 4 November 1992.

[37] *Tamil Lexicon*, vol. 2, pt 2, p. 955.

[38] *Madras Native Newspaper Reports* for week ending 28 June 1879.

[39] *Mathimosa Vilakkam*, p. 34.

[40] Vindhan, *Palum Pavaiyum* (1951, rpnt. Chennai: Star Prasuram, 1978), pp. 11 and 61.

a distinct kind of 'low' culture, the 'other' of respectable and honourable living as well as, by extension, publishing. In many ways this is reminiscent of Grub Street in London, where a similar process was at work.[41] Nearer home the 'Battala publications' of late nineteenth-century Bengal offer an analogous case, the name deriving from the poorer quarters of north Calcutta where they were produced. As Sumanta Banerjee points out, 'In respectable circles, the "Battala books" . . . were associated with dirty stories, spicy accounts of local scandals and poor print.'[42]

## Ballads and Chapbooks

Though gujili came to denote a certain class of publications, gujili books were by no means homogeneous. The catalogue of P.M. Raju Mudaliar & Sons enables us to categorize popular literature as its publishers themselves saw it and presented it to prospective buyers and readers.[43] This lists over 900 books under the following heads: religion, story books, *ammanai*, *vilasam*, plays, *kirtanais*, medicine, astrology, 'one anna books', 9 paisa books, 6 paisa books, Muslim books, *peria eluthu* (literally, 'big letter') books, and 'newly' printed books.

The category of religion consisted of a wide range of books providing paraphrases of classics like *Kambaramayanam*, *Thiruvachagam*, *Thevaram*, the many puranams, and the works of the various Siththars (medieval iconoclastic poets with supernatural powers). *Ammanai*, *malai*, and *kirtanai*, later designated as minor literary genres (*chitrilakkiyam*), were ballad forms narrating popular stories. *Nallathangal*

[41] Pat Rogers, *Grub Street: Studies in a Subculture* (London: Methuen, 1972), esp. ch. 6: 'The Grub Street Myth'. Also see Kathy MacDermott, 'Literature and the Grub Street Myth', in P. Humm, *et al.* (eds), *Popular Fictions* (London: Methuen, 1986).

[42] Sumanta Banerjee, *The Parlour and the Streets: Elite and Popular Culture in Nineteenth Century Calcutta* (Calcutta: Seagull, 1989), p. 184. Also see Kesavan, *Printing and Publishing in India*, vol. 1, pp. 283–7. For a recent study, see Anindita Ghosh, *Power in Print.*

[43] See *Puli Pocket Diary 1909* published by the same firm. This diary provides, apart from other details, a detailed list of its publications.

*Kathai*, *Eniyettram*, *Alliarasani Malai*, *Nandanar Charithira Kirtanai*, and *Rama Nataka Kirtanai* were some of the better-known books in these categories. *Vilasam* was a popular drama form, and it involved dramatizing similar stories. The *peria eluthu* books were publications set in big and easy type, targeted very specifically at a neo-literate audience. Medical books were mostly in the nature of *materia medicas*, setting forth in detail the medicinal uses of various vegetables, fruit, and herbs, apart from providing diagnosis and prognosis for a wide range of illnesses. Books of the veterinary sciences also came under this head. Works of astrology dealt with the zodiac, omens, portents, auguries, dreams, and the like. I consider these books 'ballads' and see them as distinguishable from chapbooks.

The chapbook, though produced on more or less similar lines as the ballad, differed, apart from being shorter, in one very crucial aspect: dissemination. These chapbooks were called *orana* (one anna) or *araiana* (half an anna) songbooks, after their price. The books were usually of 8 or 16 pages, in either Demy 8vo/16vo or Crown 8vo/16vo. The chapbooks dealt with themes similar to those of the ballads.

The standard stock of the chapmen consisted of invocations to 'minor' and local deities such as Amman, lullabies, *oppary* (lamentation songs), *valinadai chindu*, *kavadi chindu*, *thanga chindu*, *pura pattu*, *seval pattu*, *kummi*, etc. For instance, offering homage to one local deity, Aeral Chairman Arunachala Swamigal, I found over a dozen songbooks published through a single decade. Songs on deities could be sold all through the year, but especially during specific annual festivals in honour of these particular deities. Lullabies and opparys, which were songs sung by women at the death of their near ones, always commanded a ready sale. *Valinadai chindu*, as noted earlier, was set in the manner of a couple on a tour, either to a temple or an entertainment centre, wherein the man pointed out and described in detail various sights to his partner. *Kavadi chindu* was a song sung ritually when pilgrims carried a palanquin like kavadi on their shoulders, involving self-mortification, to the Murugan temple in fulfilment of a vow. *Pura pattu* and *valaiyal chindu* were set as a conversation, usually between two women. *Thanga chindu* and *kullathara chindu* derived their names from the recurring refrain of *thangame* and *kullathara*. *Aesal* was a genre of sarcastic praise. *Lavani* was set as a debate over whether Manmadan, the god of love, was indeed destroyed by Lord Siva or whether the destruction was only symbolic.

These songs could be religious, quasi-religious, or secular. But all played an intimate part in the everyday life of the common folk. Morals and practical tips were also sought to be inculcated in readers via these. Numerous chapbooks caution against gambling, punting, participating in chit funds, patronizing whores, etc. Chapbooks like *Kaliyuga Chindu* (by Sirumanavur Munisami Mudaliar) generally lamented the topsy-turvy nature of the world in 'modern times'. Another important kind of chapbook had to do with popular astrology. Texts like *Sahadeva Sastram* were a guide to reading omens and portents from the sighting of birds, the ticking of lizards, etc. Predictions based on the exact time of the attainment of puberty were also provided in chapbooks such as *Pendugal Jathakamennum Ruthu Nool Sastram*. Songs for occasions such as marriages, especially songs meant to tease bride and bridegroom, formed part of the stock. Songs on the horror that was the mother-in-law no doubt found ready buyers among young women.

Given the fact that they were only booklets hawked at crossroads and marketplaces, they tended to speak of topical and sensational news. A contemporary critic observed: 'Some train should meet with an accident somewhere; or somebody should commit a murder; or some woman should give birth to a monkey; or a child should be born with three heads; or some place should be gutted in a fire. Immediately, these poets will compose a song. The lilt of the song and its word order enthral the common folk. Moreover, if the poet himself were to hawk the songs at the crossroads, who from among the common folk will not buy?'[44]

Sensational news naturally formed the staple of hawkers in their day-to-day business. Local scandals, murders, curious news items—such as the inauguration of novel locomotives such as aircraft, trains, and motor cars—and epidemics interested the common folk greatly in an age when mass media had not come into being. The

[44] *Suthanthira Sangu*, 13 July 1933.

proliferation of such themes was not missed by historians. L.D. Barnett, who prepared the catalogue of Tamil books in the library of the British Museum, observed:

> during the last 20 years the growth of Tamil literature has been copious and rapid in most branches [. . .] An interesting feature is the wealth of popular ballads [. . .] which deal with a great variety of themes: the attack of the German cruiser Emden during the War, local riots and murders, the ravage of the guinea-worm, the wonders of the aeroplane, social absurdities, and many other matters of topical interest are described in rhymes which, though usually of slight literary merit, are nevertheless of real value for the light which they throw upon the thought and feeling of the masses.[45]

Songs about murder were so popular that a separate genre called *kolai chindu* (chindu on murder) came into being; hundreds of such chindus were written and published.[46] These songs narrated in detail, no doubt with embellishment, murders by cuckolded husbands, adulterous women, wayward men, and violent thieves.[47] Some chapbooks on social bandits—like Jambulinga Nadar, Santhana Thevar, and Kodukkur Arumuga Padayachi—also survive. With the start of the mass phase of Indian nationalism, chapbooks with nationalist themes also began to form part of the stock-in-trade of the chapmen, as we shall see below.

What distinguished the ballads from the chapbooks was essentially the mode of dissemination. Given the fact that the ballads were

[45] L.D. Barnett, *A Catalogue of the Tamil Books in the Library of the British Museum*, vol. 2 (1931, facsimile rpnt. New Delhi: Asian Educational Services, 1998), pp. v–vi.

[46] The murder of Lakshmikantham (1944), a yellow journalist, was extremely popular among chapmen, and numerous popular booklets were published in the mid-1940s. A good book, taking into account the rich popular material, is waiting to be written on the Lakshmikantham murder.

[47] For the text of some *kolai chindus*, see *100 Puthakam Adangiya Nuthana Inbarasa Korvai* (Chennai: n.p., 1929). For a bibliography of *kolai chindus*, see Ci.Ma. Ravichandran and Pa. Subashbose, *Tamilaga Kolaichindu: Aaivadangal* (Coimbatore: Manju Pathippagam, 2001). For a pedestrian study, see Aru. Marudathurai, *Tamilil Kolai Chindu* (Musiri: Aruna Veliyeedu, 1991).

longer and consequently more expensive, they were rarely hawked by peddlers. They were usually stocked in and sold from petty shops, or spread by the roadside. John Murdoch, whose office, the Christian Vernacular Education Society, was a stone's throw from Gujili Bazaar, observed: 'In the evening about 25 book hawkers may be seen at the bazaar, sitting behind their piles of books.'[48]

By contrast, chapbooks were usually disseminated by chapmen, who were often the authors themselves, at street corners and market-places. Such chapmen would often play on the *taeppu* (tambourine) as they sang their songs. An observer derisively dubbed them 'songsters of the crossroads'.[49] The District Magistrate of Tirunelveli gives a clearer description: 'What generally happens in such cases is this. Some hawkers who have a gift of street singing generally gather a crowd in street corners and begin to sing. The songs catch the mass and are repeated by them. There is a sale of the books to the crowd assembled.'[50] Such street singing would gather huge crowds, as happened once in Pudukkottai late in the nineteenth century. A Muslim chapman was selling chapbooks at the crossroads where a lamp post stood. Mischievous little boys perched on it, and the Dewan of Pudukkottai, A. Seshia Sastri, had to warn the chapman to take care of the lamp post.[51]

It should also be emphasized that ballads and chapbooks were not two discrete categories; there was quite a bit of overlap. As noted, chapbooks often dealt with topical and sensational issues. Selling the entire printrun of a topical chapbook while the topic was hot may not always have been possible. Interest in specific scandals and murders could not last long. By the time the next sensation came along, the earlier one was forgotten. Chapmen found an ingenious way of marketing stock left over. A bunch of dated chapbooks would be bound

[48] Murdoch, *A Classified Catalogue of Tamil Printed Books*, p. xi. Also see T.K. Chidambaranatha Mudaliar's preface, in M. Arunachalam, *Mukkudal Pallu*, p. 51.

[49] *Suthanthira Sangu*, 13 July 1933.

[50] G.O. no. 58, Pub. (Gen.), 10 January 1935.

[51] U.V. Swaminatha Iyer, *Nallurai Kovai*, vol. 3 (1938, rpnt. Chennai: U.V. Swaminatha Iyer Library, 1991), pp. 23–5.

கணபதி துணை

ஜம்புலிங்க நாடார்
துற்விளையாடற் சிந்து.

இஃது
சூளை - மாணிக்க நாயகரவர்களால்
சென்னை சூளை
ஸ்ரீ பாரதி அச்சுக்கூடத்தில்
பதிப்பிக்கப்பெற்றது.

காப்பிரைட்] 1929. [விலை அணா 1.

இப்புத்தகம் தேவையானால், எஸ். டி. மாணிக்க நாயகர்,
இராமலிங்கம் அண்டு கம்பெனி, சூளை ஜரோட், மதராஸ்.

Fig. 5: A chapbook on the legendary social bandit Jambulinga Nadar. Printed on flimsy paper, with the other side showing through.

Fig. 6: A typical illustration—from the ballad *Siruthondabathan Kathai.*

together with a new title page. These were generally referred to as *chillarai kovai* or *chillarai kattadam* (literally, assorted miscellanies). Like *festschriften* in our time, these had little if any thematic unity and fitted their description as miscellanies.[52] Sometimes thematic collections were also brought out, but they tended to be shorter, like *16 Desathathisaya Kolaikothu* (a bunch of 16 murder songs). Through this manner of putting together chapbooks they became ballad books, and were marketed as such.

The chapmen also showed great enterprise in enlarging their repertoire. The 1920s and early 1930s—just before the advent of the talkies—saw the rapid spread of gramophone records across the Tamil country. Companies such as HMV, Columbia, Odeon, etc. released scores of records based on songs sung by popular stage artistes as well as as-yet-unknown singers. The gramophone became such a phenomenon that one historian describes it as a 'music boom'.[53] Gujili

[52] See, for instance, *100 Puthakam Adangiya Nuthana Inbarasa Korvai* (New Pleasurable Assortment of 100 Books; Chennai: n.p., 1929); *200 Puthakam Onrai Chertha Pala Pattu Chillarai Kovai* (Assorted Miscellany of Various Songs from 200 Books; Chennai: n.p., 1926).

[53] Steve Hughes, 'The "Music Boom" in Tamil South India: Gramophone,

## மண்ணடி லக்ஷமையாவின்

# மர்டரின் மர்மம்.

கல்வாக்கு நீகொடடி என்ற மெட்டு.

ஆண் மனதுக் கிசைந்தவளே
மாங்குயில் போன்றவளே
வணக்க முடையவளே
வருத்தமென்ன மயிலே — மன

பெண் வருத்தப் படவுமில்லை
வாதுசூது ஒன்றுமில்லை
பொருத்தமாய் யுரைத்தகொலை
போனவழி தெரியவில்லை — வரு

ஆண் சொல்லுவேன் கேளுமடி
சிங்காரமான லேடி
கள்ளமில் லாமலடி
கருத்தாய் நீ கேட்பாயடி — மன

பெண் கட்டழகா காதலரே
கனமாய் உரைப்பீர் நீரே
இஷ்டமுள்ள நாயகரே
ஏந்திழைக் கேசொல்வீரே — வரு

ஆண் சென்ற சிலநாள்முன்னே
சேயிழையே கேளும்கண்ணே
இன்பமாய் மண்ணடிபெண்ணே
இராமசாமி வீதிதன்னில்

வளையல்சிந்து மெட்டு.

1 கன்னியாவும் ராஜமுடன்
கலந்திருந்த போது கொஞ்ச
காலத்தின்பின் வாது நேர
கட்டளையோ மாது அந்த
கட்டழக னுடனே அவள் வாழ்ந்துவந்தாள் தோது

Fig. 7: Page from a chapbook on a scandalous murder. Note the bold print.

publishers transcribed these songs and published them as chapbooks. Needless to say, these were not authorized and no copyright permission was taken to publish them. Songs from, and sometimes even the scripts of, popular plays were thus published.

In Madras, apart from Gujili Bazaar, Moore Market, Choolai, and George Town (especially Mannady) were important centres of dissemination. Choolai was crucial to the popular literature circuit, especially the chapbooks, because it was a thickly populated working-class locality.[54] Choolai was surrounded by the Binny Mills (then the largest textile mills of South India), the Tram Shed, the Central Station, and the Salt Cotaurs (where trucks were loaded and unloaded). No wonder, apart from being a major centre for chapbook and ballad production, it was also the haunt of hawking peddlers.[55] The chapmen themselves, in due course of time, came to be called 'Choolai Kavignar' (the poets of Choolai).[56]

In Madurai, Pudumantapam just across the Meenakshi Temple was another major centre of diffusion, especially for ballads. In Pudumantapam rows of bookstalls catered to the needs of the milling pilgrim crowds, especially from the nearby villages.[57]

In rural areas itinerant chapmen carried reading material to the people. Weekly markets, and temple and village festivals, were occasions for marketing ballads and chapbooks. Kasim, with lullabies and

---

Radio and the Making of Mass Culture', *The Historical Journal of Film, Radio and Television*, 22 (4), 2002.

[54] See *Namathindia Tholilalar Thalaivargalin Narpugal Prabalya Arputha Geetham* (Chennai: 1919), a chapbook which contains songs in praise of labour leaders such as M. Singaravelu Chettiar, Adikesavalu Nayagar, V. Chakkarai Chettiar, B. Shiva Rao, and T.P. Meenakshisundaram Pillai.

[55] Interview with M. Babu, son of K.A. Madurai Mudaliar, a leading popular publisher of the inter-war period, aged 56 years, Chennai, 2 June 1992.

[56] Chandilyan, *Porattangal*, p. 43.

[57] Ki. Rajanarayanan writes about how his friend 'Annachi' Kandasami Chettiar, from Koilpatti over 100 km from Madurai, bought a copy of Karaikkal Ammaiyar's early medieval poems from Pudumantapam', *Ki. Rajanarayanan Katturaigal* (Essays of Ki. Rajanarayanan; Sivagangai: Annam, 1991), p. 188.

opparys, toured the small towns and villages of Thenthirupperai, Aeral, Thiruchendur, Valliyoor, Palayamkottai of Tirunelveli district, and Nagore and Keelakkarai in Ramanathapuram district from the late 1940s well up to the early 1980s.[58] K.A. Gunasekaran writes of how, in the 1960s, people from his village of Kiranur would go to Ilayankudi town for the Saturday market and buy chapbooks along with provisions.[59]

Apart from these areas chapbooks were quite popular in the Kolar Gold Fields (KGF) of the princely Mysore State. As gold was beginning to be mined on capitalist lines in the late nineteenth century, a huge lower-caste working force from the northern districts of the Tamil country migrated to this region. (It was here that the radical neo-Buddhist movement of Ayothee Thass Pandithar found its most enthusiastic adherents.) Many of the songbooks that emanated and circulated in the KGF were addressed to a working-class audience and were sometimes replete with moral sermonizing.[60]

Chapbooks seem to have had a wide circulation in the Tamil Muslim world. Earlier we saw that there was a category called 'Muslim books' advertised by a gujili publisher. The songs of Tamil Sufis such as Kunangudi Masthan Sahib and Thakkalai Peer Muhammed Vappa were part of this repertoire. One scholar has listed over sixty chapbooks by and on Muslims.[61]

Sellers of popular literature, especially of ballads, had a field day during major religious festivals.[62] The Ekadesi festival at Srirangam, the Karthigai festival at Thiruvannamalai, the Chithirai festival at Madurai, and the Theppam festival of Mylapore were times of hectic

[58] Interview with M. Kasim, aged 70 years, Srivaikuntam, 7 November 1992.

[59] K.A. Gunasekaran, *Nagarsar Nattuppura Kathaippadalgal* (Urban Folk Ballads; Sivagangai: Annam, 1988), p. 118.

[60] I owe this information and the songbooks to Janaki Nair. For more on the KGF working class, see Janaki Nair, *Miners and Millhands: Work, Culture and Politics in Princely Mysore* (New Delhi: Sage, 1998).

[61] Semumu Muhamadali's preface to K.S. Seyedu Muhammed Annaviyar (ed.), *Nagore Pugairatha Vali Singara Oyil Chindu* (Chennai: Singai Pathippagam, 1985), pp. viii–4.

[62] Murdoch, *Classified Catalogue of Tamil Printed Books*, p. lxi.

activity. P.S. Kumaraswamy Raja, later Chief Minister of Madras and Governor of Orissa, recollecting his boyhood days (in the 1910s) gives a graphic description of the *adippura urchavam* in the famed temple town of Srivillipputtur, where scores of new stalls were set up.[63] During the twenty-day festival of *rappathu pagalpathu* during Vaikunda Ekadesi, popular publishers flocked to Srirangam. Books were spread out at the Rangavilas Mandapam and sold at fabulous discounts.[64] This came to be known derisively as 'Srirangathu pathivilai' (half rates of Srirangam).[65] Apart from travelling salesmen during festival seasons, all the major temple complexes included small bookstalls.

## Authors and Publishers

Little is known of the authors of the chapbooks except that they also peddled them. The question of authorship does not arise for the ballads as virtually all these were only the printed versions of a pre-existing folklore. The chapbooks provide us with the names of their authors, for they followed the convention of affixing signature lines in the songs. This, and the fact that through the course of the song the price of the chapbook was also often woven in, provides unquestionable evidence that the chapbooks were indeed hawked by their authors. The evidence is reinforced by the fact that quite a few chapmen, in the course of their songs, promise second instalments.[66]

Vijayapur Sabapathy Das, P. Rajagopal Naidu, T.V.R. Chinnasamy Pillai of Tirumalai, Muthialupettai V.A. Thyagaraja Chettiar, M.S. Sabjan, Pandit S. Pir Muhammed Rowthar, K.A. Madurai Mudaliar, and Choolai Manicka Nayagar are some of the songsters whose names crop up often. Sirumanavur Munisami Mudaliar seems to have been the doyen of these chapbook songsters, authoring numerous

[63] P.S. Kumaraswamy Raja, *Ilamai Ninaivugal* (Boyhood Memories; Chennai: Bharati Pathippagam, 1957), p. 46.

[64] *Ananda Bodhini*, December 1919.

[65] See the review of J.R. Rangaraju's *Rajambal* in *Amirtaguna Bodhini*, 15 August 1928.

[66] See *Janakiammal Sathi Thaimaman Kolai, Kanniyaral Kaluthu Vettunda Chinnappan Kolai Chindu*.

songs.[67] Choolai Manicka Nayagar made it a point in his chapbooks to introduce himself as Munisami Mudaliar's disciple.[68] Likewise R.B.S. Mani proudly proclaimed himself a student of T.P. Krishnaswamy Pavalar, a renowned popular playwright of his time.[69] Clearly, some of them were associated with the popular stage, as, in another instance, T.V.R. Chinnasamy Pillai is referred to by the appellation '*ayanpart*' (the one who plays the lead or best part in a play). Likewise, V.A. Thyagaraja Chettiar could be a playwright as he is referred to as *upathiyayar/vathiyar* (from 'upadhyaya', teacher or master; a term used to refer to one who wrote and trained stage actors). An advertisement in one of the chapbooks indicates that the author would 'for an advance' paint backdrops for stage plays.[70]

Information on a few of the songsters filters through because of their later involvement in (radical) politics. One of them, Nagai Saminathan, was born in a hamlet near Nagapattinam and studied only up to the third standard. The poverty of his family pushed him into working for a provision store, until he got an ill-paid job in the Nagapattinam Railway Workshop on a daily wage of Rs 0–5–4. He was 16 then, and he would read the poems of the Siththars, which were then available only in gujili editions. He also picked up the art of singing *lavani* songs from a co-worker, until a more politically conscious foreman spotted him and introduced him to the political literature of the Self-Respect Movement.[71] Gradually, he joined the

[67] See the obituary of his son's death in *Sentamil Selvi*, November 1950. For two articles on publishing by another of his sons, Siru. Muni. Natesa Mudaliar, see *Sentamil Selvi*, 5 (1–2), February–March 1927.

[68] See many of Choolai Manicka Nayagar's chapbooks in *100 Puthakam Adangiya*.

[69] See, for instance, *Nattin Nilamai Vilakkum Desabhakti Geethangal* (Chennai, 1931). Also interview with R.B.S. Mani's son B. Ramanan, who continues to deal in second-hand books in Mylapore, Chennai, 21 April 1993.

[70] *Kudalurai Cherntha Anukkampattu Chedal Muthalu Amman Sirappu*, 1914.

[71] The details of Nagai Saminathan's life are drawn from the biographical appendix in Nagai Saminathan, *Samadharma Geetham* (Chennai: Ponni, 1987).

radical left faction of the movement and later went on to join the Communist Party. He composed a number of songs set in the chapbook tradition but is chiefly remembered, if only by the Left, as the composer of the Tamil version of Eugène Pottier's 'Internationale', the popular anthem of the socialist movement.

Another chapbook man, Ve.Na. Thirumurthy (1904–1976), was born in a village near Erode and educated up to the fourth standard. He dabbled in a variety of low-paying work such as shepherding, doing menial chores in a provision store, working as a labourer in a railway workshop, farriering, haberdashering, etc. He composed and sang a variety of songs in the chindu and lavani forms. Influenced by the communist movement he picked up revolutionary themes, and Jeyakanthan remembers him singing such songs as he pushed his small haberdasher's cart on the streets of Tiruchy.[72] A historian researching the struggles of the women workers of textile mills in Coimbatore found his songs being sung in the mid-1980s.[73]

Of the author of *Kodukkur Arumugam Kolai Chindu*, Adhanur Kadhirvel, we know that he was an Adi Dravida (dalit) and occupied as an inland fisherman. He was literate.[74] 'Taeppu Kalaignar' Gurusami Das was known to everyone 'of the last generation' in the districts of Thanjavur, Tiruchy, and South Arcot. Belonging to the most backward caste of Vanniyar, he had no formal education and is known to have composed numerous songs on topical events.[75]

The lives of Nagai Saminathan and Thirumurthy illustrate the career of popular songsters, even if they are not exactly typical. With little or no education, they picked up the art of composing songs from the popular tradition, and continued to write in the same manner, even though they moved towards organized radical politics. There

[72] Jeyakanthan, *Sinthaiyil Ayiram* (Madurai: Meenakshi Puthaka Nilayam, 1987), pp. 114–16.

[73] I owe this information to M.V. Shobana Warrier.

[74] Ka. Muruganandam, 'Kodukkur Arumugam Kolaichindu', unpublished dissertation for diploma in folklore, Department of Tamil Literature, University of Madras, 1992, App. 1.

[75] Mu. Ilangovan, *Palayana Puguthalum* (Past Comes Back; Idaikkatu: Vayalveli Pathippagam, 2002), pp. 55–62.

must have been other songsters like them. Few have survived the 'enormous condescension of posterity', but the names of three have survived in a well known saying.

*Pichaikku Bhaskaradas*
*Perumaikku Sankaradas*
*Ichchaikku Muthusamy*[76]

This popular doggerel means Bhaskaradas' songs were sung even by beggars,[77] Sankaradas' songs were respectable,[78] and Udumalai Muthusamy Kavirayar wrote bawdy songs.

Apart from the fact that on many occasions many songsters printed and disseminated chapbooks, we know little about the process of production. On ballad books the information is even scantier. But it is clear that author cum publishers alone could not have sustained this vast production of popular literature. B. Rathna Nayagar & Sons, R.G. Pathy & Co., Choolai Manicka Nayagar, Sirumanavur Munisami Mudaliar, and K.A. Madurai Mudaliar seem to have been the prominent names in popular publishing. Unfortunately we have no account of them or their work. Only during the 1920s and 1930s, when this stream of publishing comes under the scrutiny of the colonial state for its handling of nationalist themes, do we get glimpses of behind-the-screen activities. In the wake of intensified nationalist activity and popular mobilization, scores of chapbooks were proscribed. On some occasions their authors, publishers, and printers were prosecuted.

[76] Surada, *Vinakkalum Suradavin Vidaigalum* (Questions and Surada's Answers; Chennai: Surada Pathippagam, 1991), p. 113.

[77] Beggars were important transmitters of popular songs. Their repertoire could be quite impressive with songs by Pattinathar, Thayumanavar, and Vallalar Ramalinga Adigal. U.V. Swaminatha Iyer describes in detail, how, in the latter half of the nineteenth century, Chandrasekara Kaviraja Pandithar recorded a brilliant *venba* from a wandering beggar. See U.V. Swaminatha Iyer, *Nallurai Kovai*, vol. 4 (1939, rpnt. Chennai: U.V. Swaminatha Iyer Library, 1952), pp. 130–6. He also says beggars sang *themmangu*, *vennila pattu*, and *para-para kanni*.

[78] Sankaradas Swamigal is now acclaimed as the father of the Tamil stage for writing popular plays and training a generation of stage actors.

These rare moments of colonial intervention provide insights into the processes by which chapbooks were produced.

When the author and publisher of *Bhagat Singh Kirtanamrutam* was prosecuted in 1931, it transpired that V. Nataraja Pillai had composed a number of songs on the death of Bhagat Singh and sold them for a consideration of only Rs 4. The petty bookstall owner of Cuddalore who purchased them printed 3,000 copies as a booklet. This printer was an illiterate widow who owned a small press managed by her brother. Since the author was also personally pushing the sales of the chapbook, it is likely that he was paid a commission. During the hearing he confessed that he never meant to write anything seditious and produced, as proof, some of his earlier compositions in praise of the King Emperor and the Governor of Madras.[79]

In the case of another chapbook on Bhagat Singh, it emerged that T.S. Kanakaṣabai of Tenpathi wrote and published 4,000 copies of it. The chapbook was printed in a small press which made only Rs 4 from the entire transaction. Kanakasabai pleaded that he wrote solely with a view to make some money, and he swore his intentions were never seditious.[80]

In yet another case the printer of a chapbook, once again on Bhagat Singh, happened to be a humble compositor in a local press who had opened a small outfit called Vedavalli Press. The Commissioner of Police remarked that he was 'a man of no status'.[81] In another case the Commissioner of Police, Madras, after his enquiries over the publication of *Arrestu Pattu* (containing songs about the arrest of Congress leaders), described the author K.T.R. Venugopal Das as 'a professional writer of songs', and K.A. Madurai Mudaliar, its printer/publisher, as 'a petty book seller'.[82]

The producers of chapbooks were small-time publishers whose occupation in the world of print did not fetch them a sufficient living.

[79] Judgement in C.C. no. 11/1931, District Magistrate's Court of South Arcot, in G.O. no. 1054, Pub. (Gen.) (Confdl), 12 October 1931.

[80] Judgement in C.C. no. 9/1931, District Magistrate's Court of South Arcot, in G.O. no. 1069, Pub. (Gen.) (Confdl), 8 August 1932.

[81] G.O. no. 1041, Pub. (Gen.) (Confdl), 8 October 1931.

[82] G.O. no. 2535, Pub. (Gen.) (Confdl), 29 December 1940.

So they hawked a variety of things, much like the haberdashers of early modern Europe. P.M. Raju Mudaliar & Sons described themselves as 'Book and Medicine Sellers, Gold Gilded German Silver Jewellers, Rubber Stamp Makers, Publishers of Annual Diaries and General Commission Agents.'[83] Many of their chapbooks also advertised the products they dealt in. Choolai Manicka Nayagar regularly advertised hair oil, Japanese silk scarves, oil for turning grey hair black, antidotes for scorpion bites, and soaps usable for depilation.[84]

> Well Known! Panacea!
>
> AYAKKANTHA THIRAVAKAM
>
> Friends, this wonder drug cures a surprising number of dreadful diseases. Thousands have used this to their satisfaction. This inimitable drug is an elixir for bodies weakened by disease and 'bad company'. It is prepared by the English method and is very pleasurable to the palate. Chronic coughs are alleviated with just two doses . . . Grey hair turns black . . . dropsy cured; smarting of the eyes and exhaustion of the limbs relieved. It makes faces glow, drives away fatigue. It's an appetizer. It elevates the spirit, strengthens the nerves, infuses new blood into the body, cures diseases caused by the imbalance of humours.

The variety of vocations they dabbled in shows that these producers of popular literature led a precarious existence. It must be remembered that chapbooks were sold cheap, sometimes as cheaply as 3 paise each. In several cases the chapbooks earned them, quite literally, their daily bread. Consequently they fiercely defended their 'right', such as this was, over 'copy'. Most of the texts they produced were not copyright material, and in any case copyright could not be enforced because of tedious legal processes within the colonial judiciary, especially for low-value goods. Yet they often claimed copyright over their publications. As Murdoch remarks, 'A considerable number of native books now bear on their title pages, "Registered Copyright". This is

[83] *Puli Pocket Diary 1909*.
[84] *Arul Nadai Palani Andi Pandaram Pattu* (Chennai, 1927).

always printed in English being considered more effective in that language. Sometimes it is expressed "Rehistered", "Coby right", "Copy write", & c.'[85]

Songsters also devised other means to protect their work. The usual device was to warn readers about 'corrupt' versions sold by other vendors. For instance, the publisher of *Navajavan Bharata Kirtanamrutam* (1931), in a note to an elegy on Bhagat Singh's death, said, 'In other books, this song is full of errors. For example, it says *kaluthai aruthathale*. Bhagat Singh was hanged and not beheaded. So we have corrected it to *nerithathale*. Moreover, we have corrected the alliterative forms and preambles along the right lines. Those who have memorized the earlier faulty version should now correct themselves.' An extra stanza was also added, which, it was claimed, was not to be found in other songbooks.[86] Likewise, Choolai Manicka Nayagar made it a point, in almost all his publications, to print a few lines cautioning against 'corrupt' editions as well as editions not published by his press.[87]

Naturally, such warnings and notices did not always have the desired effect. Competitors continued to publish the 'same' texts and make their living. More dire threats had then to be issued. A publisher called V.R. Elumalai Pillai put up the following verse in one of his publications:

> If he has been begotten
> by a chaste woman and a single man,
> he will not think of pirating my book.
> But if he has been born
> to a wretched widow cohabiting with three hundred men
> he will not hesitate to do so.[88]

J. Purushottama Naidu avowed that anyone who pirated his *Gramophone Swarasahitya Sangitha Thirattu* (4th volume, Madras, 1930)

[85] Murdoch, *A Classified Catalogue of Tamil Printed Books*, p. lxii.

[86] For similar advertisements, see *Bangalore Audhi Hindu Vinoda Sabha/ Periya Indira Sabha* (Chennai, 1900), wrapper information.

[87] See the chapbooks bound in *100 Puthakam Adangiya.*

[88] *Uppu Satyagraha Pattu* (Chennai, 1931).

would be deemed his concubine's son. Likewise the songster of *Angara Padukolai Alankara Chindu* issued this memorable warning: 'They who print or cause to get printed this book may be considered my sons, or they are despicable men who eat cows, or are impotent eunuchs.'[89]

There were any number of such instances. They indicate not only the desperation of chapbook producers to fiercely protect their means of livelihood, but also in some ways their worldview and values.

## The Elite and the Popular: Some Aspects of Interaction

Our discussion of popular literature, its production and consumption, brings us to the vexed question of the relationship and interaction between elite and popular culture. It is necessary to explore some aspects of the interaction and set it in the context of the hegemonic project of the Tamil middle class.

### *Nationalism and the Chapbooks*

There is, first, the handling of nationalist themes in chapbooks. This provides us with an illustration of an elite ideology diffusing into the lower strata of culture. It emphasizes the vitality that the latter possessed, a cultural energy which enabled it to appropriate elite culture.

From around the beginning of the Non Cooperation Movement in 1919 there began to flow a steady stream of chapbooks on nationalist leaders, non-cooperation, picketing, khaddar, temperance, and such other Gandhian themes. Gandhi was immensely popular among the songsters. Other leaders to receive attention were Motilal Nehru, C.R. Das, and in later days Subhas Chandra Bose and Jawaharlal Nehru. When Bhagat Singh was martyred, numerous chapbooks were published; in fact his fame may even be said to have eclipsed the Mahatma's.[90] As one colonial official said, 'This adulation of Bhagat

[89] Quoted in Aru. Marudathurai, *Tamilil Kolai Chindu*, p. 51.

[90] For a list of chapbooks on Bhagat Singh, see Supa. Veerapandiyan, *Bhagat Singhum India Arasiyalum* (Chennai: Kanimuthu Pathippagam, 1985).

Singh is definitely objectionable.'[91] Similarly, songs were composed when prominent Congress leaders were arrested. Consequently *arrestu pattu* (song of arrest) even became a distinct genre.

Lest it be thought that this was a nationalism of the Congress Party, a few caveats are in order. The nationalism of the chapbooks was a nationalism reworked by the songsters of the crossroads in harmony with popular mentalité. The leaders lionized in the chapbooks were portrayed as noble men, akin to venerated saints, with little regard for fact or the specificities of the individual leader. A song on one nationalist leader could well hold good for another. The elegies on Bhagat Singh would often be prefaced by an invocation of the Mahatma despite their differing ideologies and conflicting programmes.[92] For instance, in the *Mahatma Gandhi Khaddarananda Pattu* (*circa* 1929) the songster, Choolai Manicka Nayagar, claimed that khadi was the garment of Dadabhai Naoroji, Gopal Krishna Gokhale, Swami Vivekananda (who were all long dead before the introduction of khadi), and V.O. Chidambaram Pillai (who was opposed to the very concept of khadi). The songster made further claims.

> Khaddar will solve the problem of childless parents.
> Khaddar will absolve sins committed.
> Khaddar is close to the heart of chaste women.
> Khaddar drives away all diseases.
> Vedic khaddar dispels all evils and sins.
> O, women of Bharat buy khaddar, worn by our forebears.

The iconography used in the chapbooks is even more interesting. Gandhi in his turban (after his return from South Africa in 1915) in traditional Gujarati clothes was the image used most often to represent the Mahatma, even in the 1920s and 1930s, well after he had discarded it for the simpler dhoti and upper cloth.[93] We also find type-made blocks of Lord Krishna with his consorts in an elegy on

[91] G.O. no. 910, Pub. (Gen.) (Confdl), 7 September 1931.

[92] *Bhagat Singh Thookku Alankaram* (Mannargudi, 1931).

[93] For some such pictures, see *Mahatma Gandhi Dhyanam*; *Swarajya Bhavana Seeman Pandit Jawaharlal Geethamum Swarajya Thilagamum*; *Sentamil Desiya Geethangal.*

Bhagat Singh![94] In a chapbook on C.R. Das we find a picture of Gandhi, flanked on the one side by Pillaiyar (Ganesha) and Krishna, on the other destroying Kali, the snake, with no image of C.R. Das himself![95] Considering that making blocks was relatively expensive, gujili publishers found it convenient to recycle blocks. They also took frequent recourse to 'type-made' blocks—readymade blocks of small size cast in metal by type foundries. These were handy and hardy, and using them small printers could summon a range of images, such as those of Pillaiyar, Murugan, Amman, as well as religious symbols, floral designs, arabesques, etc. They were used extensively in job printing—of bill books, marriage invitations, funeral notices, visiting cards, etc. (and are in use to this day), and evidently gujili publishers found them very convenient for their purposes.[96]

The advertisements published in nationalist chapbooks were even more curious. Books like *Kokkokam* (a manual of sex), *Mathimosa Kalanjiyam* (a compendium on frauds), *Aan Pen Marma Rahasyangal* (on the secrets of man and woman), *Nija Pulugan* (funny stories about a prolific liar), etc. were frequently advertised in these chapbooks.[97] Some even thought it fit to advertise Madana Sanjivi Thathu-pushti Lehyam, an aphrodisiac,[98] and an ointment for venereal diseases, apart from drugs for fungal infections and antidotes for scorpion bites.[99]

Not only the colonial state, the nationalists too were baffled by this mixture of rhyming songs set to dramatic tunes, badly printed on flimsy paper, with incongruous and crude iconography, and 'immoral' advertisements. The colonial state, though it proscribed and confiscated scores of nationalist chapbooks, hardly ever prosecuted their

[94] *Bhagat Singh Thookku Alankaram*, 1931.

[95] *Ceeyardas Sirappu Deseeya Geetham* (Chennai, 1919).

[96] See A.R. Venkatachalapathy, 'Art in the Type Foundry: The Cultural Uses of Typemade Blocks in Colonial Tamilnadu', *Nunkalai*, March 1999.

[97] See, for instance, ibid.; *Mahatma Sirappu enum Gandhi Pattu*, 1931; *Swarajya Geetham*, 1931; *Motilal Pattu*, 1931; *Sardar Bhagat Singh Uyirvidutha Parithapa Geetham*, 1931; *Sentamil Desiya Geethangal*, 1931.

[98] *Mahatma Sirappu enum Gandhi Pattu*, pt 1 (Chennai, 1931).

[99] *Swarajya Geetham*, pt 1 (Chennai, 1937).

authors and publishers. As the Tamil Translator to the Government of Madras remarked of one such chapbook, 'The names of the different authors are not known [. . .] No information is also available as to whether it is worthwhile prosecuting the authors of these petty songs.'[100] And another official said of a similar work, 'The pamphlet is largely bunk and need not, I submit, be proscribed.'[101] There was no consistency in the government policy on nationalist chapbooks. This was quite understandable given the colonial state's lack of comprehension of even some of the elementary aspects of a chapbook—as the following remark by the Tamil Translator testifies: 'The title of the book is *Desiya Oonjal, Nalangu, Khaddar, Madhu Vilakku* and not *Gandhi Adigal Viruppam Niraiveruga*, which is only a prayer printed on the wrapper of the book.'[102] This reveals the difficulties in comprehending chapbooks from a perspective tuned to elite books. The title page of chapbooks looked so cluttered, with an array of titles, subtitles, slogans, advertisements, decorative borders and incongruous type-made blocks that it bewildered the elite.[103]

The nationalist chapbook came under the scrutiny of nationalists too, and their condemnation was no less damning than the colonial state's. As a contemporary observer remarked in the nationalist organ *Suthanthira Sangu*:

> People who are not qualified to write proper 'national songs' are composing national songs by the basketful. A song when Motilal dies, a song when Deshbandhu dies, a song on the [indentured labourers of] tea estates: nationalist songs like this are legion. If these songsters didn't manage to describe that the national leader in question was born on such and such a year, such and such a date and died on such and such a date after achieving such and such things, their heads would burst. If they start a song with the word '*thungam*', they have to continue to rhyme it with '*mangam*', '*chengam*', '*vangam*' and '*dangam*', whether

[100] G.O. no. 995, Pub. (Gen.) (Confdl), 19 July 1932.

[101] G.O. no. 1050, Pub. (Gen.) (Confdl), 10 October 1931.

[102] G.O. no. 995, Pub. (Gen.) (Confdl), 19 July 1932.

[103] The awkward footnote references to popular literature in this chapter perhaps bear testimony to this.

such words have any meaning or not [. . .] We and our national leaders should somehow escape from the danger of these poets of the crossroads.[104]

So, then, the nationalism of the chapbooks was not the high nationalism of annual Congress meetings and the All India Congress Committee, but the 'low' nationalism of the gujili—a nationalism reworked by songsters and chapmen. Their Gandhi had more in common with the Gandhi of the Gorakhpur peasants than with the Gandhi of Rajagopalachari or Bipan Chandra.[105] Thus cultural diffusion from the top down could never be straight and simple, the elite dictating terms to the people: a tabula rasa on which anything could be impressed. If an elite ideology reached to the lowest echelons, it was through a process of appropriation by the lower classes which made that possible.

### *The Appropriation and Sanitization of Popular Texts: Elite Poets and Popular Literature*

The relationship between elite and popular traditions was one of mutual interaction and not a one-way traffic. If the high nationalism of the Congress variety was reworked by the songsters of the crossroads, the elite tradition too picked up much from popular tradition.

Let us begin with Subramania Bharati, who drew heavily on popular verse forms to express himself. A prosodic classification of his complete poems reveals that of the total of 2,267 poems that comprise his collected works, no less than 794 are in the chindu metre, the dominant verse form used in the chapbooks and ballads.[106] This amounts

[104] *Suthanthira Sangu*, 13 July 1933. For a similar critique of nationalist songs on the popular stage, see Aakkur Anandachari, *Sriman S.G. Kittappa Charithiram* (A Life of S.G. Kittappa; 1933, rpnt. Senkottai: Kittappa Prachuralayam, 1938), p. 107.

[105] For different perceptions of Gandhi, see Shahid Amin, 'Gandhi as Mahatma: Gorakhpur District, Eastern UP, 1921–2', in Ranajit Guha (ed.), *Subaltern Studies III: Writings on South Asian History and Society* (Delhi: Oxford University Press, 1984).

[106] *Bharati Padalgal: Aaivu Pathippu*, App. 10, pp. 1162–86.

to about 35 per cent of his entire poetic output, making it the verse form employed most frequently by Bharati. He was not unfamiliar with popular literature and chapbooks and had commented, though only adversely, upon them. Bharati consciously drew upon popular ballads like *Nandanar Charithira Kirtanai,* arguably a 'classic' of the ballad market, *konangi pattu,* the song of the soothsayer, etc. His career coincides with the 'moment of departure' of nationalist discourse in India,[107] and is best understood in this context. He consciously used popular forms to rally the subaltern classes for the nationalist project, and as he says in the dedication to his *Panchali Sabhatham* (1912): 'Simple words; a simple style; an easily grasped rhythm; a lilt liked by the common people—anyone who writes an epic with these qualities today will actually give new life to our mother tongue . . . It must be easily comprehensible to all Tamil people familiar with book reading, if only for a year or two . . .'[108] Bharati's target is clear, and his description is possibly the best one can give of the nature of popular literature and its consumers. Little attention has so far been paid to the influence of the popular tradition on Bharati, but researchers focusing on the popular are on the wrong track when they seek (rural) folkloric inspiration for Bharati, even though such focus is a welcome corrective to the earlier concern with Bharati's debt to the classics. There is a good book waiting to be written on Bharati and the world of popular publishing.[109]

Bharati was not alone in drawing from this tradition. Bharatidasan, who modelled himself on Bharati, wrote on similar lines, and his early works are best described as chapbooks.[110] But Bharatidasan's later evolution took a different path. Harking back to a pre-Aryan, classical Tamil past, he rejected the 'corrupt' urban folklore of the

[107] See Partha Chatterjee, *Nationalist Thought and the Colonial World: A Derivative Discourse?* (New Delhi: Oxford University Press, 1986), ch. 2.

[108] *Bharati Padalgal: Aaivu Pathippu,* App. 2, pp. 1038–9.

[109] It should be remembered that a number of Bharati's poems were reprinted by chapmen. See, for instance, *Desiya Oonjal, Nalangu, Khaddar, Madhu Vilakku* (Ambasamudram, 1932).

[110] See, for instance, *Khaddar Rattinappattu* (Puducherry: Author, 1930); *Thondar Valinadaippattu* (Puducherry: Author, 1930).

chapbook tradition, even as he drew from the 'pure' and 'pristine' rural folklore.[111]

Namakkal Ramalingam Pillai presents a more interesting case. Popularly known as Namakkal Kavignar, he was the official Congress poet from the time of the Civil Disobedience Movement until his death in 1972. His autobiography tells us that his ideas on poetry germinated on the songs of Sankaradas Swamigal, Udumalai Charabam Muthusamy Kavirayar, and Santhanakrishna Naidu, all of whom wrote extensively for the popular stage and were published in the gujili.[112] 'I could grasp the tunes of the stage songs only because of the singers behind the screen. And I'd often write songs keeping Uraiyur Mohideen Sahib's rhythm in mind', he says.[113] Before he moved to the nationalist stage Namakkal Ramalingam Pillai wrote a number of songs for plays by the popular dramatist S.G. Kittappa. His songs were also reprinted in chapbooks.[114] No wonder a critic of the time derisively remarked: 'He has written a number of *pandaram* [mendicant songsters] songs which will regale the common folk. He does not possess any sublime poetic qualities.'[115]

Another instance of elite–popular interaction can be seen in the work of T.P. Krishnaswamy Pavalar. Pavalar's father T. Ponnuswamy was a student of Sodasavadhanam Subbaraya Chettiar, who was tutored by none other than Mahavidwan Meenakshisundaram Pillai. Pavalar studied Tamil under G. Vadivelu Chettiar, a leading traditional scholar at the turn of the twentieth century. Pavalar was very active in the popular stage, and wrote numerous plays and songs.[116] One of his students, R.B.S. Mani, was a leading chapbook publisher

[111] See, for instance, his songs in *Isaiyamudhu* (Puducherry: Kuyil, 1952).

[112] *En Kathai* (My Story; 1944, rpnt. Chennai: Palaniappa Bros., 1977), pp. 132–3.

[113] Ibid., p. 134.

[114] See *Mahatma Gandhi Khaddarananda Elappattu* (Chennai, 1929).

[115] T.M.C. Ragunathan, *Ilakkiya Vimarsanam* (Literary Criticism; 1948, rpnt. Madurai: Meenakshi Puthaka Nilayam, 1980), p. 77.

[116] Details of T.P. Krishnaswamy Pavalar drawn from M.P. Sivagnanam, *Krishnaswamy Pavalar Valkai Varalaru* (Chennai: Punkodi Pathippagam, 1988).

operating from Moore Market. In every publication of his, R.B.S. Mani proclaimed he was a student of Krishnaswamy Pavalar.[117]

Pulavar Kulandai offers the most elaborate case of the elite appropriation of popular literature. Born in 1906, he did not attend regular school and was self-taught. Even in his boyhood he excelled in writing imitative songs. When hardly 20 years of age, he wrote chapbooks like *Kanniyamman Chindu*, *Nallathambi Charkkarai Thalattu*, *Veerakumaraswamy Rathorchava Chindu/Kavadi Chindu/Valinadai Chindu.*[118] From such 'lowly' beginnings, he acquired a remarkable scholarship, not only in literature but also in grammar and prosody. By the 1930s he was deeply influenced by the Dravidian Movement. He wrote much verse, but the work that brought him fame, and proscription also, was *Iravana Kavyam*. This is a classic of the Dravidian Movement, which stands *Kambaramayanam* on its head, making Ravana the hero. The rich texture of the work, abounding in literary allusion, reveals his immense scholarship.

Our present concern is with two manuals of prosody that he authored. In *Yappathigaram*, first published in 1957, he devoted separate sections to describe kummi and chindu (the chapbook verse forms par excellence), probably the first grammarian to do so in some detail. His *Thodaiyathigaram* deals with chindu in even more detail.[119] This 350 page book devotes no less than 70 pages to the elaboration of the grammar of chindu.[120] Kulandai classified it into 27 types, and prescribed the norms regarding its composition in terms of syllables, feet, and metre. He also quoted from scores of chapbooks and ballads, which in itself presents a fantastic inventory of popular literature, to illustrate his prosodification of chindu: probably the only time a scholar deemed it fit to cite these as authorities.

[117] See, for instance, *Nattin Nilamai Vilakkum Desabhakti Geethangal* (Chennai, 1931).

[118] Details of his early life are drawn from the biographical introduction in Kulandai, *Iravana Kavyam* (1946, rpnt. Erode: Vela Nilayam, 1971).

[119] Kulandai, *Yappathigaram* (rpnt. Chennai: Pari Nilayam, 1991), pp. 97–111.

[120] Kulandai, *Thodaiyathigaram* (Chennai: Pari Nilayam, 1967), pp. 257–326.

In a deft manoeuvre to further appropriate and integrate these popular songs into the mainstream of Tamil classical literature, Kulandai highlighted features which, in his view, were common to both traditions. He wrote of oppary, quoting a passage from it: 'This is a song sung by women who are illiterate and have never touched a book in their lives. It is sung when someone close to their heart—father, mother, or husband—dies. Look closely at the alliteration of this oppary or *alugani chindu*, as it is called.'[121] Or, of another popular song: 'In this *komali pattu* [the song of the buffoon] referred to as a folk song, the alliteration far surpasses the alliteration of even a good literary work. How enjoyable this song is, to read!'[122]

### *Sanitizing Popular Texts*

During the early part of the twentieth century another process of appropriation was also at work. Elite scholars began to carefully select texts from the popular market, sanitize them, make them respectable, and include them into the Tamil classical canon whose construction was nearing completion in the 1930s and 1940s.[123] This attempt at sanitization came at the end of a process which started in the latter part of the nineteenth century, when ancient Tamil texts, long considered lost, were retrieved from palm-leaf manuscripts. The publication of these texts was a major preoccupation of scholars and publishers, especially during the age of patronage. As this project neared its end, the need to complete the classical canon was felt most deeply. U.V. Swaminatha Iyer, towards the end of a long career which had began in the age of patronage, started to devote more attention to 'minor' literature. There is evidence to suggest that, once the major part of his life work was complete, he felt the need to turn to 'lesser' works. As one scholar from Jaffna wrote to Swaminatha Iyer, 'the works, of the Siththars, unattended to by elderly scholars, are now carelessly printed by some and they abound in mistakes. There are many more

[121] Ibid., p. 12.

[122] Ibid., p. 265.

[123] A.R. Venkatachalapathy, 'The Making of a Canon: Literature in Colonial Tamilnadu', in *In Those Days There Was No Coffee*.

which need to be searched for and printed. If even the *Thirumandiram*, which is so well preserved, has so many distortions, need I say more about the uncared-for Siththar texts?'[124] Swaminatha Iyer did indeed turn his attention to 'lesser' works, though not those of Siththars. For instance, he obtained a copy of *Thenthirupperai Makaranedumkulaikathar Pamalai* from a cook;[125] he was greatly impressed by the poetry, but, finding its text 'corrupt', he acquired other versions and published a clean edition.

Thiru.Vi.Ka. set forth his ideas about this in his 'clean' edition of *Pattinathar Badragiriyar Padalgal* (1923): 'Many of those who publish such texts and commentaries are more concerned with their business and profit making, and less with aspects of language and spelling. The commentaries written by some late lamented scholars are in the clutches of gujili market publishers. In these days, when Tamil scholarship and Tamil development are on the wane, one should be grateful for those who publish books without misprints.'[126]

The Saiva Siddhanta Mahasamajam and the Saiva mutts of Dharumapuram, Thiruppanandal, and Thiruvavaduthurai likewise reprinted in neat editions the Saiva classics of *Thevaram, Thiruvachagam, Thirumandiram*, etc., which were collectively called the Thirumurais. The editions of the Mahasamajam were not only cheap but especially known for their meticulous editorship and fine printing, apart from scholarly aids like indexes, glossaries, concordances, and cross-references. A wide range of scholars, cutting across sectarian lines and personal jealousies, cooperated in these ventures.[127]

M. Arunachalam, who was for some time associated with the Mahasamajam, edited and published *Mukkudal Pallu*,[128] *Seekali Pallu*, etc. S. Bhavanandam Pillai brought out editions of ballads like *Alliarasani Malai* and *Eniyettram*. The noted writer G. Alagirisamy

[124] Kandiah Pillai to Swaminatha Iyer, 7 November 1931, U.V. S. Papers.

[125] (Chennai: Author, 1939), see editorial preface.

[126] Reprinted in *Kumari Malar*, 33 (10), January 1977.

[127] See *Siddhantam*, 9 (3), March 1936.

[128] It may be remembered that T.K. Chidambaranatha Mudaliar's review of this book, quoted extensively in the earlier sections, is a barely concealed attempt to invest the edition with authority and baptize it for the classical canon.

published a neat edition of the ever-popular kavadi chindu of Annamalai Reddiar.

Many of these works were accommodated into the Tamil classical canon as *chittrilakkiyam* (literally, 'minor literature')—an appendix to *perilakkiyam* ('great literature'). This process is by no means complete, as newer texts are still being sanitized and published by elite publishers, though not all have met with equal success.[129]

## Silencing the Popular Press

From the early 1940s, the popular press was slowly eroded. Rapid social and economic changes after World War II, the rise of the middle class, and, more importantly, the emergence of mass media took their toll.

As Chandilyan said of his early days as a journalist in *Swadesamitran* in 1935, describing the days when he published sizzling news of crime and judicial proceedings in detail: 'As cases like the "Kuppubai Rape Case" and the "Gramini Murder Case" were all conducted in Tamil, I was able to write about them more openly and in greater detail than the English dailies [. . .] In those days a poet from Choolai used to compose songs on such cases and sell it the same evening. As I reported every line, including the cross-examination, he was not left with much to do.'[130]

The birth and growth of the popular daily *Dina Thanthi* was perhaps the single largest factor working against the chapbook. Its coarse and rustic style, and its choice of topical and catchy news probably caught the fancy of the lower orders bred on chapbooks and ballads. From the time it appeared in 1942, *Dina Thanthi* grew phenomenally. As the Collector of Madurai reported in 1956, 'The *Dinathanthi* is a paper widely read, particularly by the lower ranks of the community because it contains sensational news and sexual

[129] See, for instance, Aranga Srinivasan, *Kavadi Chindum Kavignan Varalarum*; Tha. Kovendhan (ed.), *Siththar Padalgal* (Songs of Siththars; Chennai: Poompuhar Prasuram Press, 1976).

[130] Chandilyan, *Porattangal*, p. 43.

stories.'[131] That even a mass-produced daily had to draw on popular tradition to sustain itself not only goes to show its vitality but also underscores the incomplete nature of middle-class hegemony. A significant chunk of the mass media, thus, seems to have functioned away from the hold of the middle class.

Even now, popular literature is far from dead, even if it has lost much of its former vigour. The chapbook tradition has metamorphosed into cinema songbooks, wherein the lyrics of popular cinema are reduced to print much in the same format as in the earlier chapbooks.[132] Though they are not hawked, they are sold almost exclusively in petty shops selling betel leaves and cigarettes. Ballads are still being written and performed. Recently, K.A. Gunasekaran published the texts of a dozen such urban folk ballads composed between 1950 and 1980, one of which speaks of the Skylab incident![133] The firms of B. Rathna Nayagar & Sons and Sri Srinivasa Press (of K.A. Madurai Mudaliar) are still functioning, though they are not part of the mainstream, with few from the world of the middle class being aware of their existence. They are content with reprinting the odd title from their backlist, and they have their own, if narrow, channels of distribution. In the last two decades, the shops of Madurai Pudumantapam have ceased to deal in popular literature and now sell only educational books and stationery.

The continuing, if muted, existence of this tradition, along with the persistence of the popular mode of reading, exposes the incomplete

[131] G.O. no. 1783, Pub. (Gen. B), Secret, 17 May 1956.

[132] For Bharatidasan's fulminations about how the songbooks massacred his lyrics for the film *Balamani* (1936), see his *Manudam Pottru* (In Praise of Humanity; Chennai: Poompuhar Pathippagam, 1984), pp. 303–4.

[133] K.A. Gunasekaran (ed.), *Nagarsar Nattuppura Kathaippadalgal*. The Skylab incident refers to fears in July 1979 that an American satellite, which was allowed by NASA to disintegrate and fall to earth, would fall on people's heads in India. In the event it fell into the Indian Ocean, with bits littering Western Australia, leading to Australia fining the US government $ 400 for littering!) Also see S. Pothi Reddy's analysis of the ballad on the Danushkodi Cyclone, 1964, 'Dhanukkodi Nattupura Puyarpadalgal', unpublished M. Phil. dissertation, Madurai–Kamaraj University, 1981.

nature of middle-class hegemony in Tamil society. Though middle class intellectuals have for long attempted to silence this tradition by condemning it and even appropriating and sanitizing it, they have been largely unsuccessful. Another pointer to this is the fact that even the vitality of popular literature was tapped not by the middle class but by *Dina Thanthi*—which was as loathed by the elite as popular literature.

# 6

# Policing the Book

No history of the book would be complete without an account of the role of the state. So I will here explore the colonial state's policy and policing of the book. I look first at the administrative structure built to monitor the book, and related enabling legislations. Then I offer an account of the documents and data generated through the administering of the regulating acts. The mechanisms of control devised by the state are then delineated, followed by two small sections on the state as patron and guarantor of copyright. The actual policing of the book is studied under two heads: the moral and the political. The moral domain concerns the attempts of the state to control the publication of erotic and prurient literature. The political seems subdivisible into three rubrics: the literature of the nationalist, Self-Respect, and communist movements.

## The Acts and Administration

Though the restrictions on native ownership of printing presses and their publishing activity were removed by Metcalfe's Regulation of 1835, and there was consequently considerable growth in the output of the Tamil presses, the colonial government had no systematic method of keeping track of publishing activity.[1] During the 1857 Revolt it seems to have been mandatory for every publication to bear the name and address of the printer,[2] which probably helped exercise

[1] Murdoch, *Classified Catalogue of Tamil Printed Books.*

[2] John Murdoch, 'Duty of Government with respect to Vernacular Literature in India', nos 45–8, Edl, 19 March 1867; also reprinted in Murdoch, *Classified Catalogue of Tamil Printed Books*, pp. lxii–lxxii.

a modicum of control. Given the fact that the impact of 1857 was minimal in South India, this regulation did not have any perceptible effect in the generation of records and the consequent creation of knowledge about Tamil books.

The first systematic effort to compile data on Tamil books was made by John Murdoch,[3] a Scottish Protestant missionary. In 1865 he compiled and published *A Classified Catalogue of Tamil Printed Books*, the first such, and one which provides a very useful account of the nature of publishing, printing, typography, and distribution during the age of patronage. It may be no exaggeration to say that this work has formed the basic, if not the sole, source for much of the extant writings on nineteenth-century Tamil publishing. In this catalogue Murdoch appended a detailed note on the duty of the government with respect to vernacular literature, and the note was also separately sent off to the government.[4]

In the *Catalogue*, no doubt speaking from his experience of preparing it, Murdoch deplored the lack of adequate and reliable statistics on literary output in the vernacular languages. His complaint revolved around two issues: first, the voluntary returns filed by the native presses were incomplete because the managers were either suspicious of the government's intentions or looked upon it as causing unnecessary trouble; second, what little information was collected was not, in most cases, accessible to the public. To rectify this Murdoch called for a catalogue of existing books, and then 'require, by law, annual returns from all presses' about every sheet that a press printed, on pain of penalty. From these returns, Murdoch suggested, regular annual returns should be prepared.[5]

[3] John Murdoch (1819–1904) was engaged in the formation of the Christian School Book Society (1854), later renamed the Christian Vernacular Education Society (1858) and then again as the Christian Literature Society for India (1891). He also produced the *Catalogue of the Christian Vernacular Literature of India* . . . (Madras: Caleb Foster, 1870). For more details on his life, see Henry Morris, *The Life of John Murdoch* (1906, rpnt. Madras: Christian Literature Society, 1995).

[4] See nos 45–8, Edl, 19 March 1867.

[5] Murdoch, *Classified Catalogue of Tamil Printed Books*, pp. lxii–lxxii; also nos 45–8, Edl, 19 March 1867.

Three considerations weighed in Murdoch's mind. First, he felt the patronizing need that 'the interest of literature' be served, which would happen if 'the antiquaries and historians of India, in future generations, should have the means of inspecting the earliest efforts of the Press and of recording its gradual progress.' Second, there was a moral need—to keep a check on the 'vile character' of books when it came to sexuality and related norms. Third, a political need: 'it was doubtless incumbent to watch any premonitory symptoms of an impending outburst.'[6]

J. Talboys Wheeler, bureaucrat and official historian of Madras, in his 'Memorandum on the Registration of Vernacular Publications',[7] while broadly reflecting concerns similar to those voiced by Murdoch, felt that a mandatory registration of publications would be unsuccessful. Instead, he suggested the purchase of three copies of every book and the publication of its title in the official gazette. He felt that 'the object of the Government should [. . .] be more literary or educational, than political.'

Out of the deliberations that the memoranda of Murdoch and Wheeler evoked was born the Press and Registration of Books Act (XXV of) 1867. This imperial act provided for the compulsory submission of three copies of every book, printed or lithographed, to the government along with a statement providing the following details: title of the book; language; name of author, translator or editor; subject; place of printing and publication; name or firm of printer and of publisher; date of issue from the press; number of pages; size of the book; number of the edition; number of copies printed; sale price; and name and address of copyright owner.[8]

A new office of the Registrar of Books was created to receive the books forwarded by the several District Registrars of Assurances, who were the local officers in charge of accepting submissions made by the printers. Initially, the Director of Public Instruction held additional charge as Registrar of Books, but owing to his persistent complaint that his duties were already too onerous he was relieved of

[6] Murdoch, *Classified Catalogue of Tamil Printed Books*, pp. lxix–lxxii.
[7] Nos 45–8, Edl, 19 March 1867.
[8] Nos 54–5, Edl, 24 September 1867.

the additional charge.[9] The Registrar of Books was a part-time job held by an officer of the government, usually of the education department, either in addition to his duties or after his retirement.[10] His essential qualification was the ability to read and write at least three vernacular languages of the Madras Presidency. The first registrar was V. Krishnamachari—he was 74 when he died in harness in 1907; he was a writer and editor who dabbled in creating a system of shorthand for Tamil. He was succeeded by M. Rangachariar, Professor of Sanskrit and Comparative Philology at Presidency College, Madras, and fluent in English, Tamil, and Telugu.[11] A.C. Pranatharthihara Iyer, a retired Inspector of Schools, had apart from the above languages a smattering of Malayalam as well.[12] He was 76 when he was forced to retire from his office in 1934.[13] C.N. Saravana Mudaliar, Senior Tamil Translator to the government with experience of over seventeen years in that position, succeeded him at his own request.[14] But soon he gave up, taking leave preparatory to retirement, as he had work for eighteen hours a day 'even on holidays'—'physically impossible [. . .] without seriously impairing [. . .] health or without detriment to efficiency'.[15] He was succeeded by Bhavani Shankar Rao Nirody, Kannada translator to the government.[16]

The duties of the registrar consisted of supervising the work of a clerk who made entries in a tabular form from the returns furnished by printers. The registrar had to then examine the books submitted for registration and form an estimate of their value regarding matter and style, and to keep an eye on possible immoral or seditious ideas expressed in them. Considering the variety of languages (about fourteen) in which books were published in the Madras Presidency, the registrar's was no easy task. Out of such examination he was

[9] Ibid.
[10] G.O. no. 737, Pub., 1 September 1928.
[11] G.O. no. 135, Home (Edn), 6 February 1917.
[12] Ibid.
[13] G.O. no. 306, Pub. (Gen.), 24 March 1934.
[14] Ibid.
[15] G.O. no. 1764, Pub. (Gen.), 28 October 1935.
[16] G.O. no. 1180, Edn & Pub. Health, 2 June 1936.

expected to prepare quarterly catalogues of books, and, at the end of the year, an annual report consisting of statistical tables analysing book production and a review of it.[17]

To assist him in these tasks, the registrar had a meagre staff of one head clerk who also doubled up as 'librarian' of the huge collection of books accumulated through mandatory submission under the 1867 Act, three clerks who read the books, one typist, one attendant, and two peons. This workforce remained stagnant from 1911 to 1935.[18] Given the fact that the post of registrar was held by a pensioner, or as an additional charge, the work of administering the act no doubt suffered. More often than not there was a delay in the submission of quarterly catalogues and annual reports. When explanation was sought for such delays, the registrar would often provide a long litany of his preoccupations. For instance, V. Krishnamachari once explained that, as secretary of a committee to scrutinize school books, he had to examine, page by page, 120 books and record his remarks, as well as serve on another committee to revise the Madras Municipal Act.[19] The Director of Public Instruction (under whom the registrar functioned) once complained, 'There was a time when it was very difficult to get the late Rangachariar [the Registrar of Books] to keep the quarterly lists up to date.'[20]

With the changing political situation, and the gathering force of the national movement, additional work with considerable political sensitivity and responsibility was assigned to the Registrar of Books. The Indian Press Act of 1910, fashioned by the colonial state in the aftermath of the Swadeshi Movement to check the growth of nationalist literature, was largely monitored by the registrar. He was 'expected to get a foretaste of the objectionable publications' and report to the Commissioner of Police.[21] And, as Registrar M. Rangachariar remarked, the act made him 'also a kind of confidential censor of books.'[22]

[17] Nos 3–5, Edl, 2 August 1875.
[18] G.O. no. 322, Pub. (Gen.), 23 February 1935.
[19] Nos 33–4, Edl, 12 March 1874.
[20] G.O. no. 135, Home (Edn), 6 February 1917.
[21] G.O. nos 314–15, Judl (Confdl), 13 July 1910.
[22] Ibid.

With the Indian Press (Emergency Powers) Act 1931, to counter the Civil Disobedience Movement, the duties of the registrar continued to increase.

In the wake of the Depression of the early 1930s, and the consequent need to cut expenditure, when the Retrenchment Committee suggested the abolition of the post of Registrar of Books the government, perhaps despite wanting to, could not accept the recommendation as it felt 'The duties which the Registrar has to carry out are statutory and they cannot therefore be suspended.'[23] Similarly, it accepted the views of the registrar regarding the staff of his office and turned down the Retrenchment Committee's proposal of reduction against the persuasive arguments of the finance department.[24] Of course, the colonial government juggled with other alternatives: reconciling financial aspects with political interest, it combined the office of Senior Translator to Government with that of Registrar of Books because, it was contended, their functions were not dissimilar.[25]

It is in this context of aged, part-time officers holding charge as registrars, their enormous workload, and their limited staff that the information collected under the various acts, especially the Registration of Books Act 1867, can be estimated, and the nature of control exercised by the colonial state over book publishing studied.

## Annual Reports and Quarterly Catalogues

The Registrar of Books prepared quarterly catalogues of books, and then, based on these catalogues wrote an annual review with some rudimentary statistical analysis. The quarterly catalogues were based on the returns filed by printers giving various details about the books and their producers. In an additional column, for remarks, the registrar was expected to make some critical comments.

The annual review classified the books under various heads, ranging from biography, history, law, literature, mathematics, medicine,

[23] G.O. no. 426, Pub. (Confdl), 14 March 1932.

[24] G.O. no. 322, Pub. (Gen.), 23 February 1935.

[25] G.O. no. 1764, Pub. (Gen.), 28 October 1935; G.O. no. 1180, Edn & Pub. Health, 2 June 1936.

philosophy, religion, natural sciences, moral sciences, and travel. Books were also classified language-wise, and whether they were educational or not. The registrar also commented on the general tone of the literary output during the year, with especial regard to its moral and political content.

As one looks through the reports over the years it is clear that, gradually, the report becomes stereotypical, with nearly identical comments being repeated year after year. The statistical tables too border on the absurd when elaborate subject-wise classification is made for languages in which hardly a handful of books had been published.[26] Instances of bureaucratic stupidity become transparent: a rubric titled 'Miscellaneous' takes up as much as 20–30 per cent of the total while heads such as travel, biography, and history often show next to nothing.[27]

The Government of India, which received these reports forwarded by the Government of Madras, often pulled up the provincial governments for the poor quality of their reports. As the Assistant Secretary, Home Department (Books) of the imperial government put it, 'these reports consist almost entirely of descriptions of books taken from quarterly lists published in local gazettes, of short summaries dealing chiefly with figures, and a number of tables showing the languages in which they are written.'[28] He laid the blame on those who prepared the review for its poor quality, who 'from want of general information (especially as regards foreign literature) have little or no sense of the proportionate value of the books.'[29] In short, he wanted nothing less than a review to match the one of continental literature published in the *Athenaeum*!

The Government of Madras, no less condescending, remarked that 'the vernacular literature of this Presidency differs widely from the continental literature reviewed in the *Athenaeum* being, by

[26] See, for instance, Review and Analysis of Books (1885), nos 296–7, Edl, 17 May 1886.

[27] See, for instance, Review and Analysis of Books (1878), nos 5–7, Edl, 2 June 1879.

[28] G.O. nos 398–9, Edl, 28 August 1900.

[29] Ibid.

comparison, uninteresting and wanting in originality.'[30] But keeping in view the imperial government's requirements, the Government of Madras entrusted the task of writing the annual review to the Director of Public Instruction, who, being an Englishman, could, with his 'critical training', be expected to have a sense of 'the proportionate value of things'![31]

But, given the multiplicity of languages in which books were published in the Madras Presidency, a new arrangement was worked out. The Registrar of Books was now to submit weekly, to the Director of Public Instruction, books that he considered worthy of special enquiry. These were to be forwarded to competent reviewers for their comments, which would be taken note of while preparing the quarterly catalogues and the annual review.[32] Under this new scheme the annual review appeared under the name of the Director of Public Instruction, without any noticeable change in the quality of the reviews, they having been virtually prepared by the registrar, as before. But the Government of India appreciated them and said 'they are far superior to those prepared in other provinces.'[33]

With the phenomenal increase in the volume of book production over the years, and the monotony of the annual reviews, the quarterly catalogues and annual reviews were seen by the colonial state to provide diminishing returns. In 1924 the Government of India abolished the publishing of the quarterly catalogues in the gazettes as it involved 'unnecessary expenditure and serves no useful purpose'.[34] By the early 1920s, the annual reviews had long outlived their usefulness. As an official of the public department, Government of Madras, remarked in exasperation, when he came to know that the Registrar of Books submitted two reports, one for the calendar year and one for the official year, 'What report goes to the Government of

[30] Ibid.

[31] Ibid.

[32] Ibid.; G.O. no. 612, Edl, 28 November 1900; G.O. no. 644, Edl, 12 December 1900.

[33] G.O. no. 426, Edl, 28 July 1904.

[34] G.O. no. 25, Pub., 10 January 1924.

India on this subject now? And for what period? And how is the material for it derived? If the report for the calendar year is prepared by the DPI [Director of Public Instruction] from material supplied by the Regr. of Books, why should this report of the Regr. be abolished? And what is the object of the report for the official year anyway?'[35]

Nobody seems to have been clear about what the reports of the registrar were for. They clearly lacked direction and purpose, and, as the Deputy Secretary of Education and Health (Books) of the Government of India confessed, the statistics were just used to put in some figures in the *Moral and Material Progress Reports of India.*[36] By 1923 the annual reviews were abolished, though bare statistical tables continued to be prepared.[37]

This, then, was the kind of knowledge created by colonialism as it went about the task of benevolent policing in the domain of book production. The annual reviews were prepared by overworked, superannuated registrars with inadequate staff. The statistical tables produced were of dubious quality and more-than-dubious utility. The categories used to classify books were basically Eurocentric, which hindered more than helped understand the output of the Tamil presses. In general it may be said that the colonial state's system of acquiring and processing data lacked both sane direction and competent personnel. This, read in conjunction with the weak and inadequate mechanisms of control used by the state to police the book, delineated below, highlight paradoxically both the limitations of the colonial state and the limitless idiocies of some of its bureaucratic structures.

## Mechanisms of Control

The colonial state's mechanisms of control were far short of adequate. The Registration of Books Act 1867, which was the lone regulating act until the Press Acts of 1910 and 1931 were passed, lacked sufficient teeth to enforce its provisions. This inadequacy came to light only in the wake of the Swadeshi Movement, decades after the act was passed.

[35] G.O. no. 419, Pub., 4 July 1921.
[36] G.O. no.152, Pub., 27 February 1923.
[37] Ibid.

As the Registrar of Books remarked, 'many printers seem to consider their compliance with the provisions of the Act with regard to delivery of books to be more a matter of favour than of duty enjoined by a specific enactment of an Imperial Act.'[38] For instance, the registrar once found a printer submitting fifty-three books and pamphlets with a statement saying they were all published in the preceding two months; of course the registrar could do nothing about it.[39]

The office of the registrar was so weak that sometimes this official could not even compel the publisher to countersign the statutory memorandum signed by the printer. He had to seek the government's help, and ultimately had to leave the publisher alone as it was found that it was *ultra vires* of the registrar to compel the publisher to countersign.[40]

Given this state of affairs, evasion of the provisions of the act was widespread. As the registrar observed, not a single District Registrar of Assurances, the man on the spot, had brought to his notice any evasion in the seventeen years since the amendment of the act in 1890.[41] Many of the district registrars were found to have 'no knowledge even of printers in the district', and consequently could 'exercise no check whatever, over them.'[42] As E.F. Thomas of the education department put it candidly, 'The District Registrar as a receiver and forwarder of books is a confessed failure.'[43]

The police were also not in a position to prevent evasion and assist the registrar as these offences were non-cognizable, and, consequently, the police were in the same position as the District Registrars of Assurances and Registrar of Books.[44] Even on the rare occasion when evasion was detected, the judicial process was protracted and the penalty meagre. For instance, K.S. Kadirvelu Nadar, proprietor of Vijaya Vikatan Press, Royapuram, Madras, was fined only

[38] G.O. no. 258, Edl, 30 April 1909.
[39] Ibid.
[40] G.O. no. 222, Edl, 9 March 1912.
[41] G.O. no. 258, Edl, 30 April 1909.
[42] Report of District Magistrate, Coimbatore, in ibid.
[43] Notes in ibid.
[44] Report of Commissioner of Police, Madras, in ibid.

Rs 10–8–0 by the Chief Presidency Magistrate for failure to deliver copies of some books that had been printed.[45]

The Government of Madras was no doubt perturbed by the 'slack state of things'. It asked the various district magistrates to suggest ways to work the act in a 'more satisfactory manner'. The district magistrates were more or less unanimous in the view that there was widespread evasion. The observations of the Acting District Magistrate of Trichy typified their response: 'I have not had the time to discover any actual cases of default but it certainly does seem probable that books are not properly reported; especially as, without some system of check, no punishment is likely to follow. I am also told that this is the case, though I have not been able to discover definite instances.'[46]

Given the political situation in the immediate aftermath of the Swadeshi Movement, the district magistrates generally agreed that the police should be involved in the surveillance and control of publications.[47] The District Magistrate of Tanjore went a step further and advocated the exercise of political censorship, and added that the 'District Magistrate is excellently fitted by virtue of his other functions and responsibilities, to supervise such a censorship.'[48] While many other district magistrates shared this view, the matter of inadequate staff to handle the new responsibilities was raised.

In light of the views expressed by the district magistrates, the government toyed with the idea of regular inspection of presses by the magistracy and police. It also contemplated the organization of Official Translators under the Criminal Investigation Department (CID) to translate political literature for purposes of surveillance. In an attempt to tighten the system, it also sought to coordinate the various arms of its regulatory agencies. The district magistrates were asked to provide the Registrars of Assurances with up-to-date lists of printing presses, which would enable them to keep track of their activity.[49]

[45] G.O. no. 1212, Judl (Confdl), 10 May 1916.

[46] G.O. no. 258, Edl, 30 April 1909.

[47] See, for instance, the reports of the District Magistrates of Coimbatore and Madurai in ibid.

[48] Ibid.

[49] Ibid.

It is quite likely that, for the first time in Madras Presidency, the CID was used for policing the book. The Madras Police Abstracts of Intelligence show that CID men kept track of nationalist and seditious literature. How effective the CID was is not certain. But given its small, untrained workforce,[50] its effectiveness must have been quite limited. Perhaps they did instil a sense of caution, among the Swadeshi leaders at least, of being shadowed by CID men. In any case, the CID was extremely unpopular, and among the nationalists was not well regarded for its sleuthing abilities. As the *Indian Express* wittily remarked when the Madras Provincial Cooperative Union Library was raided and all books on Russia seized, 'If we must have a Criminal Intelligence Department, it is time that a little more emphasis is laid upon intelligence.'[51]

It was only with the passing of the Indian Press Act in early 1910 that more systematic attempts were made to exercise control over political literature. The Government of India was generally unhappy with the existing mechanisms of control.[52] Therefore, through the Press Act it required all presses to deposit security (unless waived by the local magistrate), and also authorized provincial governments to confiscate any printed material containing prohibited matter. The mode of enforcing the act emphasized the need for prompt examination of printed materials to detect objectionable matter.[53]

But this act meant little in the Tamil publishing world. In 1910 and 1911,[54] less than eight publications were banned under the act, while no further forfeiture orders were issued until the

[50] G.O. no. 205, Judl, 4 February 1910. David Arnold's admirable work on the colonial police in Madras makes no mention of its role in the surveillance of the book trade. *Police Power and Colonial Rule: Madras, 1859–1947* (Delhi: Oxford University Press, 1986).

[51] Clipping from *Indian Express*, 10 February 1937, in G.O. no. 414, Pub. (Gen.) (Confdl), 26 February 1937. It is said that when in the 1940s the Annamalai University's library was purged of leftist literature, all communist books, including the anti-communist ones, were removed!

[52] Letter no. 1272, Judl (Confdl), 25 August 1910.

[53] G.O. nos 314–15, Judl (Confdl), 28 February 1910.

[54] G.O. nos 1681–2, Judl (Confdl), 19 July 1915.

Non-Cooperation and Khilafat movements (1919–22). Perhaps the act's biggest success was the virtual silencing of Subramania Bharati, who was forced into exile and deprived of the means to publish his works. Between 1910 and 1914,[55] though forty-three presses were asked to furnish security under section 3 of the act, even such demands were not always backed by political compulsions or perceived threats to the state, only betraying the class and colonial prejudices of the officials. For instance, one T. Kanniah Nayudu was ordered to pay a security of Rs 1,000 'as his educational qualifications were limited to a meagre knowledge of Tamil and he was considered unfit to be a keeper of a press.'[56] Similar was the fate of one Parthasarathi Mudaliar, who was a compositor and wanted to start a small press.[57] K. Muhammed Ibrahim was asked to furnish security 'as he was a cooly with no property and possessed only a meagre knowledge of Tamil.'[58] Security was demanded from Saiyid Ali Sahib not only for the usual reason that he was 'unfit to manage a press' but also that the proposed location of his press was 'a dwelling house occupied by his gosha [secluded] women to which access could not be freely obtained.'[59] One C.A. Natesa Mudali was asked to deposit security as he had earlier been convicted of publishing obscene books,[60] in contravention of the provisions of the act which provided only for the control of seditious literature. Ultimately, so marginal was the operation of the act in the Madras Presidency that an official of the judicial department said 'there is little to comment on in these reports [on the working of the Indian Press Act 1910] [. . .] and the reports show that the Act has been applied with leniency as well as with discretion.'[61]

Important to our present concern is the fact that no new administrative mechanism was evolved to keep an eye on the book

[55] G.O. nos 190–1, Judl (Confdl), 27 January 1914.

[56] G.O. no. 1068, Judl (Confdl), 14 May 1915.

[57] Ibid.

[58] G.O. no. 1212, Judl (Confdl), 10 May 1916.

[59] Ibid.

[60] Ibid.

[61] Ibid.

trade. The usual methods of surveillance were adopted, and it is evident that the Government of Madras was well aware of this lethargic state of affairs. When, in 1920, the Government of India decided to discontinue certain precautions regarding the detention of objectionable literature imported into India, a public department official jotted down the following crisp note on a detailed draft put up on implementing the Government of India decision: 'Practically the only action taken on [the] letter [. . .] from the GoI [Government of India] was to tell certain officers to be extra watchful. They have probably forgotten all about it now [. . .]'[62]

Even after the passing of the Indian Press (Emergency Powers) Act 1931, which re-established a system of security demands and enhanced the state's powers to confiscate publications, the weak administrative structure remained.[63] As late as 1931 the Commissioner of Police complained that he had little opportunity to acquire a number of objectionable books because they were all being sent to the Registrar of Books. He had had to rely on informal sources to acquire some of them, and these he then passed on to the CID. It was only after this complaint that the registrar was ordered to bring seditious publications to the notice of the police.[64]

From 1934 the government laid down new procedures to strengthen its control of literature. Pressed by the need to take prompt action, it ordered the registrar to bring seditious literature to its direct notice, instead of to the concerned district magistrates or the police commissioner, as was earlier the case.[65] This was in addition to the CID's work of forwarding to the government books suspected of containing seditious matter.

Such constant tinkering with the mechanisms of control underscores their inherent weakness. An interesting incident throws this weakness into sharp relief. In 1907 *Swadesa Chindu* was published

[62] G.O. no. 86, Pub., 12 February 1920.

[63] The Press Act of 1910 was repealed in 1922 by the Press Laws Repeal or Amendment Act XIV of 1922, though the power to order confiscation was retained. See G.O. no. 51, Pub. (Confdl), 14 June 1922; and G.O. no. 1116, Pub. (Gen.) (Confdl), 28 October 1931.

[64] G.O. no. 1280, Pub. (Gen.) (Confdl), 17 December 1931.

[65] G.O. no. 1198, Pub. (Gen.) (Confdl), 29 November 1934.

from a small press in Komaleswaranpettai, Madras. This chapbook on the Swadeshi Movement did not come to the notice of the government until the Inspector of Customs at the port of Danushkodi confiscated a copy of it from a Jaffna passenger on his way to Chidambaram. And this 'ephemeral' chapbook was banned in 1932, a quarter of a century after its publication when it was no longer in print or circulation![66]

The weakness of colonial mechanisms of control over publishing is also reflected in the nature of data in government records. The abilities of the official translators, on whom the government largely relied to form an estimate of objectionable works, were especially limited. P.S. Sivaswami Aiyer's parenthetical remark: 'The opinion of the Translator, however good a scholar he may be (which is perhaps more than what can be said of Translators generally) . . .' testifies to this.[67] Likewise the Registrar of Books, commenting on a Tamil translation of Mahadev Desai's *Bardoli Satyagraha* by Va.Ra., a leading man of letters, described the translator as 'one Va.Ra.'[68] Consequently, the records generated by the colonial state provide little in terms of hard data about the publishing world. Historians of the book in India are not as fortunate as Robert Darnton, who laid hands on dossiers maintained by a police inspector of the *ancien régime* on hundreds of eighteenth-century French authors.[69]

The weakness of the colonial state machinery, certainly greatly in evidence in its attempts to police the book, runs against nationalist romanticizations of the repression let loose by an all-pervasive colonial state gazing at potential sedition from its panopticon. The presence of the colonial state was far from being ubiquitous and, in the domain of publishing, approximated to the notion of being a rather 'limited Raj'.[70]

[66] G.O. nos 958–9, Pub. (Gen.) (Confdl), 11 July 1932.

[67] G.O. no. 1344, Judl (Confdl) 3 July 1913.

[68] G.O. no. 1521, Pub., 17 September 1935.

[69] See Robert Darnton, *The Great Cat Massacre and Other Episodes in French Cultural History* (Harmondsworth: Penguin, 1984), ch. 4, 'A Police Inspector Sorts His Files'.

[70] This being a notion expounded in Anand A. Yang, *The Limited Raj* (Delhi: Oxford Univeristy Press, 1989), esp. pp. 225–39.

### State Patronage

In two other areas, patronage and copyright, the colonial state played a marginal role *vis-à-vis* book publishing even as compared to its incomplete policing of seditious publications.

The state extended a limited amount of patronage to authors and publications that were in its view 'deserving'. In an exceptional case of government assistance U.V. Swaminatha Iyer was awarded a grant of Rs 1,000 to pursue his publication programme.[71] But such monetary grants were rare, the usual mode of assistance being to sanction the purchase of some copies of books deserving support: as we saw earlier, M.V. Ramanujachari's Mahabharatam translation received some succour from the government, due not least to his persistent efforts.[72]

Such support was not only rare and limited, it was never really substantial. Nor was the scheme of assistance systematized. As late as 1918, towards the fag end of the age of patronage, the Government of Madras confessed that

> No general rules regulating the extension of Government patronage to authors of books have been prescribed. Each application for patronage is dealt with on its own merits. The Government may patronize an author [sic.] either by giving him an honorarium or by purchasing as many copies of the book as are required for the use of Government institutions and libraries [. . .] It has been held that Government patronage should be restricted to books which are worthy of production and the cost of production of which is out of all proportion to the probable sale.[73]

### Copyright

If the state had no general rules for the extension of patronage to books, the same could not be said on the issue of copyright. Copyright was of course a novelty in the Indian context. Without the means for (mechanical forms of) multiple reproduction, the question of

[71] G.O. no. 600, Edl, 6 September 1905.

[72] See G.O. no. 393, Edl, 14 April 1915; G.O. no. 835, Edl, 3 August 1915 and G.O. no. 543, Edl, 12 May 1914.

[73] G.O. no. 182, Home (Edn), 13 February 1918.

copyright did not arise. With the advent of print, however, the issue of copyright began to emerge. There was naturally considerable cultural misunderstanding, even perplexity as Thomas Trautmann suggests, when 'the idea of copyright [was] possibly being introduced in South India for the first time' by the colonial government in Madras.[74] When the Madras Government sought to acquire the copyright of a Telugu dictionary produced by Mamadi Venkayya in the early 1810s, it offered 1,000 star pagodas, a not insubstantial sum, as recompense. However, Venkayya demanded perpetual pension and rent-free land in the vicinity of Masulipatnam![75] Similarly, when the College of Fort St George acquired the copyright of the Tamil translation of *Vignaneswariyam: Vivakara Kandam*, the deceased translator's brother demanded '1,000 Pagodas for building a Charity Choultry and also to grant a Shrotriem village for the purpose of completing the said building [. . .] and also for the continuance of charity dispensation there.' His reason: 'I would gain a great reputation and the Honourable Company an everlasting fame for this high act of Concession.'[76] Evidently copyright and patronage seemed synonymous to native literary producers.

The Government of India passed a few acts on copyright during our period. Act XX of 1847 provided for the award of damages for infringement of copyright.[77] The 1867 Registration of Books Act provided for a payment of Rs 2 which gave the regular registration the force of registration for copyright.[78] Consequently the Registrar of Books, apart from preparing the usual quarterly catalogue of publications, also made ready a similar list of copyright registrations. His annual report was usually wound up with some dry statistics about registrations of copyright and inane remarks on how the increase in their numbers reflected a growing awareness among native printers and publishers.[79] This separate quarterly catalogue of copyright was

[74] Trautmann, *Languages and Nations*, p. 147.

[75] Ibid., pp. 147–9.

[76] Madras Public Consultations, 11 September 1815.

[77] Nos 114–15, Edl, 15 July 1882.

[78] No. 254, Edl, 7 August 1867.

[79] See, for instance, Annual Reports for 1886 and 1889, in nos 305–6, Edl, 21 June 1887 and nos 221–2, Edl, 17 March 1890.

later abolished at the instance of the Government of India: even the bureaucracy considered it superfluous. In its place a new column for copyright was incorporated into the quarterly list of books registered.[80]

This whole business of copyright registration was little more than a farce. The government itself was aware that 'The fact that copyright is registered does not "secure" copyright, which subsists equally before and after registration and need not necessarily be possessed by the person who registers proprietorship [. . .]; the entry in the book of registry or in the catalogue does not do more than serve as prima facie proof [. . .]'[81]

Confusion marked the functioning of the Registrar of Books for he occasionally met objections when copyright was being registered. But more numerous were the cases wherein, during the course of registering books under the 1867 act, he found the prevalent practice of inserting formulae like 'Copyright Registered' on the title page of the book when they had not been actually so registered.[82] The Advocate General, P.S. Sivaswami Aiyer, reiterated the view that registration of copyright only provided prima facie evidence of proprietorship which could be rebutted by other evidence. Regarding the wrongful insertion of 'Copyright Registered' on the title page, he was of the view that though it was morally objectionable it was not punishable under the Indian Penal Code.[83]

The Government of India passed a new Copyright Act in 1914.[84] This was modelled on the English Act.[85] The Government of Madras played little part in the deliberations preceding the passing of the act. As Murray Hammick of the education department frankly confessed when the draft law came to him for comments, 'I don't desire to add anything. It is a subject on which I know very little.'[86] What ultimately emerges is that copyright was marginal to Tamil publishing. As

[80] G.O. no. 35–6, Edl, 23 January 1902.

[81] G.O. no. 166, Edl (Confdl), 22 March 1902.

[82] G.O. no. 111, Edl, 25 February 1909.

[83] Ibid.

[84] G.O. no. 612, Edl, 26 May 1914.

[85] G.O. no. 1150, Edl, 4 December 1913.

[86] G.O. no. 782, Edl, 26 August 1912.

J. Talboys Wheeler commented in his 'Memorandum on the Registration of Vernacular Publications', 'In this country, it is scarcely necessary to say that conditions of publishing are altogether different: the sale is small, the price is small, and there is little, if any, distinction between copyright and non-copyright. Authors being in general satisfied with the glory of having their works printed.'[87]

In a colonial economy and society, wherein a middle class had not quite emerged and a literary market had not developed, books were not worthwhile commodities. Consequently, copyright was hardly ever an issue. Even in the case of popular publishing, where the books meant their daily bread to their producers, other means were resorted to in order to secure 'copyright'.[88]

## Policing the Book

In light of the foregoing discussion on the various acts of the colonial state and the mechanisms of control it evolved to keep an eye on the publishing world, what of its actual policing of books?

### *Eroticism and Expurgation*

The missionary impulse of the British Raj, which it gave out as a kind of benevolent paternalism, impelled it to not only enforce political control but also police the morals of the colonized. In the Madras Presidency the government's attention turned to supposedly morally objectionable and obscene works. It was customary for the Registrar of Books to end his annual reports with a comment on the 'moral and political tone of the vernacular literary output'.[89]

[87] Nos 45–8, Edl, 19 March 1867.

[88] For a rare instance of copyright infringement being taken up judicially, see *Ananda Bodhini*, August 1917. N. Munisami Mudaliar successfully sued P.T. Masilamani Mudaliar, a printer, for infringing his copyright in his annual almanac. The Presidency Magistrate, George Town, Madras, awarded damages of Rs 20, or three days' simple imprisonment in case of default.

[89] See, for instance, Annual Reports for 1895 and 1896, G.O. no. 125–6, Edl, 5 March 1896 and G.O. nos 133–4, Edl, 5 March 1897.

That Christian missionary pressure was behind the colonial state's 'crusade against erotic works' is evident.[90] There was a consistent demand by missionaries for the diffusion of secular and morally correct literature in India.[91] The most strident attack on government policy towards vernacular literature and education was launched by John Murdoch. His attack centred on the government system of education, which was 'professedly based on principle of perfect religious neutrality'.[92] His criticism of obscenity in literature was part of his overall critique of oriental culture which was seen to be pagan and anti-Christian:

> Probably few Europeans in India are aware of the vile character of some of the productions of the Native Press. The lowest savages on the face of the earth have not utterly lost all feelings of decency—there is generally a shred of clothing, however small, on the body. But Indian authors, in some cases, seem to have sunk beneath this level. In a Tamil poem, a portion of which was prescribed for examination by the Madras University, there is a glowing description of what cannot be named [. . .] The scenes which took place in the bridal chamber are related at length in another part of the poem above mentioned [. . .] There are whole treatises of a still worse character.[93]

Murdoch's criticism was specially focused on textbooks, and he even authored a pamphlet, 'The Idolatrous and Immoral Teachings of Some Government and University Text Books'. 'While all Christian allusions have been struck out of Government school books', he lamented that 'every inculcation of idolatry has been retained.' To the argument that similarly obscene passages were to be found in the Western classics, he retorted that 'English precedent may be adduced

[90] Note of H.A. Stuart, Member of Governor's Council, in G.O. no. 874, Judl (Confdl), 6 May 1913.

[91] See, for instance, communication of Rev. James Johnston, Secretary of Christian Vernacular Education Society for India, in no. 598, Edl, 22 August 1890. Also, communication from Rev. W. Meston, Secretary, Madras Missionary Conference, G.O. no. 1703, Judl, 25 October 1905.

[92] Nos 47–50, Edl, 29 March 1871. Also see Bishop Caldwell's note, ibid., for similar views.

[93] Nos 45–8, Edl, 19 March 1867.

for almost every iniquity under the sun'! Refuting the argument of literary merit, he was at his missionary best: 'the greater the beauty of the diction, the greater the mischief.'[94] In sum, then, he advocated the expurgation of objectionable passages and suggested making selections instead of prescribing the full text. He himself set an example, as head of the Christian Vernacular Education Society, by issuing a series of bowdlerized editions.[95]

This moral concern was shared by the emerging English educated Indian elite. The *Combaconum Athenoeum* took serious exception to the prescription of Adi Parvam of Mahabharatam, with its description of miscegenation and the genealogies of various rishis, for the matriculation examination. It called upon the government, 'who occupy the place of father to the children concerned', to remedy their grievance.[96] Similarly, C.W. Damodaram Pillai excised all eleven occurrences of *algul* (old Tamil for 'the mound of venus') from his edition of the Sangam classic *Kalithogai*, keeping students 'of government institutions' in mind.[97] The new breed of teachers was embarrassed by such passages. U.V. Swaminatha Iyer recollects how he refrained from teaching an erotic passage in *Prabodha Chandrodhayam* to his students and gave as an excuse the opinion that no question would be asked on it in the university examination. Much to his consternation the examiners set questions from that very passage![98]

[94] For the text of this pamphlet, see nos 16–18, Edl, 10 December 1874.

[95] For the list, see Murdoch, *Classified Catalogue of Tamil Printed Books*, pp. 212–14.

[96] For the relevant extract from *Combaconum Athenoeum*, August 1872, see no. 3, Edl, 1 October 1872. For government action on this issue, see nos 6–7, Edl, 1 November 1872. The prescribing authorities in the university were of course in a spot. Earlier, when the Panchatantra had been prescribed, there had been an outcry that 'it was a book of tricky morals'!

[97] *Kalithogai* (Chennai: Author, 1887), Preface.

[98] Swaminatha Iyer, *Nallurai Kovai*, vol. 3, pp. 40–3. Ultimately it turned out that the students answered the question quite well, as, out of curiosity, they had carefully read the untaught passage! For an instance of a student asking uncomfortable questions during the course of a class lecture on an erotic work, and how his teacher V.G. Suriyanarayana Shastri tackled it brilliantly,

Apart from government action against 'immoral' passages in textbooks, the earliest incident we have of intervention in the sphere of morality is the case of *Dambachari Vilasam*. This was a play written by Kasi Viswanatha Mudaliar, a retired tahsildar and Brahmo Samajist. The eponymous hero is a fop who comes to the city to study, is seduced by a courtesan, and consequently ruined. The book was first brought to the notice of the government by the Registrar of Books, who sought to prosecute the actors and producers of the play. The Senior Magistrate of the Town Police observed that 'there was no office under the [Madras] Government in the position of a censor analogous to that of Lord Chamberlain' and dismissed the case with costs.[99] The government, overruling the advocate general's advice, had proceeded with the case 'to ascertain whether the law is so powerless for the repression of outrages against public decency as is supposed, in view of its amendment if necessary.'[100]

After this prosecution we find a lull in the government's moral policing of books, or else its actions went unreported. In the first decade of the twentieth century we find occasional references to some action against obscenity in print. The state was particularly concerned at the practice of sending en masse price lists of cures for impotence and venereal diseases addressed to students. It ordered the postal authorities to intercept and forward these to the CID, along with seditious literature.[101] The state was also perturbed by 'indelicate and indecent advertisements [which] lower the tone of the public press', and wrote confidentially to journals like *Vikataratinam*, *Vaisya Mitran*, *Dravidabhimani*, and *Hindunesan*, persuading them to desist from advertising aphrodisiacs and the like.[102] In fact an

---

see *Parithimal Kalaignar Noottrandu Malar* (Centenary Souvenir of V.G. Suriyanarayana Shastri; Madurai: V.S. Swaminathan, 1970), p. 112.

[99] No. 71, Edl, 28 February 1873. For details of the case, also see no. 306, Edl, 1 November 1872; no. 5A–C, Edl, 5 February 1873. For a full account, see A.R. Venkatachalapathy, 'The Colonial State as Moral Police: The Case of *Dambachari Vilasam*, 1872–73', forthcoming.

[100] Ibid.

[101] G.O. no. 1273, Judl (Confdl), 25 August 1910.

[102] G.O. no. 1804, Judl (Confdl), 5 September 1913.

official of the education department actually took the trouble to cut out such advertisements ('out of curiosity', as he put it) from respected dailies like the *Hindu* and the *Madras Standard*, and wondered if the government should provide them patronage.[103] In some cases, books considered particularly obnoxious were seized by the CID and destroyed, and the booksellers and publishers prosecuted.[104]

It was not until the early 1910s that any serious debate on the question of what precisely constituted obscenity and how to suppress it was raised. When the Government of India sounded out the provincial government on the International Agreement for the Suppression of Obscene Publications signed at Paris in May 1910, it was smug in its reaction: obscene publications were 'almost entirely in the vernaculars and without illustrations' and therefore it did not feel the need for adopting an international agreement.[105]

But very soon there was a sea change. By 1912 the government action on the eighteenth-century Thanjavur Maratha court poetess Muddu Palani's *Radhika Santwanamu*, edited by the redoubtable Bangalore Nagarathnamma and published by the reputed publisher Vavilla Ramaswami Sastrulu & Sons, had in the face of opposition within the Telugu literary world became a *cause célèbre*. The government not only confiscated copies, it also launched a prosecution. Government action against some well-regarded Tamil literary works, namely, *Kavadi Chindu* and *Viralividu Thoothu*, and Telugu literary works like *Bilhaneeyamu*, on grounds of obscenity in 1913 was considerably coloured by this case.[106] A spate of protests against the government's move ensued. A public meeting of 'Tamil Pandits and English-educated men of standing, deeply interested in the study of Tamil literature' was conducted to condemn the prosecution. The meeting insisted that *Kavadi Chindu* was a religious work and had no intention of exciting sexual passion. The classical nature of

[103] G.O. no. 186, Edl (Confdl), 29 March 1911.

[104] See, for instance, G.O. no. 208, Judl (Confdl), 1 February 1911.

[105] G.O. no. 680, Judl (Confdl), 26 April 1912.

[106] G.O. no. 348, Judl (Confdl), 4 March 1912. See V. Sriram, *The Devadasi; and the Saint: The Life and Times of Bangalore Nagarathnamma* (Chennai: EastWest Books, 2007), for more on this celebrated case.

*Viralividu Thoothu* was emphasized, and it was contended that the book exposed in unmistakable terms the evils and dangers of an immoral life. A general demand was put forward that the prohibition of such books would spell disaster for Tamil literature. In short, the 'ancient and literary' character of the works was underscored.[107]

The Madurai Tamil Sangam submitted a similar memorial opposing the government's attempt, going a step further by using theological arguments: 'One of the ancient methods of representing the human soul and Almighty Providence is by characterizing their relation as similar to that subsisting between a man and a woman drawn to each other by the force of reciprocal love and by viewing the birth, sufferings, and sorrows of the mundane existence of human beings as analogous to the painful consequences of separation between such lovers.'[108] One P. Narayana Iyer of Madurai, in a personal communication to P.S. Sivaswami Aiyer, Member of the Executive Council, came down heavily on the police action: 'If the standard of morality as understood by the ignorant police is to fix the standard of Tamil literature, I can simply say that our plight is a sad and contemptible one.' He expressed the fear that if the police were allowed to have their way, even religious classics like *Thevaram*, *Nalayira Divya Prabandam*, *Tiruvachagam*, and *Tiruppugal* could be banned.[109]

Professor M. Rangachariar (the former Registrar of Books), and G. Venkataranga Rao, Chairman of the Telugu Board of Examiners, University of Madras, put forward the case for Telugu books. Given their proximity to the state and its discourse, they argued their case in terms more convincing to the state: 'The standard of taste which determines the amount of openness in erotic description, which may be held to be appropriately permissible, is apt to vary from time to time in every country, and is also affected by the idiosyncrasies of particular writers and also their patrons and clientele [. . .] it cannot be conducive to the best interests of literary scholarship and the

[107] Memorandum submitted by S. Somasundaram Pillai, *et al.*, in G.O. no. 289, Judl (Confdl), 11 February 1913.

[108] Ibid.

[109] Ibid.

knowledge of the history of literary art to interfere with the integrity of artistic work produced by competent authors.'[110] In their perceptive analysis they added that literary works should not be judged through translation in a foreign tongue, as the state was in fact doing: 'the very process of translation adds a touch of vulgarity or broadness to description.'[111] In an attempt to be more convincing they even argued their case by citing parallels from Western literature. P. Narayana Iyer drew attention to the 'Song of Songs of Solomon' in the Bible,[112] while M. Rangachariar and G. Venkataranga Rao referred to the eroticism in the works of Calallus, Tribulus, Ovid, Chaucer, Marlowe, and Shakespeare.[113]

Despite these vehement protests, South Indian middle-class intellectuals shared many of the basic assumptions about morality held by the British. Their arguments were set within the discourse of Victorian morality, with all its cultural and class prejudices.[114] Both colonial rulers and middle-class intellectuals shared a certain kind of contempt for 'the lower orders'. If J.N. Atkinson of the public department remarked, 'There is a material difference between publishing cheap editions [of obscene books] for sale to general public and the bringing out of a very limited edition at high price for the use of scholars',[115] middle-class intellectuals only laboured the same point more stridently. As scholars of the Madurai Tamil Sangam put it, the books in question were 'written in an abstruse style and [. . .] intended to be read only by Tamil scholars and by others who

[110] G.O. no. 348, Judl (Confdl), 4 March 1912.

[111] Ibid.

[112] G.O. no. 289, Judl (Confdl), 11 February 1913.

[113] G.O. no. 348, Judl (Confdl), 4 March 1913. A.G. Cardew, the Chief Secretary, termed the attempts to draw parallels as 'absolutely preposterous'. See G.O. no. 944, Pub. (Confdl), 2 August 1912.

[114] For similar responses from the Bengali intelligentsia, see Sumanta Banerjee, 'Bogey of the Bawdy: Changing Concept of "Obscenity" in 19th-Century Bengali Culture', *Economic and Political Weekly*, 18 July 1987. Also see his *The Parlour and the Streets*.

[115] G.O. no. 944, Pub. (Confdl), 2 August 1912. For similar views expressed by A.G. Cardew, see the same file.

have attained a high degree of proficiency in the knowledge of Tamil.'[116] Intellectuals who conducted the public meeting to condemn the prohibition of the books made the defence of their privileged position even more elaborately:

> Such works were written for the benefit of particular sections of humanity and to suit the different ages and were not intended for the general public. The press did not then exist and books were not within the reach of the common public. They were written only to benefit the learned, the devoted and so very limited circles of men, whose minds these passages of rare occurrence cannot poison. It is very wrong to suppose that the minds of well educated and pious men will be turned by such occasional passages [. . .] If the Police wish to protect the minds of the common people, the right books that they have to direct their efforts against are the low-priced Tamil novels that are daily coming out of the press. They have also to attack the many advertisements wherein most indecent pictures of the fair sex are made to meet the eye of the man in the street, for these are the things that poison the common mind.[117]

Despite their shared assumptions, this chorus by middle-class intellectuals surprised colonial officials. Their arguments cut no ice with the bureaucrats: 'We have had before us a very surprising spectacle of highly respectable Indian gentlemen solemnly writing to Government on the ground that they occur in classics . . .',[118] said one of them. This stemmed from the colonial perception of vernacular literature, and here it seems justifiable to invoke Edward Said and point out how clearly the perception was defined by the vision of Orientalism. In the comments of British officials within the government documents we find 'an almost uniform association between the Orient and sex'. As Said points out, this association is a 'remarkably persistent motif in Western attitudes to the Orient . . . [which is] singularly unvaried.'[119]

The debate served to reinforce the Orientalism of colonial

[116] G.O. no. 1344, Judl (Confdl), 11 July 1913.
[117] Clipping from the *Hindu*, 31 July 1912, in ibid.
[118] G.O. no. 1344, Judl (Confdl), 3 July 1913.
[119] Edward Said, *Orientalism* (London: Routledge, 1978), p. 188.

officialdom but a clearly-laid-out procedure for handling obscene publications also emerged from it. Given the hostility to using the police for these purposes, the government entrusted the task to the CID. While the power to order prosecution of 'all modern writings which are so obviously obscene as to call for immediate suppression' was given to the Deputy Inspector General of Police, similar powers for action against the classics were given to the Inspector General, who was expected to keep in mind the following considerations: works published not later than the seventeenth century should not be prosecuted unless it appeared from the circumstances of publication that the object was to appeal to prurience and attract readers by presenting obscene ideas; facts like whether the language was archaic or not, whether the style was abstruse or clear, etc., were also to be taken account of.[120] In the specific case of *Kavadi Chindu* and *Viralividu Thoothu*, the former was not banned; and of the latter only expurgated editions were permitted.[121]

The broad policy and procedures set by the Government of Madras in 1913 stood the test of time. For instance, in 1927, Vavilla Venkateswara Sastrulu got into trouble for selling unexpurgated versions of certain classics. Given his standing and repute, he rallied testimonials from a wide range of 'respectable men' such as university syndicate members, professors, and scholars, and tried to get the government's orders revoked.[122] A deputation of eminent persons waited on the governor and presented a detailed memorandum with a scholarly analysis of 'Obscenity in Literature' discussing the various views on obscenity, drawing their ammunition from English literature, British law, Indian treatises, etc. But the government declined to interfere, considering the 'definite principles' it had laid down in 1913.[123]

[120] G.O. no. 1344, Judl (Confdl), 3 July 1913.

[121] Ibid. For reviews of the expurgated edition of *Viralividu Thoothu*, see *Kumaran*, 21 June 1928; *Swadesamitran*, 25 May 1929. Many years later, in 1949, when the Tamil scholar Roya. Chockalingam republished the book, an expurgation order was issued citing the G.O. of 1913. See G.O. no. 3397, Pub. (Gen. A) (Confdl), 7 October 1949.

[122] G.O. no. 1219, Pub. (Confdl), 25 November 1927.

[123] G.O. no. 545, Pub. (Confdl), 18 June 1928.

Consequently there was little change in government policy towards obscenity and eroticism in print well up to the transfer of power in 1947. Orientalist stereotypes of the sensual East continued to predominate and police action continued against supposedly obscene and erotic works. Orientalist colonial officials were at best patronizing. A.G. Cardew, Chief Secretary to Government of Madras, when sent certain books for action on grounds of obscenity, variously remarked:

> The objectionable passages appear to be few and even these are quite mild for an Indian writer.[124]

> A high degree of delicacy is not apparently expected in this country and an occasional reference to sexual intercourse even in rather broad terms, is possibly quite an everyday affair in native writings.[125]

> The *Taykkilavikal Talukku* seems to contain hints on etiquette for dancing girls. It does not seem to be very bad, as these native books go.[126]

More typical, though, seems the response of H.A. Stuart, Member of the Governor's Executive Council, at the end of the 1913 debate: 'I hope I shall not for a very long time be obliged to read such filth as this again.'[127]

## The State and Political Literature

The colonial state was, naturally, extremely sensitive to any threat to its existence. Its sensitivity to political opposition is most clearly evident in its response to the nationalist, Self-Respect, and Communist movements.

### *Nationalist Literature*

We have seen that the mechanisms of control devised by the Government of Madras to police the book were very limited, and that the

[124] G.O. no. 1535, Judl (Confdl), 29 July 1913.
[125] G.O. no. 1200, Judl (Confdl), 18 June 1913.
[126] G.O. no. 1198, Judl (Confdl), 18 June 1913.
[127] G.O. no. 874, Judl (Confdl), 6 May 1913.

state was far from being either all-pervasive or a panopticon. Given this, its response to political pamphleteering was essentially reactive, an impulsive effort to stop the gathering of political storms. The state's proscription orders clustered around times of intense political activity and then petered out once the storm had been weathered.

The Swadeshi Movement (1905–11) was the first period of intense political agitation with any semblance of mass mobilization.[128] As evident from the Madras Police Abstracts of Intelligence the government shadowed political leaders and writers like G. Subramania Iyer, V.O. Chidambaram Pillai, Subramania Bharati, Subramania Siva, and V.V.S. Aiyar. An attempt was also made to restrict seditious literature reaching students who were, for the first time, being mobilized for such political movements. This was done by ordering the postal authorities to hand over to the state all postal articles addressed to students as a community.[129]

But it was not until the Indian Press Act was passed in early 1910 that the government possessed the legislative powers to enforce its writ.[130] Works like *Sri Aurobindo Ghosh Charithiram* and V.V.S. Aiyar's biography of Garibaldi were banned under the act.[131] The government was especially worried by strongly worded pamphlets with marked religious overtones such as *Sadarana Varushathiya Vaikunda Ekadasiandru Sri Bhagawan Thiruvaimalarndaruliyirukkira Akgnai* (The Commandment of God on the day of Vaikunda Ekadesi in the year Sadarana [1910–11]),[132] *Ariyargalukku Oar Aptha*

[128] The classic monograph on the Swadeshi Movement by Sumit Sarkar has reappeared in a second edition with a new preface by the author and two critical essays: see idem, *The Swadeshi Movement in Bengal 1903–1908* (1973, rpnt. Ranikhet: Permanent Black, 2010).

[129] G.O. no. 758, Edl (Confdl), 10 November 1908; G.O. no. 224A, Edl (Confdl), 16 April 1909.

[130] For the various Press Acts as responses to active political agitations and movements, see N. Gerald Barrier, *Banned: Controversial Literature and Political Control in British India, 1907–1947* (Columbia: University of Missouri Press, 1974).

[131] G.O. no. 1059, Judl (Confdl), 15 July 1910; and G.O. no. 1403, Judl (Confdl), 15 September 1910.

[132] G.O. no. 581, Judl (Confdl), 30 March 1911.

*Vakkiyam* (A Word of Advice to the Aryans),[133] and *Abinava Bharata Samajathil Sernthukolla Pramanam* (Oath of Admission into the New Bharat Association)[134]—the latter two printed at the non-existent Paranginasini Achagam (The Feringhee Destroyer Press).

Especially in the aftermath of the assassination of Robert Ashe, Collector of Tirunelveli, in June 1911 there was virtual panic in the government. Subramania Bharati's *Kanavu* (Dream) and *Aril Oru Pangu* (One-sixth), 'a harmless love poem and a social reform novelette',[135] were banned for no better reason than that they were either mentioned in the correspondence or found in the possession of the accused in the Ashe murder conspiracy case.[136]

In another instance J.F. Bryant, District Magistrate of Ramnad, made unreasonable demands for security deposits for the opening of new presses under the 1910 Press Act. When, a year later, he was called upon by the government to explain his action, he replied from Dorset reminding the government of the 'considerable excitement' prevailing at the time of the Ashe murder and drew attention to the circulation of 'highly seditious matter'. 'Such being the conditions', he confessed, 'it is possible that the provisions of the Act were somewhat rigorously enforced and the opening of new presses were [sic.] discouraged in certain places—even at the risk of punishing the innocent for the guilty.'[137]

Because of the circulation of anti-British literature from the French enclave of Pondicherry, wherein Subramania Bharati, V.V.S. Aiyar, Aurobindo, and others had taken refuge, the government, apart from banning its entry into British India, also empowered the CID to detain letters and parcels suspected of containing seditious literature.[138]

[133] G.O. no. 1036, Judl (Confdl), 24 June 1911.

[134] G.O. no. 1056, Judl (Confdl), 27 June 1911.

[135] As Bharati described them in his letter to the *Hindu*, 8 October 1912; for the full text, see Venkatachalapathy (ed.), *Bharati Karuvoolam*, p. 49.

[136] G.O. no. 1588, Judl (Confdl), 11 October 1911; also G.O. nos 1909–10, Judl (Confdl), 6 December 1911.

[137] G.O. no. 1539, Judl (Confdl), 27 September 1912.

[138] G.O. no. 1211, Judl (Confdl), 27 July 1911; G.O. no. 353, Judl (Confdl), 24 February 1911; G.O. nos 953–4, Judl (Confdl), 4 May 1915.

Despite all these measures the Madras Government's harvest of banned literature during the Swadeshi phase was meagre: 3 in 1910, 6 in 1911, 1 in 1912,[139] and nothing at all in the subsequent years until the Non Cooperation Movement. The periods of lull were marked by routine annual reports on the working of the act.

While a number of publications were banned during the Non-Cooperation and Khilafat movements (1919–22), this made little impact on the Tamil publishing scene because most of the proscribed books were in Urdu, Hindustani, and languages other than Tamil.[140] During this phase, apart from proscribing books and making security demands on presses, the government blacklisted a number of presses from an indirect form of state subsidy—getting printing contracts from the state. Such blacklisted presses sometimes numbered as many as a few score.[141] Even then the government was lenient: it provided the caveat that its order be carried out with 'regard [. . .] to local conditions'.[142] What effect this blacklisting move had on the publishing scene is not clear, though presses like the Sadhu Achukkudam of Thiru.Vi.Ka. were on the list. In all likelihood the impact was minimal. Many of the presses seem to have survived. In any case, once the storm blew over, the status quo ante was more or less restored. As C.P. Ramaswamy Iyer, Law Member of the Governor's Council, remarked in 1926, 'Now that the Non cooperation movement is, to all intent and purposes dead, the bigger question may be considered as to whether it really serves any purpose to discriminate between our presses and another's.'[143]

The next phase of feverish proscription took place during the Civil Disobedience Movement (1930–3). Preceding it there was the most celebrated case: the enforced forfeiture of Bharati's poetry books following their proscription by the government of Burma, and subsequent notification of this by the Government of Madras. There

[139] G.O. nos 1681–2, Judl (Confdl), 19 July 1915.

[140] See History of Freedom Movement, vols 83, 85 and 86, Tamilnadu Archives.

[141] G.O. no. 142, Pub. (Confdl), 15 February 1922; G.O. no. 535, Pub., 23 June 1922.

[142] G.O. no. 142, Pub. (Confdl), 15 February 1922.

[143] G.O. no. 153, Pub. (Confdl), 23 February 1926.

was a public uproar and heated exchanges in the Madras legislature which finally led to annulling the proscription order. In an ingenious move publishers sold copies with the seal of forfeiture, which greatly added to their marketability. The ultimate outcome was the posthumous fame that accrued to Bharati, leading to his enshrinement as the greatest modern Tamil poet.

During the Civil Disobedience Movement hundreds of publications were scrutinized and scores banned. The Indian Press (Emergency Powers) Act 1931, gave the government special powers to act and was put to effective use. The scores of government orders that were generated through this process of political control do not reveal a fresh outlook, but as a spin-off we get some fascinating details about the world of popular publishing. This domain came to the extended notice of the government, possibly for the first time, and consequently much valuable light was thrown on it. While in 1931 only five Tamil books had to be forfeited, in 1932 no less than forty-nine were proscribed, many of these being part of popular literature.[144]

With Congress taking over office in 1937, a slight shift in government policy followed for many decades. Within months of assuming office C. Rajagopalachari (Rajaji), as Premier, revoked the ban on mild nationalist agitprop. As he remarked of books by the prolific nationalist writer and journalist M.S. Subramania Iyer: 'I know that this writer's books do not infringe the rule of violence and perhaps not even the strict bounds of the rule of sedition. They may be safely allowed and the ban removed.'[145] But Rajaji's scheme of deproscription was also selective, self-serving, and shrewd. Not only were the publications of the Self-Respect Movement excluded (see below), but, with Congress's eyes set on the Transfer of Power and its implications for stability, law and order, some strong nationalist books were not spared either. As Rajaji observed, they were 'written long ago when an active movement was going on. To put it in fresh circulation now by an order of cancellation of the old order would, in the opinion of the Government, lead to misunderstanding of the

[144] G.O. no. 1591, Pub. (Gen.), 17 July 1946; for a partial list for 1932, see Letter no. 1653, Pub. (Gen.), 22 December 1932.

[145] G.O. no. 2158, Pub. (Gen.) (Confdl), 12 November 1937.

law as to the limits of freedom of expression of opinion.'[146] Rajaji suggested that the authors 'revise their book[s] carefully with due regard to existing circumstances and apply for orders' in respect of them.[147] His actions are reminiscent of the poignant climax of Orwell's *Animal Farm*, where the excluded animals look from man to pig and pig to man and cannot distinguish between them. No wonder E.M.S. Namboodiripad complained to the Congress Working Committee in October 1937 that 'genuine Congressmen would feel sorry that the representatives of the Congress who were hitherto speaking the language of independence and struggle have begun to speak the language of "Law and Order" of the old regime.'[148]

### *Publications of the Self-Respect Movement*

From its inception by 'Periyar' E.V. Ramasamy in mid 1927, the Self-Respect Movement launched a strident campaign against Brahminism, caste, and religion. Viewing Brahminism as the primary contradiction of society, the thrust of its campaign was directed towards this. Consequently, agitation against the colonial state took a backseat and, given its links with the Justice Party, the Self-Respect Movement was often characterized as pro-British. Despite this, its publications were scrutinized by the government, and quite a few were banned on the ground that they 'excited disaffection between the various classes of His Majesty's subjects'.[149] For instance, *Suyamariyathai Sangitha Rathinam* was banned on the ground that it contained an outrageous attack on Brahmins.[150] Some works attacking Christianity from a rationalist viewpoint were also proscribed.[151] Even those that escaped proscription were seen to contain objectionable passages, but, as one official commented, 'we cannot muzzle "rational" criticism of

[146] Ibid.

[147] Ibid. For the Congress's policy during the interim government, see G.O. no. 1591, Pub. (Confdl), 17 July 1946.

[148] Quoted in David Arnold, *Police Power and Colonial Rule*, p. 218.

[149] Letter no. 369, Home, 26 April 1936.

[150] G.O. no. 58, Pub. (Gen.), 10 January 1935.

[151] For instance, *Pathirigalin Brahmacharya Latchanam*. See G.O. no. 418, Pub. (Gen.) (Confdl), 8 March 1935.

religion unless it is clearly malicious'.[152] Given the existence of a radical socialist faction (consisting of M. Singaravelu, P. Jeevanandam, Sathankulam A. Raghavan, and others) within the Self-Respect Movement, the government was wary of its literary output. For instance, when a publishing house named Karpagam Company began to issue a series of Self-Respect pamphlets, the first of which was penned by M. Singaravelu, the CID was asked to keep a watch over the other books in the series.[153]

But the *cause célèbre* of the day was the proscription of Bhagat Singh's *Naan Naathigan—En?* (*Why I am an Atheist*). Translated by P. Jeevanandam, who later emerged as the most prominent of the communist leaders of Tamilnadu, it was published (very cheaply, like all other Self-Respect books) by the Paguttharivu Noorpathippu Kazhagam (Rationalist Publishing House), an organ of the Self-Respect Movement. The spectre of Bhagat Singh's fame still loomed large in the colonial mind and the book was promptly banned.[154] Some 529 copies were seized from the Unmai Vilakkam Press, another organ of the movement, and subsequently destroyed.[155]

The government went on to prosecute Jeevanandam and E.V. Krishnasamy Naicker, Periyar's older brother and publisher of the book. Chief Secretary G.T.H. Bracken brusquely set aside the advocate general's advice not to prosecute: 'The Advocate General is hard to satisfy.'[156] Another official explained the rationale behind the prosecution: 'If this passage [. . .] is not calculated to bring government into hatred or contempt or to excite disaffection against it, I am not able to see what else can [. . .] The object of the pamphlet may be to advocate Atheism but we are not so much concerned with the object as with the intent underlying the passage and the effect it is likely to produce on the minds of its readers . . .'[157] Ultimately, on the advice of Periyar, Jeevanandam, and E.V. Krishnasamy Naicker tendered an apology and escaped imprisonment.

[152] G.O. no. 1579, Pub. (Gen.) (Confdl), 28 September 1935.
[153] G.O. no. 1456, Pub. (Gen.) (Confdl), 12 November 1932.
[154] G.O. no. 1070, Pub. (Gen.) (Confdl), 22 October 1934.
[155] Report of the District Magistrate of Coimbatore, in ibid.
[156] G.O. no. 211, Pub. (Gen.) (Confdl), 2 February 1935.
[157] Ibid.

With the assumption of office by the Congress, the Self-Respect Movement was in for worse. In the context of the revocation of proscription on some publications, Periyar wrote to the government asking for both revocation of proscription and return of seized copies of his *Kudiarasu Kalambagam.*[158] Rajagopalachari, the Premier, wrote a shrewd note on the file: 'This is a "test application". So the orders should give reasons for rejecting the application. The petitioner may be informed that copies of proscribed books are generally destroyed after 3 months and cannot be returned and that the book contains passages (seriously) provocative of great class hatred and highly offensive general allegations against whole classes of people and consequently the order cannot be reversed.'[159] Similarly, especially in the context of the anti-Hindi agitation launched by the Self-Respect Movement, Rajaji ordered that the publishers of Self-Respect books 'attacking particular castes and communities' be *orally* warned.[160] No wonder Periyar reacted viciously in his *Kudi Arasu.* In a characteristically hard hitting editorial he exposed the hollow claims of the Congress regarding freedom of expression and condemned the partisan handling of revocation orders by the Rajagopalachari ministry. Periyar demonstrated that only Rajagopalachari's own caste men and stooges had profited from the government's orders.[161] And in fact rigorous state control over the Dravidian Movement's publications continued to be exercised by various Congress ministries from the mid-1940s through the 1950s.

### *Communist Literature*

The spectre of communism haunted the colonial government, especially during the 1930s. Though the actual strength of the Communist Party may not have warranted such paranoia, the government's surveillance of communists and their activities amounted to a

[158] G.O. no. 999, Pub. (Gen.) (Confdl), 13 June 1935.

[159] Note by Rajaji, 13 October 1937, in ibid. The word 'seriously' is struck off by Rajagopalachari as an afterthought.

[160] The word 'orally' has been inserted by Rajaji—an afterthought perhaps—to conceal the extra-legal character of his instructions. Note dated 13 August 1938, G.O. no. 1417, Pub. (Gen.) (Confdl), 17 August 1938.

[161] *Kudi Arasu,* 24 October 1937, editorial.

witch-hunt. Graham Shaw's detailed study of colonial control over books in India, based on the files of India Political Intelligence, is largely concerned with the red sceptre haunting Europe.[162] When, in 1934, the Retrenchment Committee recommended a reduction in staff for the Registrar of Books, the government not only accepted the registrar's plea against this on grounds of burgeoning publishing activity but also raised the bogey of communism. An official of the Public department remarked: 'as communist doctrines seem to be becoming increasingly popular there can be no relaxation at present in the strictness of scrutiny.'[163] The Chief Secretary affirmed: 'We have been tightening up our scrutiny of publications very definitely and insisting on special advance reports on communist literature generally.'[164]

Not surprisingly, the Government of Madras wholeheartedly welcomed the 'Communist Notification' of the Government of India which prohibited the import of literature emanating from the Comintern and its affiliates, and reprints thereof.[165] Shaw mentions attempts to ship in communist publications through Pondicherry with variable success. And among booksellers who imported books from leading left-wing publishers he lists in detailed appendices a few from the Tamil country.[166] Though some communist publications were banned, some presses harassed, and a few libraries searched,[167] the harvest far from matched the paranoia.

Our discussion of the colonial state and its policing of books shows that the state was marginal to the world of Tamil publishing. Despite

[162] Graham Shaw, 'On the Wrong End of the Raj: Some Aspects of Censorship in British India and its Circumvention, 1920s–1940', in Abhijit Gupta and Swapan Chakravorty (eds), *Moveable Type: Book History in India* (Ranikhet: Permanent Black, 2008).

[163] G.O. no. 322, Pub. (Gen.), 23 February 1935.

[164] Ibid.

[165] G.O. no. 1227, Pub. (Gen.), 24 September 1932.

[166] Shaw, 'On the Wrong End of the Raj', pp. 161–5.

[167] See G.O. no. 1619, Home (Confdl), 3 August 1936; G.O. no. 414, Pub. (Gen.) (Confdl), 26 February 1937.

being armed with wide-ranging legislative powers, its administrative structure and mechanisms of control were weak. As a consequence the state was not a dominating presence within the Tamil publishing scene. The Registrar of Books, on whom the state relied heavily for information on publications, produced reviews and statistics of dubious value. Hardly any worthwhile knowledge about Tamil publishing was generated. Contrary to what Tapti Roy argues with reference to Bengal, where there was not only colonial policing but also an 'internalization of discipline' by the Bengali elite, the government of Fort St George managed to exercise very little control over literary production.[168] Consequently, the impact of censorship in revolutionary England, for instance, cannot be compared to that in the Tamil context—though this is not to underestimate fear of the colonial police among the native subjects. As Christopher Hill argues in the context of the English Civil War, censorship was so powerful that it even enforced a sort of self-censorship among authors.[169]

In Tamilnadu, though a number of books were banned, few literary producers were persecuted or prosecuted or even subjected to direct censorship. There were none of the celebrated court cases that are the staple of histories of the book elsewhere: as Robert Darnton puts it, 'Not that they [the colonial state] impounded or imprisoned on a great scale.'[170] The colonial secret police was also rather weak: the CID in the Madras Presidency numbered only 29 in 1907 and increased to 55 in 1910.[171] In this situation, recourse to princely states and French enclaves was also limited. There is evidence to suggest that a few books were pirated from Karaikkal, part of the French

[168] Tapti Roy, 'Disciplining the Printed Text: Colonial and Nationalist Surveillance of Bengali Literature', in Partha Chatterjee (ed.), *Texts of Power: Emerging Disciplines in Colonial Bengal* (Minneapolis: University of Minnesota Press, 1995).

[169] Christopher Hill, 'Censorship and English Literature', in *The Collected Essays of Christopher Hill*, vol. 1 (Brighton: Harvester Press, 1985).

[170] Robert Darnton, 'Literary Surveillance in the British Raj: The Contradiction of Liberal Imperialism', *Book History*, vol. 4, 2004, p. 168.

[171] Richard J. Popplewell, *Intelligence and Imperial Defence: British Intelligence and the Defence of the Indian Empire, 1904–1924* (London: Frank Cass, 1995), p. 73.

territory of Pondicherry, to evade copyright. As the Registrar of Books observed, copyright was 'violated by native printers [. . .] especially in Karaikkal, with impunity, pirated editions of government school books in particular having been largely published there for sale in this presidency.'[172] An official CID memo conceded that of the number of obscene publications circulating in the presidency 'some of which no doubt found their way to Pondicherry and any obscene book published in Pondicherry very soon attracts notice outside.'[173] At the height of the Swadeshi Movement the government conceded 'the straggling character of the Pondicherry frontier and the opportunities it affords for evasion of customs and post office restrictions';[174] and again, 'the circulation through the post from Pondicherry is exceedingly easy.'[175] However, from the available evidence it is apparent that the government was not losing much sleep over it. During the Civil Disobedience Movement a customs inspector of Nagapattinam, upon seizing a Tamil pamphlet published from Karaikkal, observed to his superior, the Collector of Customs, that 'the necessity for printing such pamphlets in a small Tamil press in the French territory when there are better facilities for printing them in British India even at less cost forebodes the mischievous intentions of the authors.'[176] The enquiry following this seizure reveals the weakness of the surveillance. The British consulate in Pondicherry reported that there could be no arresting on French territory; a warrant for complicity in the distribution of printed matter on British soil was essential, and even then no extradition was possible. In this situation, 'It is merely a question of entente with the French police. Our CID men inform them of the existence of the warrants and they inform the CID men, or our police when there are no CID men that the wanted man is about to leave French territory.'[177]

Perhaps, only Subramania Bharati and a few other Swadeshi writers, such as V.V.S. Aiyar and Mandayam S. Srinivasachari, were

[172] Nos 296–7, Edl, 17 May 1886.

[173] G.O. no. 680, Judl (Confdl), 26 April 1912.

[174] G.O. nos 314–15, Judl (Confdl), 28 February 1910.

[175] G.O. no. 1211, Judl (Confdl), 27 July 1911.

[176] G.O. no. 546, Pub. (Gen.) (Confdl), 8 April 1932.

[177] G.O. no. 836, Pub. (Gen.) (Confdl), 4 June 1932.

exceptions. Bharati was shadowed closely during his exile in Pondicherry and had to consent to unofficial 'censorship' for a brief period on his release from prison in end-1918.[178] During World War II some presses and publishers moved to the native state of Pudukkottai, not for political reasons but to circumvent government restrictions on launching new periodicals in the wake of acute paper shortages.

Though M.S. Subramania Iyer complained to Rajaji that the proscription of his books frightened press keepers and his readers,[179] this did not seem to have prevented him publishing dozens of books. Even with obscene and erotic books, an area in which the colonial government could claim a reasonable amount of success, for every book it banned or expurgated scores of others circulated freely.

[178] Letter of Bharati to Parali Su. Nellaiyappa Pillai, 21 December 1918 in Padmanabhan (ed.), *Bharatiyin Kadithangal*, pp. 67–8.

[179] G.O. no. 2158, Pub. (Gen.) (Confdl), 12 November 1937.

# 7

# Readers, Reading Practices, Modes of Reading

Having looked at publishing structures, agencies, varieties, and state interventions in the domain of the book, we reach an important figure missing so far in our picture: the reader—the consumer for whom the book was produced. So, here I explore the social composition of readers and chart evolving reading practices as well as modes of reading.

## Readers and their Social Composition

Who read? How many people read? These apparently simple questions are the most difficult to address and answer satisfactorily. The rise of the novel is what first brings readership into discussion and analysis. From all the evidence it is clear that, with the growing volume of novels, there was a great expansion in readership, leading away from patronage publishing for a select readership towards an expanding book market. But with the limited research in this area so far it is dangerous to hazard a guess as to printruns and sales figures—the only reliable ways of estimating the readership for books. It is even more hazardous to generalize about readership based on one class of books, the novel.

We found earlier that most novels, even those by the most popular writers— for instance J.R. Rangaraju's *Chandrakantha* (5th impression) and *Rajambal* (9th impression), Arani Kuppuswamy Mudaliar's *Aboorva Chintamani* (3rd impression)—all had printruns of only a thousand copies each,[1] a figure that persists to this day. But these novels were frequently reprinted, testifying to their popularity. J.R. Rangaraju led in this area: by 1927 his *Rajambal* had seen 22 impressions, *Rajendran* 9, *Varadarajan* 2,[2] giving a combined sale of about 70,000 copies for these titles. Even at a conservative estimate of four readers a copy, this amounts to a substantial readership—given the literacy rate of the period. It should also be borne in mind that works by Arani Kuppuswamy Mudaliar, Vaduvur Duraiswamy Iyengar, Vai.Mu. Kothainayaki Ammal, and S.S. Arunagirinathar were sold in even larger numbers.

The circulation figures of contemporary periodicals too could help us make a calculated guess on readership numbers. At the end of the first year of its existence *Ananda Bodhini* claimed a total of 5,000 subscriptions.[3] In 1933 *Ananda Vikatan* claimed a printrun of 50,000 copies.[4] We have figures for *Ananda Vikatan*'s circulation through agency sales alone, as distinct from subscription sales (Table 7.1). These figures show that *Ananda Vikatan* had reached every district of Tamilnadu, with a strong readership base in Madras, Coimbatore, Thanjavur, Tiruchy, Madurai, Tirunelveli, and Ramanathapuram, suggesting the wide geographical spread of popular reading materials.

However, this tells us little about the social composition of book readers; for this we need to look elsewhere. Fortunately, Maraimalai Adigal maintained an address book in which he kept a record of all those who bought his books. I was able to locate only the second of his address books, which starts with entry no. 906 dated 20 April 1923 and ends with entry no. 1852 dated 10 August 1930, giving a total of over 950 readers.[5] It is hazardous to generalize about readership based on the profile of just Maraimalai Adigal's readers. Yet, in

[1] G.O. nos 375–6, Home (Edn), 19 March 1918.

[2] See advertisements in Rangaraju, *Mohanasundaram* (Chennai: Rangaraju & Bros, 1927, 12th edition).

[3] *Ananda Bodhini*, 1 (12), June 1916.

[4] *Ananda Vikatan*, 8 (3), 26 November 1933.

[5] Address Book no. 2, Maraimalai Adigal Papers. The data in the following paragraphs are drawn from this address book unless otherwise specified.

Table 7.1

Agency Sales of *Ananda Vikatan*, 1933

| | |
|---|---|
| Madras | 2025 |
| Chinglepet | 181 |
| North Arcot | 300 |
| Salem | 455 |
| South Arcot | 581 |
| Thanjavur | 2070 |
| Tiruchy | 1022 |
| Madurai | 1441 |
| Ramanathapuram | 857 |
| Tirunelveli | 1050 |
| Nilgiris | 115 |
| Pudukkottai | 125 |
| Coimbatore | 3435 |

Source: *Ananda Vikatan*, 10 June 1933

the absence of any other data, this may suggest certain broad patterns. Here are some of the results of the analysis.

Of the 956 readers, 556 belonged to the Tamil districts of the Madras Presidency. As many as 202 were from Sri Lanka, 64 from Burma, and 34 from the Federated Malay States. Of the 556 from Tamilnadu, 59 were from Madras city and its environs, 48 from the cities of Tiruchy, Madurai, and Coimbatore, 139 from other towns, and 310 from rural areas, giving the lie to the generally held assumption that books were read mostly in urban areas. The educational qualifications of only 24 could be ascertained. There were 21 BAs (including five Licentiates in Teaching and four Bachelors of Law) and two MAs. Educational qualifications below graduation obviously went unrecorded because it was not customary to indicate those along with one's name. Perhaps a good number of the others were matriculates.

The occupational classification tends towards the middle class (Table 7.2). Before making hasty generalizations, we need to note that occupations were identified from the addresses given, and one cannot be quite sure except in the cases of teachers, students,

Table 7.2

Occupational Profile of Tamil Readers, 1923–1930

| | |
|---|---|
| Booksellers | 37 |
| Headmasters, teachers, and pundits | 87 |
| Merchants | 49 |
| Authors, editors and scholars | 15 |
| Students | 19 |
| Sangam secretaries | 49 |
| Bureaucrats | 14 |
| Engineers | 3 |
| Vakils | 9 |
| Doctors | 4 |
| Clerks | 47 |
| Press managers | 3 |
| Tahsildars/karnams | 2 |
| Post office employees | 9 |
| Native doctors | 6 |
| Astrologers | 2 |
| Priests and religious mutts | 16 |
| Mirasdars, zamindars, and landlords | 9 |
| Commission agents | 8 |
| Railway station vendor | 1 |
| Bangle-sellers | 2 |

*Source*: Maraimalai Adigal's Address Book no.2

merchants, and the like. In any case, teachers, clerks, and merchants predominate. More interesting is the presence of two bangle-sellers and a railway-station vendor in the list of readers. Vaiyapuri, a hawker from the Salem railway platform, bought a copy of Adigal's *Vellalar Nagarigam*. How many unsung Menocchios lurk among these is difficult to guess. This draws attention to the fact that though books are by and large social products fashioned by complex historical forces that operate within identifiable social classes, they often take on an independent existence and may reach the most unlikely hands.

From occupation to caste we tread even more treacherous ground. Surnames are tricky indicators of caste, especially in the case of 'Pillai' and 'Mudaliar'. But a tentative count of the caste surnames in Maraimalai Adigal's Address Book gives the following results (Table 7.3).

It is not very surprising that Maraimalai Adigal's books, which were most often addressed to a Saiva Vellala audience, should have been bought by so many 'Pillais' and 'Mudaliars'. 'Chettiars', especially those involved in the banking business in Burma, too were patrons of his works. (Perhaps it was a portent for what was to come. There was a surfeit of Chettiar capital flowing into the Tamil book trade during and after World War II, as many Chettiar firms had to flee from South East Asia and Burma.) That thirty-five Brahmins should figure as readers of Maraimalai Adigal's frequently anti-Brahmin books is interesting. The presence of Gounders, a dominant caste in the western region of Tamilnadu, is notable, because they have invariably gone unmentioned in studies of colonial political and social movements. There is no indication of dalit surnames. The low percentage

Table 7.3

Caste Surnames of Tamil Readers, 1923–1930

| | |
|---|---|
| Pillai | 215 |
| Mudaliar | 61 |
| Chettiar | 92 |
| Brahmins | 35 |
| Gounder | 27 |
| Yadavar/Konar | 3 |
| Padayachi | 2 |
| Reddiar | 12 |
| Achari | 6 |
| Nadar | 13 |
| Desigar | 10 |
| Naidu/Naicker | 14 |
| Udaiyar | 1 |
| Moopanar | 1 |
| Servai | 3 |
| Devangar | 1 |
| Karunigar | 2 |
| Muslims | 13 |
| Christians | 22 |

*Source*: Maraimalai Adigal's Address Book no. 2

of Brahmins apart, this broad caste profiling fits broadly with assumptions about purchasing power alongside the cultural priority accorded to book purchases, and goes some way in reinforcing them.

### The Traditional Mode of Reading

Until the turn of the twentieth century, reading practices were largely determined by the limited availability of printed materials.[6] We have little evidence of how printed books were read in the first centuries of their existence and circulation in the Tamil world—except for some surprisingly detailed documentation of how print impinged on one native convert in the early eighteenth century. This brings in the astonishing story of Rajanaiken, a poor outcast 'pariah' who lived in Thanjavur. The story comes from J. Fred. Fenger, a missionary who spent many years at Tranquebar and wrote the history of the mission in rich detail.[7]

Rajanaiken's grandfather became a Catholic at the age of 30 and Rajanaiken himself was baptized at birth. By the age of 22 he had learned to read and write. Along with his younger brother Sinnapen, he took a great fancy to reading books—mostly on palm leaf which contained 'papal histories of saints, the miracles of the Virgin Mary and a few of those of Christ.' His hunger for reading was not satiated and he tried to get more books, especially the books of Moses, from Catholic catechists through 'flattery and presents'. It was at this time, in 1725, that he met a Catholic mendicant monk, Sittananden, who possessed a printed book containing the four Gospels and the Acts of the Apostles bound together (Ziegenbalg's translation of the first

[6] For instance, see Madras Public Consultations, vol. 619, 22 February 1834, pp. 514–28, for the high subscription tariff and restrictive rules and regulations of the Madras Hindoo Literary Society for borrowing books.

[7] Fenger, *History of the Tranquebar Mission*, pp. 175–9. Fenger mentions that his account is based on Rajanaiken's own letter written in 1732. It is not clear where this letter is now. For a detailed account of printing in Tranquebar, see my 'Written on Leaves in the Malabarian Manner: Print and Cultural Encounter in Eighteenth-Century Tranquebar', *Review of Development and Change*, XIV (1–2), January–December 2009. Also see Volmer Rosenkilde, 'Printing at Tranquebar, 1712–1845', *Library* (5th series), IV (1949); Priolkar, *The Printing Press in India*, ch. 3.

part of the New Testament, 1714)—a copy probably acquired from Schultz. Apparently he could not read it himself—an important reminder that books were often meant not for reading but to stand as respected artefacts signifying authority—and had torn off the title page. After much effort he granted Rajanaiken's request to read it but warned him, 'You can keep it for your own reading, but take care that the Priest does not see it.' Rajanaiken 'used to read it all day and then from evening till midnight by a light.' When he had read it through, 'the Lord had given me great light in understanding it.' But then he was struck by a real fear: once Sittananden came he would have to return the book. 'I therefore determined to copy it all out on Palm-leaves and make a book of them, and so began to write. I copied the Gospels of St Matthew and Mark and part of Luke, but being but little accustomed to writing, my hand was so tired that I could do no more.'[8] Luckily for him, Sittananden never turned up, so Rajanaiken kept the book. A few years later, in 1727, he went to Tirukadaiyur, a village near Tranquebar, where he met a Catholic, 'Schawrimuthu', who had a small printed book—Ziegenbalg's letter addressed to all Malabarians, published in 1717. Rajanaiken claims, interestingly, that this Savarimuthu could not actually read the book but pretended to and so collected alms from his 'ignorant (Romish) hearers'! Rajanaiken promptly bought the book from him, for 'one fano'. Upon enquiry he found that Savarimuthu had got the book from German priests. Rajanaiken struck a deal and got himself other imprints from the Tranquebar press. Beginning to suspect that he was being cheated, however, he began corresponding with the German priests and finally went to Tranquebar with his brother. The first book he bought was the full New Testament. 'After I had had about six months' intercourse with them, partly by writing, partly by word of mouth, and had studied the Bible', he says, he converted to the Evangelical congregation in 1728.[9] Rajanaiken personifies the impact that print could have on people.[10]

[8] Fenger, *History of the Tranquebar Mission*, p. 177.

[9] Ibid., p. 179.

[10] The opening up of access to print that lower-caste converts had through missionary agency caused much heartburn among upper caste literati. An

Buchanan, in his record of a journey through large parts of southern India in the first years of the nineteenth century, states that there was 'a great cry for Bible'. With typical Christian make-believe he tells us that people followed him crying they did not want bread or money but 'we want the Word of God'! A missionary of Thanjavur told him there were over ten thousand Protestants in the southern districts 'who had not among them one complete copy of the Bible, and that not one Christian perhaps in a hundred had a New Testament.'[11] If this was the situation with the Bible, the near-exclusive output of the early presses, little need be said of other literature.

In this situation of the limited availability of printed artefacts and restricted literacy on account of social factors such as caste, class, and religion, a printed book was quite novel even in the mid-nineteenth century. As late as 1858 Sabapathy Navalar was describing print as '*elutha eluthu*', 'the unwritten writ'! The phrase is quite revealing of print's continuing novelty and is employed by the early editor Thiruthanikai Visakaperumalaiyar as well.[12] An incident narrated by U.V. Swaminatha Iyer bears testimony to the sense of surprise the printed book continued to evoke even in the 1870s. One day, Swaminatha Iyer happened to be reading verses from a printed copy of *Kambaramayanam* along with some fellow students at the Thiruvavaduthurai Mutt, Ambalavana Desigar, an old-fashioned scholar and teacher of Mahavidwan Meenakshisundaram Pillai, happened to walk past them. Enquiring of the book they were holding and learning it was a copy of *Kambaramayanam* he exclaimed, 'Have

---

1828-petition to the Company by upper castes from Tirunelveli complained, 'European missionaries having come to the country, sent teachers to the village and by means of books which they have newly and cunningly made and printed [. . .], many mean caste people such as pallars, parias and shanars who were as slaves [. . .], became bold and turned to the religion of Christ.' Quoted in Bhavani Raman, 'Document Raj: Writing and Scribes in Early Colonial South India' (unpublished manuscript, 2010), p. 70.

[11] J.S.M. Hooper, *Bible Translation in India, Pakistan and Ceylon* (1938, rev. edn. Oxford: Oxford University Press, 1963), p. 75.

[12] Venkatasamy, *Pathonbatham Noottrandil Tamil Ilakkiyam*, pp. 94–5.

they made a *book* [he used the English term] of it, too!' This exclamation in turn surprised the students, who could barely control their laughter at the old man's naiveté.[13] The anecdote reveals not only the novelty of the book to the older generation but also the beginnings of its penetration into the new. Having been socialized into print, young students had begun to take printed books for granted and so felt the disdain of the technologically advantaged for supposedly passé scholars brought up on palm-leaf manuscripts.[14]

As we have seen, even in the latter part of the nineteenth century palm-leaf manuscripts and printed books continued to exist side by side. Mylai Seeni. Venkatasamy's observation that printed books did not displace palm-leaf manuscripts overnight should put to rest the argument for technological determinism.[15] It is pertinent that paper, which was introduced into North India as early as in the thirteenth century, was not taken up in Tamilnadu until well into the nineteenth century. Non-Tamil words—*kaditham*,[16] *kadithasi*, *kagitham*—were used in the nineteenth century for paper until '*thal*', from 'stem/stalk', was employed by more discerning users of the language. Given the fact that palm-leaf manuscripts and printed matter could not be consumed in the same mode, conflicts arose. Traditional scholars often ridiculed new scholars who fumbled with palm-leaf manuscripts, unable to decipher them fluently. C.W. Damodaram Pillai, refuting criticisms of his editions, derisively referred to his critics as 'scholars of the printed book who know not how to hold or read palm-leaf manuscripts.'[17] Likewise U.V. Swaminatha Iyer writes that his teacher Meenakshisundaram Pillai rarely ever wrote on paper, preferring to dictate to his students.[18] A.C. Burnell, the distinguished Orientalist, observes as late as 1874 that the use of paper in South

[13] *SMPC*, vol. 2, 1940, p. 207.

[14] No wonder, one Brahmo Samajist rued that young men were being misled by the baseless allegations of Christian missionaries contained in 'clearly printed tracts'. *Thattuva Bodhini*, 1 (1), May 1864, editorial.

[15] Venkatasamy, *Pathonbatham Nootrandil Tamil Ilakkiyam*, pp. 94, 107.

[16] By the early twentieth century '*kaditham*' came to mean a letter.

[17] *Tholkappiyam–Porulathikaram–Nacchinarkkiniyar Urai* (Chennai: Author, 1885), Preface.

[18] *SMPC*, vol. 2, p. 277.

India 'is at all events very recent, and even now scarcely ever occurs except among Mahrathi colonists.'[19] It is said that Dandapani Swamigal too rarely, if ever, wrote on paper and preferred to use cadjan leaves,[20] while Ramalinga Adigal, even when he used paper, used the orthography meant for palm leaves.[21] But this was a passing generation. The new breed of students and scholars was pretty uncomfortable with palm-leaf manuscripts, and, as even U.V. Swaminatha Iyer admits, when Meenakshisundaram Pillai asked him to read from the *Thiruvidaimarudur Ula* he could read out from a palm-leaf manuscript only falteringly.[22] It was years before he acquired the proficiency required for reading manuscripts—which he then used to edit the classics.

Printed books also caused conflicts over the authority of texts. On one occasion, in the early 1870s, U.V. Swaminatha Iyer was reciting a poem from Sivaprakasa Swamigal, a well-known poet of the seventeenth century. As the recitation progressed, Meenakshisundaram Pillai corrected him on one count. When Swaminatha Iyer asserted boyishly that he was only following the printed version, there was stunned silence among the observers: a young man had dared to contradict a scholar of Meenakshisundaram Pillai's stature on the mere authority of print! Meenakshisundaram Pillai broke the ice by instructing Swaminatha Iyer: 'Print does not validate everything. People who are not proficient in the language may print anything.'[23] The authority of print was therefore never taken for granted and in fact its initial penetration into society was considerably contested.

On another occasion Meenakshisundaram Pillai was giving classes on *Periya Puranam*, the Saiva literary classic. While a student read out from the printed book, he annotated the allusions and provided glosses. When the class had progressed to the story of Kannappa Nayanar—the hunter-devotee of Siva who in his devotion

[19] Burnell, *Elements of South-Indian Palaeography*, p. 11.

[20] Interview with Tha. Kovendhan (1932–2004), editor of some of Dandapani Swamigal's works, 21 June 1992.

[21] See the facsimile edition of *Arutperunjothi Agaval* (Vadalur: Thiruvarutprakasa Deva Nilayangal, 1961).

[22] *SMPC*, vol. 2, p. 60.

[23] Ibid., pp. 92–3.

Fig. 8: Mahavidwan Meenakshisundaram Pillai (1815–1876). Legendary teacher and prolific poet-scholar. Note the palm-leaf manuscript in the foreground.

went so far as to gouge out his eyes to offer them to Siva—Meenakshisundaram Pillai stopped the lesson, observing that certain verses were missing in the printed version. He then went in and fetched a palm-leaf manuscript, and as he had pointed out, five verses were indeed missing in the print version. Naturally, his students were awestruck.[24]

Though exceptional scholars like Meenakshisundaram Pillai could often dazzle students and others by such display, they were fighting a losing battle by clinging to a traditional mode of reading and attendant reading practices which placed a premium on memory and learning by rote. Even geniuses have limits, and these limits were

[24] Swaminatha Iyer, *En Charithiram*, p. 205.

Fig. 9: Arumuga Navalar (1822–1879). Scholar, orator, champion of Saiva revivalism. Credited with introducing punctuation into Tamil. Seen here holding a printed book.

exposed by print. Before the advent of print, only a limited number of texts could be acquired for study or reference, for locating and copying them were often unrewarding exercises, particularly because their owners rarely ever permitted people to read or even examine them.[25] C.W. Damodaram Pillai once wrote in exasperation that it would be easier to extract the mythical ruby from the cobra than make certain owners part with their manuscripts, even just to read or copy them.[26] One reason for reluctance among owners will have been

[25] For an interesting anecdote on how one of Meenakshisundaram Pillai's students tricked the zealous owner of *Sivadarumotharam* into parting with it for a few days, see *SMPC*, vol. 1, pp. 208–15.

[26] C.W. Damodaram Pillai, *Kalithogai* (Chennai: Author, 1887), Preface.

that copying was an expensive process involving a great deal of time and energy. The early eighteenth-century Danish missionaries observed that 'Transcribing was to supply the Place of the Press, which as it required more Hands, so it increased also the Cost considerably';[27] they added that 'One of the most expensive Branches of the whole Undertaking, was the transcribing of Books for the Use of their Schools . . . For this End they sometimes employ'd Four, Five, Six, or more Kaṇakappel, or Transcribers.'[28] Murdoch recollected Rev. Peter Percival telling him, in the early part of the nineteenth century, that a manuscript copy of Beschi's Tamil dictionary cost him nearly 10 pounds while now in 1865 a printed copy cost him only 2s. 6d![29] (It was in this context that rich Jains adopted the practice of *sastra dhanam* or the gifting of manuscripts to scholars on festive occasions.) There was the additional and legendary problem of scribal errors. Students in the traditional schools copied out the manuscripts of elementary texts—this explains the widespread occurrence of such texts during national manuscript mission searches—as did more mature scholars in monasteries. With the coming of the printed book a much larger number of standard copies of various texts began to be more widely available, and few traditional scholars could keep pace.

The limits of the traditional mode of reading are highlighted by some anecdotes in the life of Meenakshisundaram Pillai. As a teacher he was in the habit of testing new students by asking them to recite verses. On one occasion, a new recruit from Tirunelveli surprised Meenakshisundaram Pillai with a verse he had never heard of. On enquiring he learnt that the verse was from Thirikudarasappa Kavirayar's *Thirukkuttrala Puranam*.[30] On another occasion, Subbu Bharati surprised him with songs from *Kuttrala Kuravanji*, composed by the same author.[31] The latter work, especially, is now considered a

[27] *Propagation of the Gospel in the East*, pt III (London: J. Downing, 1718), p. 8.

[28] Ibid., pp. 11–12.

[29] Murdoch, *A Classified Catalogue of Tamil Printed Books*, p. xxiii.

[30] *SMPC*, vol. 1, p. 154.

[31] Ibid., p. 215.

classic and not only forms part of the school curriculum but has also been popularized as a dance drama. And to think that Meenakshisundaram Pillai was ignorant of it! Similarly, he had never read Mambala Kavirayar, his contemporary, until he was accosted with a printed copy of his verses on a visit to Pondicherry in 1867.[32] Print and the availability of a wider range of texts were beginning to seriously erode the authority even of outstanding scholars whose erudition was based on an earlier mode of reading.

In brief, though printed books began to be more easily available during the age of patronage, there was no major change in reading practices. Before the arrival of print, the concept of private reading did not exist. Given the physical disadvantages of palm-leaf manuscripts, not to speak of their limited social accessibility, special efforts had to be made to read them. Even though palm leaves were probably hardier than paper (even in those pre-acid days) palm-leaf manuscripts were unwieldy. Processed slats of dried palm leaves were cut to shape before being used for writing with a hard and pointed iron stylus, which in turn required enormous energy.[33] Given the absence of binding, a large perforation or two was made for a string to run through the leaves in order to tie and hold them together. Flipping through the leaves was impossible and the manuscript had to be carefully handled to pre-empt damage. Sometimes lecterns were used to provide support. Substances such as turmeric and soot had to be applied to the surface of the palm leaves to make the writing visible. More importantly, the orthography followed for palm-leaf manuscripts constituted a major determinant of the mode of reading. Since this orthography was not entirely standardized, and especially because dots could not be used (they would damage the leaves), a single character could be read in more than one way. Lack of page numbers was

[32] Ibid., p. 299.

[33] Swaminatha Iyer narrates an incident in Meenakshisundaram Pillai's life attesting to the speed of his verse-making and dictation. One day he overheard a student saying that Pillai could not match the speed with which he could take them down on palm leaves. The next day he dictated so many verses that the errant student finally broke down and wept. *SMPC*, vol. 1, pp. 314–17.

the norm. (It could be argued that the nature of the palm-leaf also precluded the development of calligraphy in Tamil.) Letters, words, lines, verses, commentaries, glosses, and quotations followed one another without space for breath, not to speak of the enormous scope for scribal errors. A bewildered Ziegenbalg wrote, 'there is neither comma, colon, nor semicolon, to be met with.'[34] Consequently reading a text virtually amounted to deciphering a text. This demanded a high level of scholarship, knowledge of prosody, and the possession of a vast vocabulary. Identifying the verse form alerted the reader to the length of the line with its set number of syllables and feet. Students were therefore expected to learn prosody and memorize traditional lexicons and thesauruses in verse form, called *nigandus*.[35]

Often the text had actually to be read aloud in order just to make out verses from the accompanying commentary, never mind comprehending their meaning. Print made a definite impact on verse: after the early years, during which poetry was printed in line with the palm-leaf manuscript tradition (but sometimes with a comma or asterisk to indicate line break), it was laid out in a manner that enabled easy recognition of the verse form. The alliterative pattern—of *ethugai*, *monai*, and *iyaibu*—could now be easily recognized with the indented splitting of lines. The use of a dash (though there was no uniformity in employing an en or em dash or sometimes even just a hyphen) to mark the *thanichol* (caesura) in the *nerisai venba* form was especially useful and conspicuous.

Vocalized reading could mean two things—reading to oneself and reading to an audience. Reading by rote or memorization, and intensive and meditative reading, were a corollary to this mode of reading. Such consumption of texts could not usually happen in private. There were more or less specifically defined arenas for reading. Students read under the tutelage of teachers. Scholastics read in monasteries. Arangettram was an arena where compositions were ritually premiered to an audience. Text-based discourses on religious occasions, fairs, and festivals stood on a similar footing as the arangettram. The

[34] *Propagation of the Gospel in the East*, part III, p. 30.

[35] *Swadesamitran*, 26 May 1914, reprinted in Bharatidasan, *Manudam Pottru* (Chennai: Poompuhar Prasuram, 1984), pp. 11–14.

consumption of texts in these arenas, it is evident, was aural, the audience listening attentively. Not surprisingly therefore *kelvi* (lit. to hear, hearing), and later the tautological *kelvi jnanam*, is Tamil for knowledge.

This kind of aural consumption set certain hermeneutic limitations, the interpretation being mediated by teachers, scholars, and performers, apart from scholarly aids such as verse dictionaries and thesauruses, and scholastic and religious commentaries. But the relatively easy availability of printed texts posed a serious threat to such hermeneutics. The very availability of a text in multiple copies of the same standard without any inconsistency was what underpinned the subversive potential of print. Apart from the fact that texts (in the form of printed books) could be conveniently carried on one's person, the text itself had undergone quite dramatic changes in the process of being printed. The very transcription of the text from the palm leaf to the printed page entailed a major interpretation. Print, for good or ill, not only made for a singular and definite reading of the manuscript, it also stabilized the text and gave it fixity.[36] Even though many early books resembled palm-leaf manuscripts in their layout, the very fact of transcription amounted to a decipherment and fixing of orthography.[37]

The introduction of punctuation, credited to Arumuga Navalar (much like Vidyasagar for Bengali), made it possible to scan the line silently, or even glance through the pages, a virtual impossibility with palm-leaf manuscripts.[38] Interestingly V.G. Suriyanarayana Shastri (Parithimal Kalaignar)'s early discussion of Navalar's

[36] No wonder the Tamil scholar T.T. Kanakasundaram Pillai commented on the imminent publication of an important classic: 'To think that *Chilappadhikaram* will be available in printed form shortly, obviating the need to cry over cadjan leaves, gives me unutterable joy.' Letter to U.V. Swaminatha Iyer, 3 June 1890, U.V.S. Papers.

[37] Murdoch, writing in 1865, says that 'A whole sentence was written as if composed of one word. About twenty years ago, the Madras Bible Soceity resolved to print each word separately and in its natural form, without change or addition of letters . . .', Murdoch, *A Classified Catalogue of Tamil Printed Books*, p. xxxii.

[38] V.G. Suriyanarayana Shastri, *Tamil Mozhiyin Varalaru* (A History of the Tamil Language; Chennai: G.A. Natesan, 1903), pp. 124–5.

innovation follows deliberations over the vexed issue of *sandhi* (conjugation) and the controversy over splitting it while printing verse. In his view punctuation marks contributed to 'clarity and speed'. While the introduction of punctuation was controversial only in relation to verse, he noted that 'nobody would object to it in prose' and added categorically that 'Considering everything there is no reason to object to [the introduction of] punctuation marks. Even those who would object have not objected. Therefore there is little doubt that punctuation will soon be adopted and fully practised. Undoubtedly, special benefits will accrue to Tamil.'[39] V.P. Subramania Mudaliar, writing a few years earlier, had noted that the practice of introducing space between words and various punctuation marks had been adopted from 'English conventions'.[40] A contemporary guide to punctuation stated, '[Punctuation marks] are signs used to add clarity to sentences and verses [. . .] If punctuation marks are properly learnt and used in the right contexts, sentences and verses may not only be better understood but will also be more elegant [. . .] Rules [for punctuation] are not to be found in any Tamil grammar—*Nannool*, *Thonnool* or *Tholkappiyam*. Therefore, it has become necessary to list the various marks and their appropriate uses.'[41] By the end of the nineteenth century similar handbooks on printing had been prepared. A brilliant example comes from C.V. Munisami Nayudu of the Madras Government Press, whose catechism had coined a number of words for printing terms, including punctuation.[42]

Vocalization retarded speed; reading without articulation enabled the reading of many pages and saved energy. While the handiness of printed volumes made it possible to read in isolation, the changed

[39] Ibid., p. 125.

[40] Preface to the Tamil translation of *Paradise Lost* (1895), reprinted in *Sandhi Kuriittu Vilakkam* (Chennai: S. Rajam, [1957/8]), p. 37.

[41] *Vasaga Kurigal* (Punctuation Marks; Chennai: Madras Ripon Press, 1908, 2nd edn), Preface.

[42] C.V. Munisami Nayudu, *A Catechism of Printing in Tamil, Part I* (Madras: C. Narahari Nayudu, 1892). His coinages were based on Tamil roots rather than Sanskrit ones, and many of them seem to have been assimilated into the Tamil language, even though it is nearly impossible to attribute authorship. Some other coinages remain worthy of adoption.

format of the printed text enabled readers to scan lines without reading aloud. By the end of the nineteenth century the book was recognized, in its physical aspect, as ready for silent reading. What was now required was a literary genre suited to silent reading, a social class with the requisite mental equipment and sensibility, and the prioritization by individuals within that class of leisure time for reading. So the transition that we spoke of earlier entailed not merely a shift from patronage to the market but also from one way of reading to another, or a shift from the ear to the eye.[43] The appearance of the novel and the emergence of the middle class led to the silent mode of reading in Tamil society.

## The Silent Mode of Reading

In the early twentieth century the novel made inroads into Tamil society and became the art form par excellence of the middle class. This middle class, especially the young within it, had been educated in modern schools and were thus not new to print, having already been socialized to read by textbooks. But their curiosity for reading material was often aroused by sundry non-educational matter. Printed advertisement notices, especially of plays which were extremely popular in the early part of the twentieth century, probably provided the first extra curricular reading material for young students. C.A. Ayyamuthu recollects, how, as a young boy in Coimbatore, he would run after carts from which drama notices and leaflets were distributed to the sound of band music, and how he was thrilled by such reading material.[44] Bharatidasan writes of his excitement on seeing a notice for a gramophone record performance with the now-well-known picture (the HMV logo) of a dog sitting beside a huge funnel-shaped speaker and a turntable.[45] Namakkal Ramalingam Pillai was even

[43] Marshall McLuhan, *The Gutenberg Galaxy: The Making of Typographic Man* (Toronto: University of Toronto Press, 1962), pp. 26–8.

[44] *Enathu Ninaivugal* (Memoirs; Chennai: Vanathi Pathippagam, 1973), p. 99.

[45] *Puduvai Murasu*, 25 May 1931, reprinted in Bharatidasan, *Manudam Pottru*, p. 89.

more captivated by a drama notice—he began to copy it out of a picture during class hours and was punished by his teacher for inattentiveness.[46]

This, then, was the generation which was drawn to the novel growing rapidly in popularity from the 1910s. We have seen the character of these novels: they were written in a popular style with action, thrill, suspense, and titillation in ample measure. This was a heady mix for new readers. V.K.R.V. Rao, the distinguished economist and institution builder, recollects that as an eleven-year-old, studying in the third form at the American Arcot Mission School, Tindivanam, he 'became a voracious reader both in Tamil and in English. I read the *Count of Monte Cristo* and *Oliver Twist* and *Tales from Shakespeare* in Tamil translations or adaptations before I read them in English. It was during this period that I developed my passion for detective stories, first in Tamil by reading Arni Kuppuswami Mudaliar's novels . . .'[47] M.M. Ismail, noted as a judge and man of letters, remembers reading scores of novels as a high school student in Nagapattinam in the 1930s.[48] Ka.Naa. Subramanyam recollects that 'In the two years [1921–3] I spent at my grandfather's, I must have read three or four hundred novels—at least that is my impression. If someone asks, "Were there so many novels in those days?" I'd say, "Yes, I think so."'[49] Clearly, readers of that time perceived a surfeit of novels, and felt the urge to read them all.

But given the nature of the novels and the disciplinarian attitude of parents and elders to such reading material, young readers had to be surreptitious to overcome such moral policing.[50] Consequently even the possession of a forbidden novel—usually in demy octavo

[46] Pillai, *En Kathai*, pp. 44–6.

[47] S.L. Rao (ed.), *The Partial Memoirs of V.K.R.V. Rao* (New Delhi: Oxford University Press, 2002), p. 34.

[48] M.M. Ismail, *Ninaivu Chudar* (The Flame of Memory; Chennai: Vanathi Pathippagam, 2001), p. 17.

[49] Ka.Naa. Subramanyam, *Muthal Ainthu Tamil Novelgal* (The First Five Tamil Novels; Chennai: Amudha Nilayam, 1957), p. iii.

[50] Ka.Naa. Subramanyam, *Padithirukkireergala? 2* (Have you Read these Books?; Chennai: Amudha Nilayam, 1958), p. 104.

and printed on cheap newsprint with plain colour wrappers and a title handset on letterpress—was the reason for secret pleasure.[51] Once a novel was acquired, it had to be quickly consumed away from the watchful eyes of elders. Solitude combined with both the necessity and the urge to read fast contributed greatly to speed-reading in silence. As a young boy, Kalki read J.R. Rangaraju's *Rajambal* by an oil lamp and slept only in the wee hours. He tells us he read Natesa Sastri's *Thikkattra Iru Kulandaigal* foregoing lunch.[52] Ka.Naa. Subramanyam recollects that reading J.R. Rangaraju made one unmindful of sleep, thirst, and hunger.[53]

This absorption in fiction led to a complete identification with the characters and events in the novel, which in turn was predicated on reading in silence and solitude. As Kalki remarked: 'How startled we were when Rajambal was murdered! And when Govindan brought her back alive, at the end of the story, how happy we were! If an election had been held then, and Detective Govindan and Lokmanya Tilak had both contested it, I'd have certainly voted for Govindan.'[54] The experience of Ki. Savithiri Ammal sounds similar. As a young girl, when she read Natesa Sastri's *Thikkattra Iru Kulandaigal*, she empathized completely with the two lost children, Radha and Alamu, experiencing all their adventures and tribulations. So completely was she absorbed in the story of A. Madhaviah's *Padmavathy Charithiram* that she felt a great urge to go to Triplicane (then a suburb of Madras) and meet Padmavathy and Narayanan, the leading lights of the novel.[55]

Such belief in the 'reality' of novels indicates a new type of relationship developing between the book and the reader, a cultural

[51] Ka.Naa. Subramanyam, *Muthal Ainthu Tamil Novelgal*, p. iii.

[52] Kalki's foreword to R.K. Narayan, *Swamiyum Snehidargalum*, p. i; also *Ananda Vikatan*, 17 February 1934, quoted in Sunda, *Ponniyin Puthalvar*, pp. 61–2.

[53] Ka.Naa. Subramanyam, *Padithirukkireergala? 2*, p. 104.

[54] *Ananda Vikatan*, 17 February 1934, quoted in Sunda, *Ponniyin Puthalvar*, pp. 61–2.

[55] 'Nan Paditha Muthal Kathaigal' (The First Stories That I Read), *Bharatamani*, September 1944.

phenomenon new in Tamil society. The personae that readers encountered in these novels were not the supernatural or fantastic beings of ballads and epics but 'real' people of flesh and blood, set in real places and not in some cloud-cuckoo land. The novels seemed so thrilling because they mirrored the lived experiences of their readers. Novels that portrayed this reality became, not surprisingly, the dominant art form of the middle class. As Kumudhini declared: 'For various reasons, my world is small. But books are one of the greatest wonders of the world. More than half of my life's happiness has come from books.'[56] Ka.Naa. Subramanyam also says these novels, especially those by Vaduvur Duraiswamy Iyengar, brimmed with subtle titillating suggestions designed to excite adolescent fantasies.[57] Kalki's confession, in a rare moment of indiscretion, provides further evidence on this score: 'Some time ago, I chanced to read a couple of recent Tamil novels. Oh, I cannot express my horror. Before I could get past a few pages, I felt as though I was rolling in the gutter. Well, even if one rolls in the gutter, one can cleanse oneself with soap. But the filth that dirties the mind is not cleansed as easily. Only after a few nights' sleep did I feel sufficiently clean.'[58]

If even an avowedly Gandhian writer could feel sexually disturbed by the novels, need we say more about adolescent readers! Ra.Ki. Rangarajan, popular writer and an editor of the mass-selling weekly *Kumudham*, recollects in his autobiography an instance within a Vaduvur Duraiswamy Iyengar novel: an advocate and a courtesan brushing against each other while travelling on a bullock cart, combining 'some openness and some suggestion'. This remained in his memory over half a century.[59] Young readers such as Ra.Ki. Rangarajan may have felt no guilt and perhaps indulged their fantasies freely: such fantasies were very much a part of the experience yielded by silent reading.

The silent mode of reading gradually emerged as a distinct, if not

[56] 'En Puthakangal' (My Books), *Kalaimagal*, vol. 7, May 1935, p. 439.
[57] *Padithirukkireergala? 2*, p. 68.
[58] *Ananda Vikatan*, 10 June 1933.
[59] Ra.Ki. Rangarajan, *Avan* (He; Chennai: Gangai Puthaka Nilayam, 2001), p. 46.

dominant, mode of reading. This is highlighted by the contrasting reading practices of old and new generations. While Ka.Naa. Subramanyam read aloud from the *Bhagavatham* to his grandmother, he slipped out to read novels alone, in silence.[60] Pammal Sambanda Mudaliar, the popular playwright, read out religious works to his aging mother.[61] M.M. Ismail recollects that his uncle would retell stories from Vaduvur Duraiswamy Iyengar's novels at bedtime to the family as they gathered around.[62] The case of the grandmothers of Indira Parthasarathy and Sujatha is even more interesting. They listened to the novels of Arani Kuppuswamy Mudaliar, Vaduvur Duraiswamy Iyengar, and Vai.Mu. Kothainayaki Ammal as they were read out by their grandsons.[63] Apart from the fact that this is an inversion of the grandma's tale—the grandmothers becoming the recipients of stories narrated by grandchildren—the grandmothers of Sujatha and Indira Parthasarathy suggest that the literary genre (here, the novel) did not of itself determine the mode of reading. As Roger Chartier has argued, the same reading materials could be appropriated for differentiated and plural uses.[64]

Studies indicate that silent reading existed in Greece even by the fifth century BC. The passage from St Augustine's *Confessions* where he refers to reading without the movement of lips is well known. However, there isn't a shred of evidence on the existence of non-vocalized reading in Tamil intellectual history.

Closely associated with the rise of the silent mode of reading was reading as a leisure-time activity. N.R. Sridharan, B.A., the hero of Kalki's *Thyaga Bhoomi*, relaxes over a Charles Garvice novel, lying in bed and fantasizing about his future wife.[65] Or, as Kumudhini

[60] Ka.Naa. Subramanyam, *Muthal Ainthu Tamil Novelgal*, p. ii.

[61] Pammal Sambanda Mudaliar, *En Suyasarithai* (My Autobiography; Chennai: Author, 1963), p. 8.

[62] Ismail, *Ninaivu Chudar*, p. 17.

[63] Indira Parthasarathy (interview), *Subamangala*, June 1993; Sujatha, 'Thoranathu Mavilaigal', *Kalki Deepavali Malar*, 1992.

[64] Roger Chartier, *The Cultural Uses of Print in Early Modern France*, Introduction.

[65] Kalki, *Thyaga Bhoomi*, p. 23.

portrays the ideal setting for reading: 'Monsoons. This is the season I like the most. One cannot go out anywhere. There are few household chores to attend to. No visitor is likely to come and disturb our peace. On such occasions I sit beside the bookshelves through the day.'[66]

There was thus a close association between being alone, and reading in silence at leisure. Only a person like Padmasani, married to a professor, with two schoolgoing children, could have the leisure to read so many novels and other books and yet remember them.[67] The novelist Krithika, wife of a high-ranking ICS officer, also found ample time to read extensively.[68] Criticism of women reading novels was frequent and can be culturally decoded as the male gaze turning into a frown against what men subconsciously recognized as an emancipatory trend which might lead 'their' women who knows where.

Very quickly, the habit of reading on trains caught on. A travelogue writer found many persons reading stories as they travelled on a train.[69] Another observer found passengers glancing through books lost in thought, unmindful of the gossip of fellow travellers.[70] T.K. Chidambaranatha Mudaliar found some passengers even more relaxed: they smoked cigarettes while reading Kalki's stories.[71] By the 1920s Higginbothams, a major European-owned bookselling firm based in Madras city, had a wide network of outlets (which survives to this day) at most railway stations. Later in the day, *Swadesamitran* joined the fray. Ka.Naa. Subramanyam recollects having bought novels at the Thanjavur Railway Station,[72] while Chandilyan claims to have made effective use of the *Swadesamitran* bookshops to quickly sell off his first collection of short stories.[73] Reading on an Indian train, though, barely qualifies as a leisure-time cultural practice.

[66] 'En Puthakangal 4', *Kalaimagal*, vol. 9, June 1936, p. 476.

[67] 'Remembered Books', *Indian Review*, November 1946.

[68] Krithika, *Vasavechwaram* (Chennai: Nool-Agam, 1991 [2nd edn]), Afterword, pp. 162–3; 165.

[69] *Jananandini*, October–December 1891, reproduced in A.K. Chettiar (ed.), *Tamilnadu* (*Payana Katturaigal*), p. 48.

[70] *Anandaguna Bodhini*, 15 June 1926, reproduced in ibid., p. 73.

[71] Preface to Kalki, *Kanayaliyin Kanavu*, p. x.

[72] *Ilakkiya Chathanaiyalargal*, p. 189.

[73] Chandilyan, *Porattangal*, p. 54.

Unlike European trains, those in India were cramped and notorious for their discomfort: not the ideal setting for relaxed reading.

Reading as a leisure-time practice also meant that reading was often extensive and desultory, whereas the earlier mode was often intensive (especially given the limited availability of books) and concentrated, involving the exertion of one's mnemonic faculty. Kumudhini admitted that as a young girl she read a book in its entirety but that as she grew old she read only the prefaces of books.[74] R.K. Narayan, an aspiring author living in Madras, observed:

> Let none conclude [. . .] that I am a voracious reader. It is not necessary [. . .] to get lost in the contents of a book. My main delight I derive by turning a page of a journal here, passing on to something else next, and making a mental note to read such and such an article at a later date; but I regret to confess that I have seldom done so. By the time I am back there again a new issue of a journal is on the table or the note has gone out of my mind [. . .] Browsing over the pages of a book here and a book there [. . .] is a pleasure [. . .][75]

This then is the testament of a reader produced by the silent mode of reading. Such reading came to be practised by an increasing tribe of middle-class readers; a perceptive observer remarked: 'A new trend is growing presently in the dailies, weeklies, and monthlies being published in Tamil. Only "light" matters are given importance as though to suggest that periodicals are intended for spending leisure time and for relaxation.'[76] No wonder A. Subramania Bharati identified these readers (especially, of novels) as 'a whole lot of butlers who know not how to spend their free time, lazy men whiling their time away at choultries [charitable inns], unemployed loafers, jobless women, menstruating women with nothing worthwhile to do in their ritual seclusion, shopkeepers without business, and others of their ilk.'[77]

[74] *Ananda Vikatan*, 1 September 1932.

[75] 'On Libraries', *Hindu*, 23 September 1951, reproduced in *The Hindu Speaks: On Libraries* (Madras: Kasturi & Sons, 1992), p. 92.

[76] Review of *Jayabharati* in *Manikkodi*, 15 December 1936.

[77] A. Subramania Bharati in his preface to Vai.Mu. Kothainayaki Ammal, *Shanbaga Vijayam*, p. 4.

The newly acquired zeal of middle-class readers to possess books, whether these were read in their entirety or not, was another new phenomenon. Maraimalai Adigal arranged and rearranged books on his shelves with a kind of narcissistic pleasure:: 'I have really a very wonderful selection of the best books on every subject of Philosophy, and the valuable books are many; it is a source of genuine intellectual pleasure to have in one's possession so many admirable books.'[78] This despite the fact that his 'wife is not in good terms with me on account of the money I spend buying books.' But: 'What am I to do! I have an unusual craving for buying new books.'[79]

Such craving was by no means peculiar to Maraimalai Adigal; it crossed Kumudhini's mind as she surveyed her bookshelves: 'There are all kinds of books on the shelves. I cannot even figure out how they reached there. I have not read quite a few of them. It is also doubtful that I will ever read them. The almirah is full. Only if some of the books there are cleared out can space be found for new additions. But I haven't the heart to part with them. I don't know which ones to discard.'[80]

Considering that middle-class readers sometimes bought books for no better reason than that they were cheap,[81] no wonder such dilemmas became commonplace. Parting with a prized collection could be traumatic. When Deenadayalu, the protagonist of Natesa Sastri's eponymous novel (1902), is forced by pressing financial need to sell off all his books for Rs 400, it feels 'like selling off children during times of famine'.[82]

Visits to libraries perhaps provided vicarious satiety to readers who wanted to possess books but did not. One reader confessed he hung

[78] *MD*, 30 September 1914.

[79] *MD*, 8 December 1906. Also see article by V. Narayanaiyar in *Tamilar Nesan*, December 1918.

[80] 'En Puthakangal 4', *Kalaimagal*, vol. 9, June 1936, p. 476. Kumudhini would have profited from reading Orhan Pamuk's essay 'How I got Rid of Some of My Books'!

[81] Ibid., p. 479.

[82] Natesa Sastri, *Deenadayalu* (1902, rpnt. Chennai: Sangam Books, 1985), p. 99.

about libraries unashamedly and 'trespass[ed] into any place that proclaims itself to be a free reading room and library.' The book's physical beauty becomes the source of aesthetic pleasure: 'The faint aroma of gum and calico that hangs about a library is as the fragrance of incense to me. I think the most beautiful sight is the gilt-edged backs of a row of books on a shelf. The alley between two well-stocked shelves in a hall fills me with the same delight as passing through a silent avenue of trees. The colour of a binding cloth and its smooth texture gives me the same pleasure as touching a flower at its stalk.'[83]

By the 1920s and 1930s, by which time silent reading among the middle classes was quite the norm, there was an increasing demand for and access to books. The Madras Library Association was founded in 1928 to foster the library movement in the Madras Presidency. It was this movement that nurtured S.R. Ranganathan, inventor of the Colon Classification system. Some of the consistent demands of the movement were for increased public spending on libraries, a wider network of public libraries, and free and easy access to libraries for everyone.[84] This period also saw the spawning of many 'libraries' which were public forums doubling as reading rooms, established by the nationalist and Self-Respect movements.

With reading growing apace, book reviews became a staple part of the diet offered by periodicals. Quite a few articles also began now to draw attention to the poor quality and often misleading nature of book reviews. Pudumaippithan, in his characteristic style, warned that such reviews would end up disappointing enthusiastic readers and ultimately kill the nascent reading habit.[85] Parallel to this

[83] R.K. Narayan, 'On Libraries', p. 92.

[84] Contemporary periodicals teem in articles about the library movement. For some of them, see *Bharati*, June–July 1932; *Kumaran*, November 1923 and 18 January 1934; *Suthanthira Sangu*, 20 July 1933; *Bharatamani*, 17 February 1939. *The Hindu Speaks: On Libraries* is a useful volume which reproduces many of the articles published in the *Hindu* on the library movement.

[85] *Manikkodi*, 15 August 1937. For more on book reviews, see Kalki, *Ettikku Potti* (1930, rpnt. Chennai: Tamil Pannai, 1965), pp. 157–67; *Kumaran*, 30 July 1927, sub editorial.

criticism was the stigma attached to borrowing books instead of buying them, it being felt that book loans harmed the book trade as a whole. The number of humorous pieces on this growing habit of borrowing books is considerable.[86]

By the end of our period silent reading had become so dominant that attempts were made to codify it. S. Satyamurti, a conservative Congress leader, while in prison during 1941, wrote a series of letters to his daughter, Lakshmi. They are homilies and pontifications on various aspects of middle-class life and culture. Of them at least three are devoted to books and reading practices. First, Satyamurti prescribes the right manner of reading: 'There are certain ways of proper reading. You should habituate yourself to them. You must read with the right posture. To read in a sitting position is best. When we are lazy, we occasionally read lying down. It is not advisable to do so; it is bad for the eyes. We should also ensure that adequate light is available when reading. At night we should read using an electric light [. . .] There should not be too much light either.'[87] Coming to the reading materials themselves, Satyamurti suggested a mix of great literature consisting of the Indian epics, Shakespeare, Kamban, Tulsidas, the English romantic poets, Kalidas, Valmiki, and Bhavabhuti.[88] Novels were to be read only 'on trains or when there is no other work to do or to relax the mind.'[89] Apart from training in the classics, he advocated the study of psychology, history, religion, geography, and the sciences. He also suggested the right approach to a study of these disciplines: 'It is not possible to attain expertise in all these subjects. Nor is it necessary. It is enough if you make a preliminary study and get a general understanding of them. If you do this, you will be able

[86] *Amirtaguna Bodhini*, 16 July 1932; *Bharatamani*, May 1945; Kalki, *Alai Osai* (1953, rpnt. Chennai: Vanathi Pathippagam, 1983), Preface; Kalki, *Ettikku Potti*, pp. 26–35.

[87] *Arumai Puthalvikku* (To My Dear Daughter; 1945, rpnt. Chennai: Bharati Pathippagam, 1988), pp. 249–50. Lakshmi (1925–2009), married to the well-known bookseller K. Krishnamurthy, launched the pioneering Tamil book club Vasagar Vattam in 1965, and published many memorable books.

[88] Ibid., pp. 54–7, 247.

[89] Ibid., pp. 54–5.

to follow newspapers and magazines in an intelligent and serious fashion.'[90] Satyamurti also advised regular visits to libraries,[91] as well as the use of notebooks to jot down notes while studying.[92] His advice on the use of a dictionary, to be kept by the side while reading,[93] is interesting because, in the earlier mode of reading, students were expected to memorize verse dictionaries before proceeding to tackle literary texts.

The reading practices codified by Satyamurti were novel in Tamil society, in marked contrast to the earlier mode with its emphasis on intensive and exhaustive study, preferably within just one field. The new mode involved consuming reading materials in solitude and silence, by scanning lines on the printed page. This also fashioned a new sensibility in tune with changing times and the changing needs of the middle class. This stentorian passage sums up what books meant to this class: 'Books are silent teachers; they act as consoling friends in our worries; they are philosophers when we are in a confused state because of critical situations; they are beacons of light showing us the nature of the world; they are cenotaphs of the past, mirrors of the present, and prophets of the future.'[94]

## Modes of Reading and the Incomplete Hegemony of the Middle Class

The reading middle class, being a product of colonialism, was congenitally weak. It harboured hegemonic aspirations but was never able to achieve hegemony within Tamil society. We have briefly looked at some aspects of this failed hegemony *vis-à-vis* popular publishing. The consumption of popular literature was in marked contrast to the modes of reading (especially silent reading) involved in elite literature.

[90] Ibid.

[91] Ibid., p. 245.

[92] Ibid., p. 250.

[93] Ibid., 28 July 1941, p. 247. For a humorous article on reading the dictionary, see Thi.Ja. Ranganathan, *Pozhuthupokku* (Passing Time; 1942, rpnt. Chennai: Kalaimagal Kariyalayam, 1953).

[94] V. Govindan, 'Puthakamum Vithakamum', *Sakti*, March 1941.

The audience for popular literature was wide, it was not restricted to buyers alone. By contrast books in the elite sphere had to be possessed, at least for a while, in order to be read. A whole range of people listened to songsters as they went about their shopping in the marketplace or tarried at crossroads. It is difficult to assess the experience of a crowd, but to hold a crowd some at least of the songs will have been enthralling: we know that some actually wept when a song was exceptionally poignant.[95] The crowds would generally thin once the song was over and the sale of chapbooks began. The dispersion would be complete when the chapman moved to the next convenient point to start his performance all over again.

Given the location of marketplaces and crossroads and their environs, the lower orders were the predominant buyers and consumers of chapbooks. Perhaps the reach of the ballads was a little restricted, these being usually consumed in small group readings. Curious little boys, running an errand for their mothers, were some who cut across class lines to devour the literature of the street.[96]

The survival of chapbooks is itself a story. None of the book collections of scholars and elite personalities that I've seen contains chapbooks or ballads. A handful of antiquarians saved some for posterity and these surviving chapbooks are not individual booklets but compiled *chillarai kovai*s, indicating the chapbooks bought by the common folk were little more than ephemeral. It is a difficult task to reconstruct the experience of the common reader. And as regards the elite, if they ever read popular literature it was either for its novelty or so that they might condemn it for not being elite. When Thi.Ja. Ra(nganathan) wrote, 'from my boyhood days, I have read many kinds of books on my own accord, without anybody's compulsion or suggestion—from *Alliarasani Malai* and

[95] Interview with M. Babu, 2 June 1992, Madras.

[96] R. Muthukumaraswamy (b. 1936), interviewed on 15 June 1991, recollected in vivid detail how as a little boy he used to stand in the crowds listening to the songs. The Mannady intersection and the Armenian Street crossing, in George Town, Madras, were important nodal points even as late as the early 1940s. In popular parlance these songsters were therefore called Mannady Kavirayar (Poets of Mannady).

*Kavadi Chindu* to *Nalavenba* and *Thiruvaimoli*',[97] he was only bragging of the width of his interests, which reached down to the 'lowest' rungs of literature.

Very rarely do we find common readers as possessors of books. After the beginnings of the mass phase of the nationalist movement, the customary examination of passengers on the way back from abroad, especially Sri Lanka, was intensified. A more thorough baggage examination yields some documentary evidence of common folk owning books. Through the 1920s and 1930s there are numerous instances of passengers apprehended with proscribed literature, and virtually all of them were chapbooks on nationalist themes, such as *Mahatma Gandhi Arrestu Pattu*, *Desiya Geetha Thirattu*, and elegies on Bhagat Singh. Nationalist chapbooks were only a small fragment of the repertoire of popular literature, but in the absence of similar data on other classes of chapbook we must perforce generalize based on this class of chapbook.

Danushkodi was an important point on the sea route to Sri Lanka. People on their way back from earning a livelihood in the tea, coffee, and rubber estates of Sri Lanka, and some of the less unfortunate employed in odd jobs in the service sector, thronged to Danushkodi. During the 1920s and 1930s the Inspector of Customs often came across proscribed literature in their baggage, and promptly confiscated it. This was reported to the Government of Madras, and enquiries about the persons found in possession of such literature were made by the district magistrates of their native districts. These reports on the social and political background of such people throw some light on popular readers.

In July 1932, five persons arriving from Sri Lanka were found possessing proscribed chapbooks like *Congress Pattu*, *Desiya Geetha Thirattu*, *Gandhi Dhyanam*, *Mahatma Gandhi Mahimai*, and *Kallukkadai Mariyal*. They were all coolies in the Kandy estates; at least one of them was an Adi Dravida (dalit), and another an Odda (a working-class caste traditionally occupied in digging wells and

[97] *Eppadi Eluthinen* (How I Wrote; Madurai: Sakti Kariyalayam, 1943), p. 61.

laying roads). Much to the surprise of the District Superintendent of Police, who conducted the enquiries, not one of them was literate or had any political antecedents—'not politically inclined', 'nothing against their character', as expressed in the 'prose of counter-insurgency'. In yet another classic case of colonialism denying subjecthood to the lower orders among the colonized, he blamed 'the maistries and kanganies in the several estates of Kandy who used to dabble in politics are selling these objectionable and unauthorized leaflets to their illiterate coolies at a high price and make a good profit out of the collections. The coolies who are all illiterate buy these books not out of choice but on pressure.'[98] What is being crucially missed here is the fact that consuming a popular text was not contingent on the ability to read alone: there could exist other modes of 'reading' which did not require 'literacy'.

Apart from the indentured labourers of the estates, we also find men with petty jobs apprehended by customs officials for possessing proscribed literature. There was one S.M.N. Maraicar and his brother from Nagore, who 'eke[d] out their livelihood by selling caps worn by Mohammedans in Africa.' We learn that '[their] monthly earnings may roughly be estimated at 20–25 Rs.'[99] Twenty-three-year-old Muthuswami 'was a barber by caste and profession'.[100] So was Palani who was caught with two chapbooks on Bhagat Singh.[101] Veerannan was a servant in a tile factory at Negombo on the western coast of Sri Lanka, and Shanmugam of Tirunelveli worked in a blacksmith's forge in Colombo.[102] A. Narayanan was the son of a mason who worked in a hotel, and Srinivasa Asari was employed in a smithy.[103] A.R. Kannusamy was a petty accountant with a

[98] G.O. no. 1145, Pub. (Gen.) (Confdl), 2 September 1932. Here it may not be out of place to mention some chapbooks which portray in poignant detail the plight of indentured labourers in overseas plantations. See *Desamakkalai Nasappaduthum Theyilai Thottapattu*; *Adimaigalin Arivuvilakka Theyilaippattu*; *Rubber Thottappattu*, Madras, *c.* 1929.

[99] G.O. no. 1202, Pub. (Gen.), 20 September 1932.

[100] Ibid.

[101] G.O. no. 1242, Pub. (Gen.) (Confdl), 24 September 1932.

[102] G.O. no. 1582, Pub. (Gen.) (Confdl), 8 December 1932.

[103] Letter no. 108, Pub. (Gen.) (Confdl), 30 January 1933.

Nattukkotai Chettiar firm and lived 'with his widowed sister who lived by selling cakes and doing work in Chetty houses.'[104]

None of these seem to have had any education worth the name in the enquiry reports of the district officials. Only on one occasion that I have come across did the Joint Magistrate of Ramnad think it fit to note that C. Vellachami had 'studied third standard. Can read and write Tamil.'[105] Booksellers at Madurai's Pudumantapam would often sell songbooks to illiterate villagers who would come into their shops after a visit to the city on business or pilgrimage: they would ask the booksellers to read bits out, and upon recognizing some lines would buy the songbooks.[106]

When U.V. Swaminatha Iyer was a teacher in the Kumbakonam Government College in the 1880s he saw the Brahmin cook of one of his students reading a popular book as he waited for his master to eat.[107]

This then was the social background of the consumers of chapbooks and other popular literature. They were people from the lower orders of society: coolies, cap sellers, barbers, cooks, and petty employees with hardly a smattering of literacy in the conventional sense. Similarly, a knowledge of ballads seems to have been quite widespread at the popular level. Suddhananda Bharati reminiscing about his younger days in Sivagangai at the turn of this century says even impecunious peasants who could barely read were able to recite *Alliarasani Malai*, *Pulanthiran Kalavu Malai*, *Eluthariyum Perumal Ammanai*, etc.[108] This was especially true of women: and, as Bharatidasan observed, even illiterate women acquired a knowledge of popular ballads by listening to them.[109]

[104] G.O. no. 1145, Pub. (Gen.) (Confdl), 2 September 1932.

[105] Ibid.

[106] Based on interviews with booksellers in Madurai Pudumantapam, November 1992.

[107] Swaminatha Iyer (ed.), *Thenthirupperai Magaranedumkulaikathar Pamalai* (Chennai: Kalaimagal Kariyalayam, 1939), Preface, p. xv.

[108] *Engal Ur* (Our Village; Chennai: Kalaimagal Kariyalayam, 1957), p. 136. Originally published in *Kalaimagal* in the early 1940s.

[109] Bharatidasan in *Puduvai Murasu*, 20 July 1931, reprinted in *Manudam Pottru*, p. 101.

Knowledge of these ballads stemmed mostly from group readings. Such readings took place often, especially during ritual occasions like funerals. As no other activity could take place until the pall was removed, ballads like *Karimedu Karuvayan* were recited to keep the mourners occupied or, if it was night, awake.[110] Texts like *Chithira Puthira Nayanar Kathai*, *Vali Motcham*, and *Vaikunta Ammanai* were recited to expedite the death of those terminally ill. Here is a description of one such event in a novel by Ki. Rajanarayanan: 'Everyone sat around [the dying] Annarappa Gounder. The hurricane lantern was cleaned and the wick raised. Balarama Nayakkar, who stood watching with other men, was summoned and asked to recite *Chithira Puthira Nayanar Kathai*.'[111] Similarly, the Virata Parvam of the Mahabharata would be recited publicly, ritual fashion, when the monsoons failed. There were strict stipulations on how to recite it. It had to be recited at one go, without a break on the part of the performer, who was expected to be ritually pure.[112]

Ballads were recited or sung, not read out. To read out 'like prose' was improper and even demeaning. In an incident in another of Ki. Rajanarayanan's novels a town educated boy is the butt of ridicule because, unable to recite in a singsong manner, he reads words out flatly like prose. The boy's grandmother is so disappointed with him that she stops indulging him.[113]

If men dominated such ritual occasions, women had their own reading circles when the men were away. Bharatidasan says they would congregate 'like the inhabitants of Kishkinda'.[114] In one such reading session 'There was a lectern shaped like "x". Nachiaramma would place a heavy tome of *Kambaramayanam* in paraphrase, with the other women seated around her. She would sing at the top of

[110] I owe this information to A. Sivasubramanian, the folklorist.

[111] Ki. Rajanarayanan, *Kidai Kurunovelum Pannirandu Sirukathaigalum* (Sivagangai: Annam), 1983, p. 86.

[112] Aranga Srinivasan, *Ninaivu Alaigal* (Waves of Memories; Chennai: Vanathi Pathippagam, 1996), pp. 92–3.

[113] Ki. Rajanarayanan, *Gopallapurathu Makkal* (Sivagangai: Annam, 1990), pp. 99–100.

[114] Bharatidasan in *Puduvai Murasu*, 20 July 1931, reprinted in *Manudam Pottru*, p. 101.

her voice and, as she recited, the women would start shedding tears. Nachiaramma would wipe away her tears and continue to recite the paraphrase in a choked voice. All the while [they would] wipe their eyes and blow their noses.'[115] Such joint readings bred a sense of gender solidarity among women who often identified their problems in an oppressive patriarchal world with the plight of ballad characters like Sita or Nallathangal.

These were simple women, like Sankaranarayanavadivu, who participated in such reading sessions. Widowed early in life and having been educated only up to the second standard, she read a number of big-letter books bought for her by her brother-in-law (older sister's husband).[116] Middle-class intellectuals repeatedly criticized women for reading such ballads.[117] In Madhaviah's 1898 novel we find Savithiri, along with her friends, reading such ballads.[118] So it is not surprising to find many chapbooks addressed directly to women.

These popular modes of reading were far from being displaced by the new phenomenon of silent reading. If anything they were spreading further into domains over which the middle class had little, if any, influence, because of the mushrooming and circulation increases of the dailies. Si.Pa. Adithan, the shrewd entrepreneur and founder of *Dina Thanthi*, the largest-selling Tamil daily, observed on its inaugural day in 1942: 'Even today you can see this in the villages: parents may not be literate, [but] they listen to their literate children read out stories from the Mahabharatam and Ramayanam. In days to come they will also start listening to newspapers being read out.'[119]

Adithan's forecast was prophetic. In Ki. Rajanarayanan's novel we

[115] Ki. Rajanarayanan, *Kidai*, p. 7. See Azhagiyanayagi Ammal, *Kavalai* (Palayamkottai: Folklore Resources and Research Centre, 1998), pp. 122–7, for an autobiographical account of such joint readings.

[116] Interview with Sankaranarayanavadivu, aged 71, Kombukkarapottal, Srivaikuntam taluk, Tuticorin district, 6 November 1992.

[117] Nagai Neelambikaiyammai, 'Tamil Matharum Sirudevathaikalum' (Tamil Women and Folk Deities), *Sentamil Selvi*, 5(8), August–September 1927.

[118] A. Madhaviah, *Padmavathy Charithiram* (1898, rpnt. Chennai: Vanavil Prasuram, 1978), p. 56.

[119] *Dina Thanthi Ponvizha Malar* (Dina Thanthi Golden Jubilee Number), 1993, p. 119.

find, by the beginning of World War II, newspapers have reached the village of Gopalla. In the evenings, villagers sit on the pial of Nunnakonda Nayakkar's house as the local teacher reads the paper out loud in his 'bell-like' voice.[120] At about the same time the toddy tappers of Kanyakumari in Hephzibah Jesudasan's *Putham Veedu* slowly learn to read out newspapers and follow the affairs of the wider world.[121] As noted earlier, sensational news items and stories in *Dina Thanthi* were especially targeted at such a neo-literate, or even non-literate, audience. Even today, this situation has far from changed. *Dina Thanthi* is a standard presence in every teashop and saloon, even in urban areas, and is often read out and the news discussed.[122]

[120] Ki. Rajanarayanan, *Gopallapurathu Makkal*, p. 202.

[121] Hephzibah Jesudasan, *Putham Veedu* (Chennai: Tamil Puthakalayam, 1964).

[122] For an ethnographic account of such reading practices in present-day rural Tamilnadu, see Francis Cody, 'Daily Wires and Daily Blossoms: Cultivating Regimes of Circulation in Tamil India's Newspaper Revolution', *Journal of Linguistic Anthropology* 19 (2), 2009.

# Epilogue: Exaggerated Obituaries?

The death of the book, in the wake of the digital onslaught that was predicted, anticipated, or feared—depending on one's ideological and cultural position—in the 1990s seems exceedingly alarmist now, at the end of the first decade of the twenty-first century. Following Mark Twain we could say that obituaries of the book appear to have been somewhat exaggerated. Even though prophets of doom such as Jeff Gomez have declared that print is dead, prescient observers of book culture such as Jason Epstein and Robert Darnton expect the book to survive as codex.[1]

Even though the disintegration of the Gutenberg galaxy was prophesied by Marshall McLuhan as early as the 1960s, there is no mistaking the anxiety occasioned in the 1990s. 'Over the past few decades, in the blink of the eye of history, our culture has begun to go through what promises to be a total metamorphosis [. . .] The stable hierarchies of the printed page [. . .] are being superseded by the rush of impulses through freshly minted circuits.'[2]

However one should be conscious of the fact that the culture that Sven Birkerts mentions is Western culture. This is predicated on the Enlightenment notion of self and knowledge, and the possible disappearance of an artefact that has been valued in that culture for over half a millennium. Given Roger Chartier's perceptive statement

[1] Jeff Gomez, *Print is Dead: Books in Our Digital Age* (London: Macmillan, 2008); Jason Epstein, *Book Business. Publishing: Past Present and Future* (New York: W.W. Norton, 2001); Robert Darnton, *The Case for Books: Past, Present, and Future* (New York: Public Affairs, 2009), Introduction.

[2] Sven Birkerts, *The Gutenberg Elegies: The Fate of Reading in an Electronic Age* (Boston: Faber & Faber, 1994), p. 3.

of its centrality in Western culture—'the book has been one of the most powerful metaphors used for conceiving of the cosmos, nature and the human body'[3]—one can understand and empathize with such fears and anxieties.

However, such insights from the history of the book also point to the fact that there is no one universal history of the book. If there is no one universal history of the book it follows that there need be no single future for the book. If books have specific and contingent histories—as I hope I have demonstrated in the foregoing history of the Tamil book—it would follow that the new digital technologies will impact countries and cultures variously. The thrust of this epilogue is therefore to make a specific argument for the possible future of Tamil books and track how Tamil book publishing has fared in its engagement with digital technology.

As noted earlier, Tamil was the first non-European language to deploy movable type and printed books. The first printed Tamil book (1577), the first complete translation of the New Testament (1714/1715), the first full translation of the Bible (1796), the first extended lexicon (1912–36), and the first modern encyclopaedia (1954–68) constitute some other 'firsts' that printed Tamil can claim in relation to other Indian languages.

Such justifiably proud claims, however, conceal a host of basic problems and weaknesses that characterize the Tamil publishing world. By common consent Bengali and Malayalam, two modern Indian languages whose engagement with printing begins some two hundred years after *Thampiran Vanakkam*, are way ahead of Tamil publishing.

Despite the early origins of print in Tamil, until the mid-nineteenth century printing was a European preserve within which missionaries dominated. From the later half of the nineteenth century print made some inroads into Tamil society and developed organic links with indigenous society. The recovery of ancient Tamil classics and their

[3] Roger Chartier, 'Libraries Without Walls', *Representations*, no. 42, Spring 1993, p. 49.

canonization through the mediation of print had far-reaching social and political consequences. Well until the end of the nineteenth century Tamil publishing was largely sustained by forms of traditional patronage derived from zamindars, native princes, religious monasteries, landlords, and caste leaders. However, the establishment of Western-type schools and the expansion of a modern bureaucratic administration had implications for publishing. Apart from the demand for printed materials that this created, the emergence of new social classes based on education as well as the colonial occupations and professions disrupted the material foundations of Tamil publishing. By the time of World War I Tamil publishing was breaking away from patronage publishing and inching towards a faceless, impersonal market.

In the inter-war period Tamil publishing showed vitality and growth, a trend that became more pronounced during World War II. The inflationary war economy ignited Tamil publishing, a process further fuelled by the influx of Chettiar capital fleeing Burma, Indo-China, and South East Asia from both Japanese invasion and local resistance. Many of the characteristic features of Tamil books until the advent of digital technology—layout, typography, cover design, etc.—took shape during this period.

The process of state takeover of textbook publishing which started in the mid-1960s and reached a head in 1971 exposed the real foundations of Tamil publishing: the bedrock of assured textbook sales had subsidized trade books. Once again, with their characteristic myopia, publishers looked to the state without exploring ways and means to expand and reach out to a market. The outcome was the establishment of the Local Library Authority (now the Directorate of Public Libraries), which, almost as a matter of routine, bought a certain number of copies—as much as 50 per cent of the actual printrun. (Bulk orders under various government schemes such as Operation Blackboard and Anna Marumalarchi Thittam constitute periodic windfalls to publishers.) Even if this ensured bread and butter for publishers, it effectively killed creativity and innovation.

This was the backdrop within which digital technology announced its entry into Tamil publishing. The most substantial impact of digital technology in Tamil publishing has been in the field of text composition. Well until the mid-1990s the technology of print had remained unchanged. For over a century movable types, cut and cast in local foundries, were used for composition within establishments which were little more than sweatshops. Even though hot metal technologies such as monotype, linotype, and rotary were available throughout the twentieth century—and widely employed for publishing in English even in Chennai—the Tamil publishing industry rarely took recourse to them. The primary reason was the low printrun—the average print-run of Tamil books hovered at the 1,000 mark. (In fact, as shrewd cutters of cost, Tamil publishers make printers print 1,200 copies for the price of 1,000 as they claim that 200 copies are meant for free distribution to authors, reviewers, and other promotional purposes!) Among the rare occasions when the rotary was used was when C. Rajagopalachari's popular prose renditions of the Mahabharata and Ramayana were published by Sakti Karyalayam and printed at the daily Dinamani press (of the *Indian Express* Group) in the 1950s. Or, when the periodical magazine press dabbled in book publishing, they pressed their rotary machines into service. Given that the dimensions of the paper rolls used for these machines were different from the sheets that were ordinarily used for Tamil books, such books were dubbed 'unsize' in popular publishing parlance. The only major publisher to use hot metal technology—monotype in this case—was Poompuhar Prasuram, established in the mid-1970s by the owners of Eagle Press, the market leaders in the production of diaries and calendars. Printing establishments such as Maruthi Press, which had its own foundry, would employ this luxury occasionally to use freshly cast types for printing.

Another major impediment to the adoption of hot metal technology was the unwieldy nature of Tamil characters, which necessitated a vast number of types difficult to accommodate on a keyboard (a difficulty digital technology also had to encounter at the outset). Even when phototypesetting (with bromide print-outs) had made its entry in the 1980s—apart from the prohibitive costs involved both due to the process itself as well as the compulsory recourse to offset printing that this process necessitated—it was only rarely used—for instance by Cre-A publishers; Kanthalakam was one of the few firms to provide phototypesetting facilities in Tamil. Even when big publishers opted to print by the offset method, they often preferred to do the typesetting in letterpresses, taking an 'art pull' on the machine, which was then translated to printing film.

By the early 1990s the PC revolution was very much at the Indian doorstep. In the initial years progress in Tamil typesetting was tardy because good DTP software using WYSIWYG was still in the future. Only with its advent did DTP come to be entrenched. This meant the gradual folding up of type foundries such as Nelson Type Foundry and Modern Type Foundry, which were reduced to casting a limited quantity of types for small letterpresses doing job work, especially in the mofussil areas.

Computer typesetting made it imperative to switch to offset printing. Well until the mid-1990s, offset printing cost twice as much as regular mechanical printing. In a very inelastic book market this posed an insurmountable problem. In the first instance, therefore, publishers took to offset printing only for the printing of book wrappers and jackets. Earlier, artists and illustrators had designed wrappers and covers that would be printed in two or three colours via metal blocks. Emphasis was usually placed on stylistic and calligraphic writing. This did not work once offset printing could be used. Given the then prohibitive costs of scanning, plate-making, and printing, the pioneers in this field used single-colour wrappers and jackets, which were quite a novelty. Elegant black-and-white photographs were used with un-stylized typefaces. It would take a decade before multi-colour jackets adorned Tamil books. Even then, such book wrappers were printed four at a time to cut down costs—it would be no exaggeration to say that printing single multi-colour wrappers is still commercially unviable for Tamil books. Initially many publishers, rather than generate original wrapper designs, used pictures from the *National Geographic Magazine* without acknowledgement, whether they were relevant to the contents of the book or not. The dominant trend now is to download images from the web!

Composing text using digital technology had its share of teething trouble. The prime problem was the availability of suitable word-processing and DTP software. Despite various governmental and non-state initiatives, Tamil digital technology is still faced with a multiplicity of keyboards (typewriter, phonetic, and standard), with the standard keyboard 'accepted' in an international Tamil computing conference being one of many available options. A Unicode is yet to gain acceptance in Tamil, even though it seems inevitable in the foreseeable future. There is presently a plethora of encoding systems: TAM, TAB, TSCII, with each DTP software developer opting for their own encoding system. If the efforts of the Indian government's Pune-based C-DAC for Indian languages was too Devanagari-centred and impervious to Tamil needs, efforts by Tamils themselves have taken two different trajectories. If the pioneering efforts by Tamils abroad were techno-savvy in keeping with the demands of technology and the net, the fonts developed were far from aesthetic. On the other hand the development of DTP software in Tamilnadu was almost exclusively propelled by publishing needs where the elegance of fonts was given priority. After a certain stage of development, interests had become so entrenched that no compromise could be effected between the two.

The long history of Tamil fonts from the days when the earliest types were cut in Goa, Quilon, and even Halle was forgotten. In the first instance the new fonts in Tamil DTP software did not gel with existing fonts in the letterpress to which Tamil readers had been socialized for more than half a century. Even some first lessons were forgotten. The character of Tamil orthography lends itself to a slight tilt to the right, unlike roman letters, and straight typefaces do not work well. (A corollary, given this natural tendency to the right, has been the persistent difficulty of fashioning suitable and workable italics for Tamil fonts.) In the initial stages there was a medley of inelegant and unreadable fonts in use, a problem that has subsided only recently. Another outcome of the evolving digital Tamil typefaces was their independent development in Tamilnadu and Sri Lanka, not to speak of Malaysia and Singapore. While an almost universal set of typefaces had evolved in the movable type era, fonts diverged again. So much so, books produced in Tamilnadu and Sri Lanka have developed distinct appearances, a situation further complicated by the wider varieties of paper available in Sri Lanka.

The other problem that cropped up with the advent of DTP was the redundancy of compositors and the resultant new recruitment of keying-in personnel. Even though traditionally composition was a skilled manual job pursued by people with little formal education, compositors often acquired skills through their long years of apprenticeship and training. There are for instance legendary stories about M.P. Sivagnanam and Vindhan, who started their lives as compositors and later emerged as not insignificant writers. There are also many instances of compositors gaining political consciousness by reading the material they composed. Through such a training process compositors produced decent galley and page proofs even when authors—as was their wont—had not submitted acceptable press copy. Well versed in standard page layouts and elementary proofing skills, some compositors could make a page even without going through the galley stage.

Such craftsmanship is virtually absent among the new generation of computer typesetters. Basically, they get trained only in the quick keying-in of text. The falling standards of school and even college education in Tamilnadu are evident in the mess they make of the copy they key in. The absence of even elementary, useable spellchecking software for Tamil, a still persistent problem, compounds the confusion. The limited number of fonts that can be used for text composition, the non-standardization of leading, inter-word spacing, hyphenation (being an agglutinative language with a syllabary rather than a phonetic alphabet, Tamil words do not require hyphenation), etc., made for some grotesque books in the 1990s. The entire aesthetics of the Tamil book which had evolved over a period of about a century—from about the time of World War I when Tamil books began to be produced for a larger, impersonal market—nearly collapsed. The almost innumerable ways in which fonts could be manipulated created more confusion rather than being put to effective use. A new aesthetic based on digital technology emerged only by the turn of the new millennium and is far from having stabilized even now.

If the new digital technology played such havoc in printing protocols, it also provided a variety of conveniences. Theoretically at least it made proofreading a more effective and less time- and place-bound activity. Given the magnitude of the publishing industry, letterpress printing establishments were small and had very little type. Consequently it was practically impossible and commercially unviable for printers to keep the types locked up for long. The customary practice was to set the page—galleys being read at the press itself, usually by the owner—at the end of the day and deliver the page proofs to proofreaders' homes at night, then collect the corrected proofs in the morning before the press opened for the day. Few presses had the wherewithal to compose more than, say, ten formes. Legendary printing presses such as Kabeer Printing Works, Progressive Printers, and Diocesan Press which could deliver the entire manuscript in proof were few and invariably too expensive. Over the last century Tamil book publishing and printing had converged in the city of Chennai. Not only U.V. Swaminatha Iyer the great editor of Tamil classics, but also Veeresalingam Pantulu the Telugu reformer, had preferred to come to *fin de siècle* Chennai so that their publishing activities could be carried on more effectively. The centrality of Chennai began to be somewhat eroded with the rise of digital technology as publishers did not have to flock there to meet their printing needs.

With digital technology, any number of pages can be composed without worrying about locked-up type. Further, the proofs of a whole book are handled not in instalments but in full. Consequently, the tiresome task of proofreading is not bound by place or time (the contingency of the computer system crashing is of course a different matter). Even though many have been like the sorcerer's apprentice in the handling of this convenience, there is no doubting its usefulness for serious pursuits such as critical editions.

This has also had a very perceptible impact on the average size of books. While until the advent of digital technology the publishing of tomes was dreaded by Tamil publishers, they have more easily taken to it since. Combined with a perceived if not actual expansion in the book market, more bulky volumes are being published in Tamil than ever before. This has also exposed the paucity of real content in the books. How much can even a society which is fast changing and throwing up new talent produce? One recourse to offset the dearth was the republication of old and out-of-print books with cultural value. The bane of Tamil publishing—that very few books were reprinted—was almost wiped out overnight. In fact there are some publishers who print only out-of-print and out-of-copyright books. This process has been strengthened by the peculiar Tamil tradition of the state taking over the copyright of the works of many cultural icons and putting them in the public domain, thus unleashing a huge corpus of texts for unrestricted and even irresponsible use.

Offset printing for text matter became the norm only after it had become normal procedure for jackets and wrappers. With offset printing cylinder machines became completely redundant and, from the late 1990s, many printing presses began to dispose their machines off as scrap. (The opportunity this afforded for setting up a printing museum was missed.)

As a result of all these changes the face of Tamil publishing, as well as the physical aspect of the Tamil book, has changed perceptibly, if not drastically. John B. Thompson, in his comprehensive study of books in the digital age, has established that the digital revolution at least in the West is 'not so much *a revolution in the product* as *a revolution in the process*.'[4] This is evidently untrue in the Tamil context. The Tamil book, in its physical aspect—bulk, layout, typeface, etc.—has greatly changed.

This has gone hand in hand with an explosion in the number of books published. Unfortunately there is no data, reliable or unreliable, on the volume of book production in India.[5] No bibliometric analysis

[4] John B. Thompson, *Books in the Digital Age: The Transformation of Academic and Higher Education Publishing in Britain and the United States* (Cambridge: Polity, 2005), p. 405, original emphasis.

[5] Publishers in India are legally mandated, under the Registration of Books Act 1867, to submit one copy of every publication to the four national deposit libraries, including the National Library, Kolkata, a provision observed more in the breach. The National Library is expected to register the books and prepare annual bibliographies which are intended to also provide statistics regarding books published in India. These bibliographies are woefully behind schedule.

is therefore possible. But the phenomenal growth in Tamil publishing is unmistakable.

An important trend in international publishing over the last two decades has been the rise of huge publishing conglomerations which have with gargantuan appetite gobbled up many independent publishing houses via huge corporate mergers. As a result many venerable publishing houses have become little more than imprints.[6] Even though Tamil publishing is marked by the very palpable absence of corporate organization, the trend in the last decade has been the proliferation of dozens of independent publishing houses which have been riding the digital wave and that have in the process brought in fresh talent, consolidating earlier gains.

The spatial rupture between typesetting establishments and printing shops first led to the mushrooming of DTP firms all over Tamilnadu. Considering the relative cheapness of typesetting there was a major boom in such establishments in the late 1980s; Puducherry for instance catered to international publishing to a great extent. Ultimately this also paved the way for the establishment of publishing houses all over Tamilnadu—rather than these being clustered in Chennai, especially in Broadway until the early 1980s and then in Pondy Bazaar since. Until then Mercury Puthaka Nilaiyam based in Coimbatore and Annam based in Sivagangai were the major exceptions. But in the late 1990s trendsetting publishing in Tamil was spearheaded by a publishing house not in Chennai but in far-off Nagercoil, Kalachuvadu Pathippagam.

Another sign of growth is the entry of major media companies into what could be called quasi book publishing. There was of course a trend in the 1970s and 1980s towards the periodical press publishing monthly novels in newsprint. There was even a 'crime novel revolution' in the later 1980s, when there was a surfeit of pulp novels. The qualitative difference in the last few years has been the publication of well-produced works printed on mechanical glazed newsprint, often in colour, but recognizable as books and marketed as books.

[6] Andre Schiffrin, *The Business of Books: How International Conglomerates Took Over Publishing and Changed the Way We Read* (London: Verso, 2000).

The major players in this field are *Nakkeeran, Ananda Vikatan*, and *Kumudam*. In 2004 the New Horizon Media was set up with the proceeds of a thriving cricket website. Never in living memory has so much capital been infused into Tamil publishing.

The attempt of some publishers to negotiate rights for publication, a virtually non-existent practice, also shows the growing maturity of Tamiḷ publishing as well as the impact of globalization. The maturity and confidence of Tamil publishers is also materially premised on the growth and expansion of the market. Even though the expansion is somewhat exaggerated, it is not to be discounted. The crowds thronging the annual Chennai Book Fair are only one indication of growing reader interest as well as market expansion. Even though the physical network of bookselling is still weak, digital technology has extended the book market. The Tamil diaspora in the wake of the political violence in Sri Lanka and the software boom have meant that readers for Tamil books—with significant disposable incomes—are now spread across the world. There are now many online booksellers catering to their needs.

The book scene in Tamilnadu thus presents not a picture of gloom but of great promise. Tamil publishing—producers and consumers—have never had it so good. Undoubtedly, digital technology has been an enabling factor. This is of course not to push forward a monocausal explanation for a very complex phenomenon that has to take into account the effects of globalization, the structural adjustment of the Indian economy, a burgeoning middle class with considerable cultural anxiety, the unleashing of fresh talent from hitherto marginal social groups, and other such things. The book, certainly its Tamil avatar, is far from dead. The next decade may prove to be crucial to its future.

# Appendices

## 1. Tamil Book Production, 1556–1982

It is literally true to say that in Tamil all books available could be bought for less than five pounds.—**Rev. A.C. Clayton**[1]

This appendix is an attempt to quantify Tamil book production. For the first two and a half centuries the numbers put together by Graham Shaw constitute the only information available on this subject. The numbers calculated by Shaw could increase, probably marginally, with further research.

For the interregnum between 1801 to the time when systematic information came to be compiled under the Registration of Books Act 1867, the classified catalogue compiled by John Murdoch in 1865, fortuitously barely a couple of years before the act, provides some information. As this is a qualitative catalogue and the numbers do not reflect actual book production, information from Murdoch has not been collated.

As stated in Chapter 6, the Registrar of Books, Government of Madras, from the inception of the act prepared quarterly catalogues of books, and then, based on these catalogues wrote an annual review with some rudimentary statistical analysis. The quarterly catalogues were prepared based on the returns filed by printers giving various details about books and their producers. The table for the years 1871–1943 has been constructed based on these annual review and statistics. The tabulation changed over the years. Many of the records, especially for the earlier years, that I consulted in the Tamilnadu Archives were in a brittle state, and reports for some years were missing. Despite the

[1] Cited by E.T. Selby, 'The Christian Literature Society for India formerly called the Ceylon Vernacular Society, Ceylon Branch, 57th Annual Report, 1916–17'.

shortcomings this table is useful, indicating the magnitude of Tamil publishing during the colonial era.

The last section gives numbers for the years 1973–82 based on books received under the act at the National Library, Kolkata.

### *1556–1800*

According to Graham Shaw, 266 Tamil books were produced over 1556–1800. This number includes books printed in Sri Lanka.

*Source*: Graham Shaw, *The South Asia and Burma Retrospective Bibliography, Stage 1: 1556–1800* (London: The British Library, 1987).

### *1871–1943*

| Year | Periodicals | Miscellaneous | Tamil | Books published in Madras presidency (all languages) |
|---|---|---|---|---|
| 1868 | | | 171* | |
| 1869 | | | 172* | 422 |
| 1870 | | | 186* | |
| 1871 | | | 161* | 418 |
| 1872 | | | 113 | |
| 1873 | | | 250 | |
| 1874 | | | 295* | |
| 1875 | | | 280* | |
| 1876 | | | 299* | 823 |
| 1877 | | | 206 | 636 |
| 1878 | | | 338 | 824 |
| 1879 | | | 243* | 775 |
| 1880 | | | 353* | 875 |
| 1881 | | | 266* | 821 |
| 1882 | | | 204* | 731 |
| 1883 | | | 292* | |
| | Educational | Non-educational | | |
| 1884 | | | 238* | 818 |
| 1885 | 40 | 205 | 245 | 872 |
| 1886 | 52 | 224 | 276 | 930 |
| 1887 | | | 305* | |
| 1888 | | | 371* | |

| | Educational | Non-educational | | |
|---|---|---|---|---|
| 1889 | 92 | 321 | 413 | 1366 |
| 1890 | 54 | 292 | 346 | 1022 |
| 1891 | 30 | 170 | 200 | 784 |
| 1892 | 32 | 251 | 283 | 982 |
| 1893 | | | 208 | 806 |
| 1894 | 44 | 153 | 197 | 887 |
| 1895 | 50 | 152 | 202 | 925 |
| 1896 | 38 | 160 | 198 | 969 |
| 1897 | 34 | 166 | 200 | 951 |
| 1898 | | | 236* | 1057 |
| 1899 | 49 | 224 | 273 | 1184 |
| 1900 | | | 251* | |
| 1901 | | | 237* | |
| 1902 | | | 245* | 1162 |
| 1903 | | | 317 | 1217 |
| 1904 | | | 335 | 1210 |
| 1905 | | | 343 | 1237 |
| 1906 | | | 425 | 1440 |
| 1907 | | | 421 | 1574 |
| 1908 | | | 626 | 2207 |
| 1909 | | | 772 | 2704 |
| 1910 | | | 1007 | 3459 |
| 1911 | | | 1142 | 3722 |
| 1912 | | | 1269 | 4098 |
| 1913 | | | 1418 | 4318 |
| 1914 | | | 1579 | 4505 |
| 1915 | | | 1113 | 4280 |
| 1916 | | | 1093 | 4329 |
| 1917 | | | 1179 | 4537 |
| 1918 | | | 1066 | 4256 |
| 1919 | | | 1111 | 4470 |

| | Books | Periodicals | | |
|---|---|---|---|---|
| 1919–20 | | | | 3093 |
| 1920–1 | | | | 3057 |
| 1921–2 | | | 1230 | 3638 |
| 1922–3 | | | 1328 | 3760 |
| 1923–4 | | | | 4404 |
| 1924–5 | 1652 | 265 | 1917 | 5011 |
| 1926 | | | 1319* | |
| 1927 | | | 1406* | |
| 1928 | | | 1304* | |

| | Books | Periodicals | | |
|---|---|---|---|---|
| 1929 | | | 1265* | |
| 1930 | | | 1154* | |
| 1931–2 | | | | 4440 |
| 1932–3 | | | | 4460 |
| 1933–4 | 1246 | 208 | 1456 | 4749 |
| 1934–5 | 1208 | 248 | 1256 | 4428 |
| 1935–6 | 1090 | 273 | 1363 | 4062 |
| 1936–7 | 952 | 219 | 1171 | 3623 |
| 1937–8 | | | 1134 | 3675 |
| 1939 | 1182 | 232 | 1414 | 4043 |
| 1940 | 1068 | 196 | 1264 | 3567 |
| 1941 | 1112 | 183 | 1295 | 3751 |
| 1942 | 970 | 158 | 1128 | 2887 |
| 1943 | 633 | 136 | 769 | 2287 |

*Source*

| | |
|---|---|
| 1869 | Nos 42–4, Edl, 31 December 1870 |
| 1871 | Nos 27–9, Edl, 19 August 1872 |
| 1872 | Nos 2–3, Edl, 3 October 1873 |
| 1873 | Nos 24–5, Edl, 12 June 1874 |
| 1876/77 | Nos 37–9, Edl, 29 June 1878 |
| 1878 | Nos 5–7, Edl, 2 June 1879 |
| 1878/79 | Nos 348–9, Edl, 1 November 1881 |
| 1881 | Nos 926, Public, n.d., 1882 |
| 1882 | Nos 1998–9, Pub., 12 October 1883 |
| 1884/85 | Nos 296–7, Edl, 17 May 1886 |
| 1886 | Nos 205–6, Edl, 21 June 1887; nos 305–6, Edl, 21 June 1887 |
| 1889 | Nos 221–2, Edl, 17 March 1890 |
| 1890 | Nos 432–3, Edl, 9 June 1891 |
| 1891 | Nos 225–6, Edl, 14 March 1892 |
| 1892 | G.O. nos 184–85, Edl, 10 March 1893 |
| 1893 | G.O. nos 182–3, Edl, 18 March 1898 |
| 1894 | G.O. nos 185–6, Edl, 1 March 1895 |
| 1895 | G.O. nos 125–6, Edl, 5 March 1896 |
| 1896 | G.O. nos 133–4, Edl, 5 March 1897 |
| 1893–7 | G.O. nos 182–3, Edl, 18 March 1898 |
| 1898–9 | G.O. nos 114–15, Edl, 10 March 1900 |
| 1902–3 | G.O. nos 161–2, Edl (Confdl), 9 March 1904 |
| 1904 | G.O. nos 194–5, Edl (Confdl), 29 March 1905 |
| 1905 | G.O. nos 186-7, Edl (Confdl), 13 March 1906 |
| 1906 | G.O. nos 201–2, Edl (Confdl), 5 April 1907 |

| | |
|---|---|
| 1907 | G.O. nos 246–7, Edl, 27 March 1908 |
| 1908 | G.O. nos 298–9, Edl (Confdl), 17 May 1909 |
| 1909 | G.O. nos 295–6, Edl (Confdl), 26 May 1910 |
| 1919 | G.O. no. 363, Edl (Confdl), 10 June 1911 |
| 1911 | G.O. no. 416, Edl (Confdl), 14 May 1912 |
| 1912 | G.O. nos 457–8, Edl (Confdl), 20 May 1913 |
| 1909–13 | G.O. nos 558–9, Edl (Confdl), 14 May 1914 |
| 1914 | G.O. nos 530–1, Edl (Confdl), 17 May 1915 |
| 1915 | G.O. nos 528–9, Edl (Confdl), 15 May 1916 |
| 1916 | G.O. nos 626–7, Home (Edn), 12 May 1917 |
| 1917 | G.O. nos 613–14, Home (Edn), 11 May 1918 |
| 1918/1919 | G.O. nos 580–1, Home (Edn), 10 May 1920 |
| 1919–20/1922–3 | G.O. no. 764, Public, 1 Oct. 1923 |
| 1923–4/1924–5 | G.O. no. 863, Public, 11 Sep. 1925 |
| 1933–4/1937–8 | G.O. nos 1684–5, Edn. & Pub. Health (P.H.), 16 July 1938; G.O. nos 1545–6, Edn. & P.H., 24 July 1936; G.O. nos 1657–8, Edn. & P.H., 23 July 1937 |
| 1939 | G.O. nos 1426–7, Edn & P.H., 31 July 1940 |
| 1940 | G.O. no. 934, Edn & P.H.., 18 June 1941 |
| 1941 | G.O. no. 1091, Edn & P.H., 4 August 1942 |
| 1942 | G.O. no. 815, Edn & P.H., 15 June 1943 |
| 1943 | G.O. no. 899, Edn. & P.H., 12 June 1944 |

*Note*: All figures marked with an asterisk are compiled from *Tamil Nool Vivara Attavanai*, vols I–VII, 1867–1935 (Chennai: Government of Madras, 1961–1983) by R. Prakash, Roja Muthiah Research Library, Chennai. These figures include only books, not periodicals.

*1973–1982*

| Year | Tamil Books |
|---|---|
| 1973 | 1089 |
| 1975 | 675 |
| 1977 | 825 |
| 1978 | 1083 |
| 1979 | 815 |
| 1980 | 549 |
| 1981 | 787 |
| 1982 | 548 |

*Source*: National Library, Calcutta, under the 1867 act
*From*: Lokenath Bhattacharya, *Books and Reading in India* (Paris: UNESCO [1987])

## 2. Printing Costs, 1865–1925

### *Printing Rates,* circa *1865*

When natives print for themselves, the rates are low. 500 copies of a half sheet demy, containing 12 pages, cost from Rs 1 ½–2 (3s.–4s.) (exclusive of paper) if a wooden press is employed. If printed by an iron press and hot-pressed, the charge is Rs 3 ½. The terms for binding are equally low. A work containing 100–200 pages 8vo. is half bound in cloth for half an anna, or ¾ d. In this case, however, the book is stitched, not sewed. A volume of 400 pages 8vo. in the usual style of bazaar books is bound for one anna. The rates, of course, are higher for superior workmanship.

A tale or drama containing about 100 pages, 8vo. half bound in cloth, is sold for about 2 ½ anna (3 ¾ d.); works which have a small circulation are more expensive. The medium specimen of native printing is a part of the dramatic Ramayana. The work forms an octavo volume of 394 pages. The compiler paid 12 annas (1s. 6d.) for a copy. The best specimen of native printing is a part of an edition of the Kural, containing 389 pages 8vo., strongly bound in sheep. The price was Rs 1 ½ (2s. 6d.). As Europeans almost invariably are charged more than Natives, the usual selling prices are probably lower.

*Source*: John Murdoch, *A Classified Catalogue of Tamil Printed Books with Introductory Notices* (1865, rpnt. Madras: Govt. of Tamilnadu, 1968), pp. lx–lxi.

### *Printing Rates,* circa *1883*

Printing costs of Meenakshisundaram Pillai's *Thirukudandai Puranam* (32 formes: 240 + 12 pp; demy octavo)

| | |
|---|---:|
| Printing costs | 112-0-0 |
| Paper | 95-0-0 |
| Binding (800 copies) | 125-0-0 |
| Proofreading | 64-0-0 |
| Errand boy (for bringing proofs) | 2-0-0 |
| Coolie charges for carting paper and book packets | 1-0-0 |
| Postage | 2-4-0 |
| Packing materials and cartage | 3-0-0 |
| Total | 404-4-0 |

*Source*: Thyagaraya Chettiar to U.V. Swaminatha Iyer, 24 August 1883, U.V.S. Papers. *Thirukudandai Puranam* was printed with the help of Somasundara

Nayagar in Chennai at the Memorial Achukkudam. As the purpose of the letter is to complain about exorbitant rates, perhaps the above rates are on the higher side.

*Printing Rates*, circa *1925*

Printing of a book of 256 pages, paper covers

| | 100 copies | 5000 copies |
|---|---|---|
| Composition | 320 | 320 |
| Machining | 50 | 192 |
| Covers (printing & paper) | 4 | 40 |
| Paper | 20 | 800 |
| Binding | 4 | 158 |
| Total | 398 | 1510 |

*Source*: W.H. Warren, *Author and Printer* (Madras: Christian Literature Society, 1925), pp. 57–8. Warren was the Superintendent of the Diocesan Press, one of the biggest and, historically, the oldest press in Chennai. The rates here are likely to be on the higher side.

## 3. Cashbook of T.M. Press, 1916–1917

Below are entries from the cashbook of Maraimalai Adigal's T.M. Press. The entries relate to the first few months of its functioning and give an indication of the inventory and expenses involved in running a small printshop where Tamil books were printed.

| | | |
|---|---|---|
| 1916 | | |
| Nov. | Capital amount | 2,000 |
| | To Demi folio treadle machine | 945-0-0 |
| Nov. 29 | Advance for types to Swadesi Type Foundry, Chintadripet | 100-0-0 |
| Dec. 5 | 1 doz. Brass rules – 24" plain | 3-8-0 |
| Dec. 11 | 6 sets of Tamil cases – small size at Rs 4 per pair | 24-0-0 |
| | 1 English case at Rs 3 per pair | 3-0-0 |
| | 3 English upper cases at Re 1-8-0 per pair | 4-8-0 |
| | 1 Tamil rack stand | 5-4-0 |
| | 1 Tamil stand without rack | 3-8-0 |
| | 1 English rack stand | 5-0-0 |
| | 2 Wooden gallies – 8" x 24" at As 8 each | 1-0-0 |
| | Amount paid to Swadesi Type Foundry in full | 221-0-0 |
| | Trainage to compositor | 0-6-6 |
| | One month's pay advance to T.V. Ulaganatha Mudaliar | 20-0-0 |
| Dec. 18 | To printing 100 T.M. Press opening invitation | 1-1-0 |
| Dec. 23 | Types purchased from Oakes & Co., Madras | 333-13-0 |
| 1917 | | |
| Jan. 2 | One ream of 14 ½ lbs Demi paper | 5-10-8 |
| | One ream of Brilliant Yellow medium 18 lbs | 7-14-0 |
| Jan. 3 | Pay for compositor Raju from 12th Dec. 1916 | 9-11-0 |
| Jan. 31 | Salary for T.V. Voolaganatha Mudaliar | 20-0-0 |
| Feb. 3 | Salary for compositor Raju | 15-0-0 |
| Feb. 5 | To extra compositor Arunachalam | 3-8-0 |
| Feb. 28 | Salary for T.V. Voolaganatha Mudaliar | 20-0-0 |
| Mar. 1 | Advance from Pamban Kumaragurudasa Swamigal | 5-0-0 |
| Mar. 14 | Salary for compositor Raju | 15-0-0 |
| Mar. 31 | Salary for T.V. Voolaganatha Mudaliar | 20-0-0 |

*Source*: Cashbook of T.M. Press, 1916–43.

# Glossary

| | |
|---|---|
| *achukkudam* | printing press |
| *adheenam* | monastery |
| *arangettram* | ritual premiere of a text |
| *chillarai kovai/kattadam* | collection of assorted chapbooks bound together |
| *chittrilakkiyam* | literally, minor literature, indicating texts in a number of minor literary genres |
| *chindu* | popular verse form |
| *chuvadi* | (palm-leaf) manuscript |
| *gujili* | a bazaar in Chennai; a term used to denote 'low' culture |
| *khaddar* | khadi |
| *kalambagam* | minor literary form |
| *kattrucholli* | novice who assists a pandit |
| *kummi* | popular verse form |
| *lavani* | popular ballad form |
| *madam* | monastery |
| *nigandu* | traditional lexicon in verse form |
| *olai* | palm leaf |
| *oppary* | song of lamentation and bereavement |
| *panchangam* | almanac or ephemeris |
| *pathippagam* | publishing house |

| | |
|---|---|
| *payiram* | preface in verse form |
| *prachuralayam* | publishing house |
| *prachurakarthar* | publisher |
| *prasuram* | publication / publishing house |
| *sattrukavi* | preface in verse form |
| *sirappu payiram* | preface in verse form |
| *thalattu* | lullaby |
| *thala puranam* | long poetic composition on a place of religious importance |

# Select Bibliography

### (i) Government of Madras Records


Educational Proceedings, 1867–1938
Public Proceedings, 1867–1938
Judicial Proceedings, 1867–1916
Under Secretary Safe Files, 1918–38
C.I.D. Reports, 1906–7
Madras Police Abstracts of Intelligence, 1906, 1908, 1911, 1913


### (ii) Journals and Periodicals


*Anandaguna/Amirtaguna Bodhini*, 1928–9, 1932
*Ananda Bodhini*, 1916–36
*Ananda Vikatan*, 1930–3, 1940
*Bala Bharati*, 1925
*Bharatamani*, 1933–45
*Bharati*, 1931–4
*Chandrodhayam*, 1946
*Desabaktan*, 1918
*Gandhi*, 1933
*Hindu*, 1904–120
*Jnanabhanu*, 1913–15
*India*, 1906–10
*Indian Review*, 1908–46
*Janasakti*, 1938–9, 1944
*Jothi*, 1937–8
*Lakshmi*, 1923–6
*Kalaimagal* (Puducherry), 1916
*Kalaimagal* (Chennai), 1932–40
*Kudi Arasu*, 1925–38

*Kudi Nool*, 1938–40
*Kumaran*, 1922–40
*Kumari Malar*, 1945–84
*Manikkodi*, 1933–7
*Navasakti*, 1920–38
*Ooliyan*, 1933–6, 1940
*Panchamirtam*, 1924–5
*Sentamil*, 1906–20
*Sentamil Selvi*, 1923–50
*Saraswati*, 1955–62
*Sakti*, 1940–6
*Siddhantam*, 1929–45
*Sivanesan*, 1927–30
*Suthanthira Sangu*, 1930–3
*Swadesamitran*, 1906–37
*Tamil Polil*, 1924–46
*Tamilar Nesan*, 1917–23
*Thathuva Bodhini*, 1864
*Vasantham*, 1945
*Viveka Bodhini*, 1908–16
*Viveka Chintamani*, 1892–1908
*Vivekodhayam*, 1916–20

### (iii) Private Papers

(a) *Saiva Siddhanta Works Publishing Society Archive (Maraimalai Adigal Library)*

T.S. Balasundaram (Azhagaradigal), 1920–72
V.O. Chidambaram Pillai, 1900–36
Avvai Duraisami Pillai, 1943–4
M. Kathiresan Chettiar, 1924–51
M.S. Purnalingam Pillai, 1928–44
Maraimalai Adigal,
  Diaries, 1898–1950
  Letters, 1930–3
  Cashbook of T.M. Press, 1916–43
  Address Book, no. 2, 1923–30

S. Sachidanandam Pillai, 1920–8
V.P. Subramania Mudaliar, 1920–41
E.M. Subramania Pillai, 1925–47

(b) *U.V. Swaminatha Iyer Library, Chennai*

U.V. Swaminatha Iyer
Diaries, 1902–42
Letters, 1860–1942

(c) *Nehru Memorial Museum and Library, New Delhi*

V.V.S. Aiyar, 1907–1925

### (iv) Institutional Papers

Saiva Siddhanta Works Publishing Society, Chennai and Tirunelveli
Christian Literature Society, Chennai
Alliance & Co., Chennai
Madras Ripon Press, Pudukkottai
Vani Vilas Book Depot, Srirangam

### (v) Book Collections

P.N. Appuswamy Collection (at U.V. Swaminatha Iyer Library, Chennai)
Maraimalai Adigal Collection (at Maraimalai Adigal Library, Chennai)
U.V. Swaminatha Iyer Collection (at U.V. Swaminatha Iyer Library, Chennai)
S. Vaiyapuri Pillai Collection (with his daughter, the late V. Sarojini, Chennai)
P. Subbarayan Collection (at C. Vijayaraghavachari Library, Salem)
P.S. Kumarasamy Raja Collection (at Gandhi Kalai Mandram, Rajapalayam)
T.K. Chidambaranatha Mudaliar (with his grandson Deepa. Natarajan, Tenkasi)

### (vi) Bibliographies

Barnett, L.D., *A Catalogue of the Tamil Books in the Library of the British Museum*, vol. 2 (1931, facsimile rpnt. New Delhi: Asian Educational Services, 1998).
——— and G.U. Pope, *A Catalogue of the Tamil Books in the Library of the British Museum*, vol. 1 (1931, facsimile rpnt. New Delhi: Asian Educational Services, 1998).

*Classified Catalogue of Books Registered at the Office of the Registrar of Books*, vols I–V, Madras, 1961–71.

Diehl, Katherine S., *Early Indian Imprints* (New York: Scarecrow Press, 1964).

Murdoch, John, *Catalogue of the Christian Vernacular Literature of India . . .* (Madras: Caleb Foster, 1870).

———, *A Classified Catalogue of Tamil Printed Books with Introductory Notices* (1865, rpnt. Madras: Govt. of Tamilnadu, 1968).

Seethalakshmi, Ve., *Tamil Novelgal: Akaravarisai* (Chennai: International Institute of Tamil Studies, 1985).

Ranganathan, S.R. and R. Muthukumaraswamy, *Commemoration Bibliography* (Tirunelveli: The South India Saiva Siddhanta Works Publishing Society, 1961).

Shaw, Graham, *The South Asia and Burma Retrospective Bibliography, Stage 1: 1556–1800* (London: The British Library, 1987).

——— and Salim Quraishi, *The Bibliography of South Asian Periodicals: A Union List of Periodicals in South Asian Languages* (Brighton: Harvester Press, 1982).

——— and Mary Lloyd, *Publications Proscribed by the Government of India: A Catalogue of the Collection in the India Office Library and Records and the Department of Oriental Manuscripts and Printed Books, British Library Reference Division* (London: the British Library, 1985).

*Tamil Nool Vivara Attavanai*, vols I–VII, 1867–1935 (The Madras State Tamil Bibliography) (Chennai: Government of Madras, 1961–1983).

### (vii) Books and Articles

#### *Tamil*

Annadurai, C.N., *Perarignar Annavin Sorpolivukal*, 2 vols (Chennai: Poompuhar Pathippagam, 2005).

*Arasavanathu Aranilayam* (Thiruvavaduthurai: Thiruvavaduthurai Adheenam, 1962).

Arunachalam, M., *Kumariyum Kasiyum* (Thiruchittrambalam: Tamil Noolagam, 1959).

——— (ed.), *Mukkoodal Pallu* (Chennai: Tamil Noolagam, 1949).

Ayyamuthu, C.A., *Enathu Ninaivugal* (Chennai: Vanathi Pathippagam, 1973).

*Bharati Noolgal (Katturaigal)*, 4 vols (Chennai: Bharati Prachuralayam, n.d.).

*Bharati Padalgal: Aaivu Pathippu* (Thanjavur: Tamil University, 1989).

Bharatidasan, *Khaddar Rattinappattu* (Puducherry: Kalanidhi Press, 1930).

———, *Manudam Pottru* (Chennai: Poompuhar Pathippagam, 1984).

———, *Thondar Valinadaippattu* (Puducherry: Author, 1930).

Chandilyan, *Porattangal* (Chennai: Vanathi Pathippagam, 1987).

Chelvakesavaraya Mudaliar, T., *Abinava Kathaigal* (Chennai: Author, 1921).

Chettiar, A.K., *Itta Pani* (Chennai: Kumari Malar Kariyalayam, 1961).

——— (ed.), *Tamilnadu: Payanakkatturaigal* (Chennai: R. Ramachandran and A. Veerappan, 1968).

Damodaram Pillai, C.W., *Damodaram* (Jaffna: Jaffna Cooperative Tamil Books, 1971).

*Dina Thanthi Ponvizha Malar*, 1993.

*Engal Ur* (Chennai: Kalaimagal Kariyalayam, 1957).

Govindan, V., 'Puthakamum Vithakamum', *Sakti*, March 1941.

Gunasekaran, K.A., *Nagarsar Nattuppura Kathaippadalgal* (Sivagangai: Annam, 1988).

Ilankumaran, Era., *Thamarai Chelvar Va. Subbiah Pillai Varalaru* (Chennai: Saiva Siddhanta Noorpathippu Kazhagam, 1981).

———, *Thiruvaranganar Varalaru* (Chennai: Saiva Siddhanta Noorpathippu Kazhagam, 1982).

Kailasam Pillai, T., *Arumuga Navalar Charithiram* (1916, rpnt. Chidambaram: Sri Arumuga Navalar Saivaprakasa Vidyasalai Arakkattalai, 1985).

Kailasapathy, K., *Tamil Novel Ilakkiyam* (1968, rpnt. Chennai: New Century Book House, 1987).

*Kalki Ponvizha Malar*, 1992.

Kalki, *Ettikku Potti* (1930, rpnt. Chennai: Tamil Pannai, 1965).

———, *Kanaiyaliyin Kanavu* (1937, rpnt Chennai: Ananda Vikatan, 1938).

———, *Parthipan Kanavu* (Chennai: Mangala Noolagam, 1952).

———, *Thyaga Bhoomi* (1939, rpnt. Chennai: Vanathi Pathippagam, 1988).

Kalyanasundara Mudaliar, Thiru. Vi., *Desabaktamirtam* (Chennai: British India Achukkudam, 1919).

———, *Pennin Perumai allathu Valkai Thunai* (Chennai: Sadhu Achukkudam, 1927).

———, *Valkai Kurippukkal* (1944, rpnt. Chennai: Saiva Siddhanta Noorpathippu Kazhagam, 1982).

*Kamban Kavithai* (Chennai: Navayuga Prachuralayam, 1939).

Kovendhan, Tha. (ed.), *Siththar Padalgal* (Chennai: Poompuhar Prasuram Press, 1976).

Kulandai, Pulavar, *Iravana Kaviyam* (1946, rpnt. Erode: Vela Nilayam, 1971).

———, *Thodaiyathigaram* (Chennai: Pari Nilayam, 1967).

———, *Yappathigaram* (Chennai: Pari Nilayam, 1991).

Kulandran, Sabapathy, *Tamil Kristhava Vedagamathin Varalaru* (Bangalore: The Bible Society of India, 1967).

Kumaraswamy Raja, P.S., *Ilamai Ninaivugal* (Chennai: Bharati Pathippagam, 1957).

Madhaviah, A., *Padmavathy Charithiram* (1898, Chennai: Vanavil Prasuram, 1978).

———, *Thillai Govindan* (Madras: Srinivasa Varadachari & Co., 1903).

*Mahavidwan Me. Ve. Venugopala Pillai Manivizha Malar*, Chennai, 1956.

Maraimalai Adigal, *A Critical Study of 'Mullaippattu'* (Chennai: Author, 1903).

———, *Kumudavalli, Naganattarasi* (Pallavaram: Author, 1921).

Mohan, R. (ed.), *Novel Valarchi* (Chennai: Manivasakar Pathippagam, 1989).

Muthiah, Mullai (ed.), *Vedikkai Manithar Pudumaippithan* (Chennai: Mullai Veliyeedu, 1956).

Muthukumaraswamy, R., 'Tamil Noolgalil Thalaippu Pakkam', in *Tamil Vattam*, 2nd anniversary number, 1969.

Narayanaswamy, Thi.Ki., 'Periya Purana Pathippu Varalaru', *Tamil Pozhil*, 13 (4), July 1937.

———, 'Thiru Arutpa Pathippu Varalaru', *Tamil Kalai*, annual number, 1940.

*Navalar Noottrandu Malar*, Jaffna, 1979.

Ooran Adigal, *Saiva Adheenangal* (Vadalur: Samarasa Sanmarga Araichi Nilayam, 2009).

Padmanabhan, R.A., *Chitrabharati* (Nagercoil: Kalachuvadu Pathippagam, 2006, 3rd edn).

——— (ed.), *Bharati Puthayal Perumthirattu* (Chennai: Vanathi Pathippagam, 1982).

——— (ed.), *Bharatiyin Kadithangal* (1981, rpnt. Nagercoil: Kalachuvadu Pathippagam, 2005).

Paramasivam, M., *Makkal Ezhuthalar Vindhan* (Chennai: Pookkudai Pathippagam, 1983).

*Parithimal Kalaignar Noottrandu Malar*, Madurai, 1970.

Prema, R., *Vai.Mu. Kothainayaki Ammal* (New Delhi: Sahitya Akademi, 2001).

Raghavaiyangar, M., *Sentamil Valartha Thevargal* (Tiruchi: T.G. Gopaul Pillai, 1951).

Ragunathan, *Ilakkiya Vimarisanam* (1948, rpnt. Madurai: Meenakshi Puthaka Nilayam, 1980).

———, *Pudumaippithan Varalaru* (Chennai: Tamil Puthakalayam, 1951).

———, *Ragunathan Kathaigal* (1951, rpnt. Madurai: Meenakshi Puthaka Nilayam, 1980).

———, *Samuthaya Ilakkiyam* (1964, rpnt. Madurai: Meenakshi Puthaka Nilayam, 1980).

Rajarathinam Pillai, T.A., *Ci. Vai. Damodaram Pillai Avargal Charithiram* (Chennai: Author, 1934).

Ramalingam Pillai, Namakkal, *En Kathai* (1944, rpnt. Chennai: Palaniappa Bros, 1977).

Ranganathan, Thi. Ja., *Eppadi Eluthinen* (Madurai: Sakti Kariyalayam, 1943).

———, *Pozhuthupokku* (Chennai: Kalaimagal Kariyalayam, 1953).

Ravichandran, Ci.Ma. and Pa. Subashbose, *Tamilaga Kolaichindu: Aaivadangal* (Coimbatore: Manju Pathippagam, 2001).

Sambanda Mudaliar, Pammal, *En Suyasarithai* (Chennai: Author, 1963).

Sambandam, Ma.Su., *Achu Kalai* (Chennai: Tamilar Pathippagam, 1959).

———, *Achum Pathippum* (Chennai: Tamilar Pathippagam, 1980).

———, *Eluthum Achum* (Chennai: Tamilar Pathippagam, 1981).

———, *Tamil Ithaliyal Chuvadugal* (Chennai: Tamilar Pathippagam, 1990).

———, *Tamil Ithaliyal Kalanjiyam* (Chennai: Tamilar Pathippagam, 1990).

———, *Tamil Ithaliyal Varalaru* (Chennai: Tamilar Pathippagam, 1987).

Samy, Aa.Ma., *19am Noottrandu Tamil Ithalgal* (Chennai: Navamani Pathippagam, 1992).

———, *Tamil Ithalgal: Thottram–Valarchi* (Chennai: Navamani Pathippagam, 1987).

Sarojini Packiamuthu, *Viviliyamum Tamilum* (Madras: Gurukul Lutheran Theological College and Research Institute, 1990).

Satyamurti, S., *Arumai Puthalvikku* (1945, rpnt. Chennai: Bharati Pathippagam, 1988).

Sivagnanam, M.P., *Enathu Porattam* (Chennai: Inba Nilayam, 1974).

———, *Krishnaswamy Pavalar Valkai Varalaru* (Chennai: Poonkodi Pathippagam, 1988).

Srinivasa Sastri, V.S., *Meendum Vazhnthal . . .?* (Chennai: Kalaimagal Kariyalayam, 1954).

Srinivasan, Aranga, *Eluthulaga Nayaki* (Chennai: Sekar Pathippagam, 1988).

———, *Kavadi Chindum Kavignan Varalarum* (Chennai: Sekar Pathippagam, 1984).

Subramaniam, Naa., *Eelathu Tamil Novel Ilakkiyam* (Jaffna: Muthamizh Veliyeedu Kazhagam, 1978).

Subramanyam, Ka.Naa., *Ilakkiya Chadanaiyalargal* (Chidambaram: Manivasagar Pathippagam, 1985.

———, *Muthal Ainthu Tamil Novelgal* (Chennai: Amudha Nilayam, 1957).

———, *Padithirukkireergala?*, 2 vols (Chennai: Amudha Nilayam, 1957–8).

Sunda, *Ponniyin Puthalvar: Kalkiyin Valkai Varalaru* (Chennai: Vanathi Pathippagam, 1976).

Sundararajan, P.G. (Chitti) and S. Sivapathasundaram, *Tamil Novel: Noorandu Varalarum Valarchiyum* (Chennai: Christian Literature Society, 1977).

———, *Tamilil Sirukathai: Varalarum Valarchiyum* (Chennai: Cre–A, 1989).

Surada, *Vinakkalum Suradavin Vidaigalum* (Chennai: Surada Pathippagam, 1991).

Suriyanarayana Shastri, V.G., *Pavalar Virundu* (Madurai: V.S. Swaminathan, 1957).

———, *Tamil Mozhiyin Varalaru* (Chennai: G.A. Natesan, 1903).

Swaminatha Iyer, U.V., *En Charithiram* (rpnt. Chennai: U.V. Swaminatha Iyer Library, 1990).

———, *Nallurai Kovai*, 4 vols (rpnt. Chennai: U.V. Swaminatha Iyer Library, 1991).
———, *Nan Kandathum Kettathum* (rpnt. Chennai: U.V. Swaminatha Iyer Library, 1980).
———, *Ninaivu Manjari*, 2 vols (rpnt. Chennai: U.V. Swaminatha Iyer Library, 1991).
———, *Puthiyathum Palaiyathum* (rpnt. Chennai: U.V. Swaminatha Iyer Library, 1990).
———, *Sri Meenakshisundaram Pillai avargalin Charithiram*, 2 vols (1938–40, rpnt. Thanjavur: Tamil University, 1986).
Swaminatha Sarma, V., *Aval Pirivu* (Pudukkottai: Prapanjajothi Prachuralayam, 1957).
———, *Nan Kanda Nalvar* (Pudukkottai: Prapanjajothi Prachuralayam, 1974).
*Tamil Anbar Mahanadu, Tamil Puthaka Katchi Arikkai*, Chennai, 1934.
*Tamil Valarkkum Dharumapuram* (Dharumapuram: Dharumapura Adheenam, 1981).
*Thiru. Vi. Ulaganatha Mudaliar Manivizha Malar*, 1941.
Thooran, P. (ed.), *Bharati Tamil* (Chennai: Amudha Nilayam, 1953).
*Va. Ve. Su. Iyer Katturaikal* (Tirunelveli: S.N. Somayajulu, 1981).
Vaiyapuri Pillai, S., *Ilakkiya Chinthanaigal* (Chennai: Tamil Puthakalayam, 1947).
*Vasaga Kurigal* (Chennai: Madras Ripon Press, 1908, 2nd edn).
Venkatachalapathy, A.R., 'Bharatam Thanta Bhagiratar', *Kalachuvadu* 73, January 2006.
———, 'Maruthuva Agarathi Thanta Medhai', *Kalachuvadu* 85, January 2007.
———, *Mucchanthi Ilakkiyam* (Nagercoil: Kalachuvadu Pathippagam, 2004).
———, *Novelum Vasippum: Oru Varalattru Parvai* (Nagercoil: Kalachuvadu Pathippagam, 2002).
———, 'Panchangamum Railway Guideum: Naveena Tamilaga Pathippulagam', *Kalachuvadu*, January–February 2003.
———, 'Tamilil Kandana Ilakkiyam', Foreword to P. Saravanan (ed.), *Arutpa Marutpa Kandana Thirattu* (Nagercoil: Kalachuvadu Pathippagam, 2010).
——— (ed.), *Bharati: Karuvoolam* (The Bharati Treasury) (Nagercoil: Kalachuvadu Pathippagam, 2008).

——— (ed.), *Bharati: 'Vijaya' Katturaikal* (Nagercoil: Kalachuvadu Pathippagam, 2004).

——— (ed.), *Maraimalai Adigalar Natkurippugal* (Chennai: Maraimalai Adigal Pathippagam, 1988).

——— (ed.), *Va.Oo.Chi. Kadithangal* (Chennai: Sekar Pathippagam, 1984).

——— (ed.), *Pudumaippithan Kathaikal* (Nagercoil: Kalachuvadu Pathippagam, 2000).

——— (ed.), *Pudumaippithan Katturaikal* (Nagercoil: Kalachuvadu Pathippagam, 2002).

Venkatasamy, Mylai Seeni., *Pathonbatham Noottrandil Tamil Ilakkiyam, 1800–1900* (Chennai: Santhi Noolagam, 1962).

Viswanathan, Seeni., *Bharati Noolgal: Pathippu Varalaru* (Chennai: Author, 1989; rev. edn 2005).

———, *Bharati Noolgal Vivarak Kovai* (Chennai: Balaji Puthaka Nilayam, 1987).

———, *Bharati Noorpeyar Kovai* (Chennai: Vanavil Prasuram, 1981).

———, *Mahakavi Bharati Varalaru* (Chennai: Author, 1996).

——— (ed.), *Kalavarisaippaduthappatta Bharati Padaippugal*, 12 vols (Chennai: Author, 1998–2010).

### English

*An Account of the Success of Two Danish Missionaries . . .* in *The Propagation of the Gospel in the East . . .* Part III (London: J. Downing, 1718).

Anderson, Benedict, *Imagined Communities: Reflections on the Origin and Spread of Nationalism* (1983, London: Verso, 1991, 2nd rev. edn).

Arnold, David, *Police Power and Colonial Rule: Madras, 1859–1947* (Delhi: Oxford University Press, 1986).

Baker, C.J., *An Indian Rural Economy: The Tamilnad Countryside, 1880–1955* (Delhi: Oxford University Press, 1984).

———, 'Tamilnad Estates in the Twentieth Century', *The Indian Economic and Social History Review*, 13 (1), January–March 1976.

Bakhtin, Mikhail, *Rabelais and His World* (Bloomington: Indiana University Press, 1984).

Banerjee, Sumanta, 'Bogey of the Bawdy: Changing Concept of "Obscenity" in 19th Century Bengali Culture', *Economic & Political Weekly*, 18 July 1987.

———, *The Parlour and the Streets: Elite and Popular Culture in Nineteenth Century Calcutta* (Calcutta: Seagull, 1989).

Baron, Sabrina Alcorn, Eric N. Lindquist and Eleanor F. Shevlin (eds), *Agent of Change: Print Culture Studies after Elizabeth L. Eisenstein* (Amherst: University of Massachusetts Press, 2007).

Barrier, N.G., *Banned: Controversial Literature and Political Control in British India, 1907–1947* (Columbia: Missouri University Press, 1974).

Baskaran, S. Theodore, *The Message-Bearers: The Nationalist Politics and the Entertainment Media in South India* (Madras: Cre–A, 1981).

Bayly, C.A., *Empire and Information: Intelligence Gathering and Social Communication in India, 1780–1870* (Cambridge: Cambridge University Press, 1999).

Benjamin, Walter, 'The Work of Art in the Age of Mechanical Reproduction', in *Illuminations* (London: Fontana, 1973).

Bhattacharya, Sabyasachi, 'Notes on the Role of the Intelligentsia in Colonial Society: India from Mid-Nineteenth Century', *Studies in History*, 1 (1), January–June 1979.

Birkerts, Sven, *The Gutenberg Elegies: The Fate of Reading in an Electronic Age* (Boston: Faber & Faber, 1994; 2nd edn 2006).

Birn, Raymond, '*Livre et Societe* after Ten Years: Formation of a Discipline', *Studies on Voltaire and the Eighteenth Century*, vol. 151, 1976.

Blackburn, Stuart, *Print, Folklore, and Nationalism in Colonial South India* (Delhi: Permanent Black, 2003).

*Brief Account of the Measures taken in Denmark for the Conversion of the Heathen in the East Indies, A* (London: J. Downing, 1715).

Briggs, Asa and Peter Burke, *A Social History of the Media: From Gutenberg to the Internet* (Cambridge: Polity, 2005).

Burke, Peter, *Popular Culture in Early Modern Europe* (New York: Harper & Row, 1978).

Burnell, A.C., *Elements of South–Indian Palaeography* (1874, rpnt. New Delhi: Asian Educational Services, 1994).

Cavallo, Guglielmo and Roger Chartier (eds), *A History of Reading in the West* (Cambridge: Polity, 1999).

Chandrasekhar, S., *A Report on South India Reading Habits* (Madras: Southern Languages Book Trust, [1960]).

Chartier, Roger, *Cultural History: Between Practices and Representations* (Cambridge: Polity, 1988).

———, *The Cultural Origins of the French Revolution* (Durham: Duke University Press, 1991).

———, *The Cultural Uses of Print in Early Modern France* (Princeton: Princeton University Press, 1987).

———, 'Culture as Appropriation', in Steven Kaplan (ed.), *Understanding Popular Culture* (Berlin: Mouton, 1984).

———, 'Libraries Without Walls', *Representations*, no. 42, Spring 1993.

———, *The Order of Books* (Stanford: Stanford University Press, 1984).

———, 'The Printing Revolution: A Reappraisal' in Sabrina Alcorn Baron, Eric N. Lindquist and Eleanor F. Shevlin (eds), *Agent of Change: Print Culture Studies after Elizabeth L. Eisenstein* (Amherst: University of Massachusetts Press, 2007).

———, 'Texts, Printing, Reading', in Lynn Hunt (ed.), *The New Cultural History* (Berkeley: University of California Press, 1989).

———, 'Texts, Symbols, and Frenchness', *Journal of Modern History*, 57 (4), December 1985.

——— (ed.), *The Culture of Print: Power and the Uses of Print in Early Modern Europe* (Princeton: Princeton University Press, 1989).

Chartier, Roger and Daniel Roche, 'New Approaches to the History of the Book', in Maurice Aymard and Harbans Mukhia (eds), *French Studies in History*, vol. 2 (New Delhi: Orient Longman, 1990).

Chatterjee, Partha, 'The Nationalist Resolution of the Women's Question', in Kumkum Sangari and Sudesh Vaid (eds), *Recasting Women: Essays in Colonial History* (New Delhi: Kali for Women, 1988).

———, *Nationalist Thought and the Colonial World: A Derivative Discourse?* (Delhi: Oxford University Press, 1986).

Darnton, Robert, 'Book Production in India, 1850–1900', *Book History*, vol. 5, 2000.

———, *The Business of Enlightenment* (Cambridge, Mass.: Harvard University Press, 1979).

———, *The Case for Books: Past, Present, and Future* (New York: Public Affairs, 2009).

———, *The Great Cat Massacre and Other Episodes in French Cultural History* (Harmondsworth: Penguin, 1984).

———, 'History of Reading', in Peter Burke (ed.), *New Perspectives on Historical Writing* (Cambridge: Polity, 1991).

———, 'Literary Surveillance in the British Raj: The Contradiction of Liberal Imperialism', *Book History*, vol. 4, 2004.

———, *The Literary Underground of the Old Regime* (Cambridge, Mass.: Harvard University Press, 1982).

———, 'What is the History of Books?' *Daedalus*, 111 (3), 1982.

———, '"What is the History of Books?" Revisited', *Modern Intellectual History*, 4 (3), 2007.

Davis, Natalie Zemon, *Society and Culture in Early Modern France* (London: Duckworth, 1975).

Dirks, Nicholas B., *The Hollow Crown: The Ethnohistory of a South Indian Little Kingdom* (Cambridge: Cambridge University Press, 1987).

Eagleton, Terry, *The Function of Criticism* (London: Verso, 1984).

Ebeling, Sascha, 'The College of Fort St George and the Transformation of Tamil Philology during the Nineteenth Century', in Thomas R. Trautmann (ed.), *The Madras School of Orientalism: Producing Knowledge in Colonial South India* (New Delhi: Oxford University Press, 2009).

———, *Colonizing the Realm of Words: The Transformation of Tamil Literature in Nineteenth-Century South India* (Albany: SUNY Press, 2010).

Eisenstein, Elizabeth L., *The Printing Press as an Agent of Change*, 2 vols (Cambridge: Cambridge University Press, 1979).

———, *The Printing Revolution in Early Modern Europe* (Cambridge: Cambridge University Press, 1983, 2nd edition 2005).

Epstein, Jason, *Book Business. Publishing Past Present and Future* (New York: W.W. Norton, 2001).

Febvre, Lucien and Henri-Jean Martin, *The Coming of the Book: The Impact of Printing, 1450–1800* (original French 1958, Eng. trans. London: New Left Books, 1976).

Fenger, J. Fred., *History of the Tranquebar Mission* . . . (Tranquebar: Evangelical Lutheran Mission Press, 1863).

Fetter, Norman, 'The Moment of Pickwick, or the Production of a Commodity Text', in P. Humm *et al.* (eds), *Popular Fictions* (London: Methuen, 1986).

Furet, François, 'Book Licensing and Book Production in the Kingdom of France in the Eighteenth Century', *In the Workshop of History* (Chicago: University of Chicago Press, 1984).

Gates, W.R., *The Indian Printer's Guide and Handbook* (Madras: n.p., 1922).

Ghosh, Anindita, *Power in Print: Popular Publishing and the Politics of Language and Culture in a Colonial Society* (New Delhi: Oxford University Press, 2006).

———, 'An Uncertain "Coming" of the Book: Early Print Cultures in Colonial India, *Book History*, vol. 6, 2003.

Ginzburg, Carlo, *The Cheese and the Worms: The Cosmos of a Sixteenth-Century Miller* (Harmondsworth: Penguin, 1982).

Gomez, Jeff, *Print is Dead: Books in Our Digital Age* (London: Macmillan, 2008).

Guha Thakurta, Tapati, *The Making of a New 'Indian' Art* (Cambridge: Cambridge University Press, 1992).

Gupta, Abhijit, 'The History of the Book in the Indian Subcontinent', in Michael H. Suarez and H.R. Woudhuysen (eds), *The Oxford Companion to the Book* (Oxford: Oxford University Press, 2010).

Hall, Stuart, 'Cultural Studies: Two Paradigms', in Richard Collins, *et al.* (eds), *Media, Culture and Society: A Critical Reader* (London: Sage, 1987).

Hill, Christopher, 'Censorship and English Literature', *The Collected Essays of Christopher Hill*, vol. 1 (Brighton: Harvester Press, 1985).

Hoggart, Richard, *The Uses of Literacy* (Harmondsworth: Penguin, 1958).

Hughes, Steve, 'The "Music Boom" in Tamil South India: Gramophone, Radio and the Making of Mass Culture', *The Historical Journal of Film, Radio and Television*, 22 (4), 2002.

Humm, P., *et al.* (eds), *Popular Fictions: Essays in Literature and History* (London: Methuen, 1986).

John, K.J. (ed.), *Thampuran Vanakkam: Christian Doctrine in Malabar Tamil* (Calicut: University of Calicut, 2005).

Joshi, Priya, *In Another Country: Colonialism, Culture, and the English Novel in India* (New York: Columbia University Press, 2002).

Kailasapathy, K., *Tamil Heroic Poetry* (Oxford: Clarendon Press, 1968).

Kaplan, Steven L. (ed.), *Understanding Popular Culture* (Berlin: Mouton, 1984).

Kesavan, B.S., *History of Printing and Publishing in India, vol. 1, South Indian Origins of Printing and its Efflorescence in Bengal* (New Delhi: National Book Trust, 1985).

*Letter to the Reverend Mr Geo. Lewis . . ., A* (London: J. Downing, 1715).

MacDermott, Kathy, 'Literature and the Grub Street Myth', in P. Humm, *et al.* (eds), *Popular Fictions* (London: Methuen, 1986).

Mahadevan, Raman, 'Entrepreneurship and Business Communities in Colonial Madras, 1900–1929: Some Preliminary Observations', in Dwijendra Tripathi (ed.), *Business Communities in India: A Historical Perspective* (Delhi: Manohar, 1984).

Mangamma, J., *Book Printing in India: With Special Reference to the Contribution of European Scholars to Telugu, 1746–1857* (Nellore: Bangorey Books, 1975).

Martin, Henri-Jean, 'The *Bibliotheque Bleue*', *Publishing History*, vol. 3, 1978.

McDonald, Ellen E., 'The Modernizing of Communication: Vernacular Publishing in Nineteenth Century Maharashtra', *Asian Survey*, July 1968.

McLuhan, Marshall, *The Gutenberg Galaxy: The Making of Typographic Man* (Toronto: University of Toronto Press, 1962).

*Memoirs of the Madras Library Association, 1940; 1941; 1944* (Madras: Madras Library Association).

Mohanarajan, P.A., *Glimpses of Early Printing and Publishing in India* (Madras: Mohanavalli Publications, 1990).

Morris, Henry, *The Life of John Murdoch* (1906, rpnt. Christian Literature Society, 1995).

Mukherjee, Meenakshi, *The Perishable Empire: Essays in Indian Writing in English* (New Delhi: Oxford University Press, 2000).

———, *Realism and Reality: The Novel and Society in India* (Delhi: Oxford University Press, 1985).

Nambi Arooran, K., *Tamil Renaissance and Dravidian Nationalism, 1905–1944* (Madurai: Koodal Publishers, 1980).

Natesan, B., *In the Service of the Nation: A Golden Jubilee Retrospect* (Madras: G.A. Natesan, 1948).

Nayudu, C.V. Munisami, *A Catechism of Printing in Tamil, Part I* (Madras: C. Narahari Nayudu, 1892).

Oddie, Geoffrey A., *Hindu and Christian in South East India* (London: Curzon Press, 1991).

Paul, Ashit (ed.), *Woodcut Prints of Nineteenth-Century Calcutta* (Calcutta: Seagull, 1983).

Plant, Majorie, *The English Book Trade* (London: Allen & Unwin, 1965).

Playne, Somerset, *Southern India: Its History, People, Commerce and Industrial Resources* (1914, facsimile rpnt. New Delhi: Asian Educational Services, 2004).

Pollock, Sheldon, 'Literary Culture and Manuscript Culture in Precolonial India', in Simon Eliot, Andrew Nash, and Ian Willison (eds), *Literary Cultures and the Material Book* (London: The British Library, 2007).

Pottinger, David, *The French Book Trade in the Ancien Regime* (Cambridge, Mass.: Harvard University Press, 1958).

Price, Pamela, *Kingship and Political Practice in Colonial India* (Cambridge: Cambridge University Press, 1996).

Priolkar, A.K., *The Printing Press in India: Its Beginnings and Early Development* (Bombay: Maratha Samshodhana Mandala, 1958).

*The Propagation of the Gospel in the East*... Parts I–III (London: J. Downing, 1715–18).

Purnalingam Pillai, M.S., *Tamil Literature* (Munnirpallam: Bibliotheca, 1929).

Rabb, Theodore K., '"The Advent of Printing and the Problem of Renaissance": A Comment', *Past & Present*, 52, August 1971.

Ramachandran, T.N., *Sivagnana Munivar* (New Delhi: Sahitya Akademi, 1999).

Rao, Velcheru Narayana, David Shulman, and Sanjay Subrahmanyam, *Textures of Time: Writing History in South India, 1600–1800* (Delhi: Permanent Black, 2001).

Richman, Paula, *Extraordinary Child: Poems from a South Indian Devotional Genre* (Honolulu: University of Hawai'i Press, 1997).

Robinson, Francis, 'Technology and Religious Change: Islam and the Impact of Print', *Modern Asian Studies*, 27 (1), February 1993.

Rogers, Pat, *Grub Street: Studies in a Subculture* (London: Methuen, 1972).

Rosenkilde, Volmer, 'Printing at Tranquebar, 1712–1845', *Library* (5th series) IV (1949).

*Royal Commission on Labour in India*, vol. 7, pt 1, 1931.

Said, Edward, *Orientalism* (London: Routledge, 1978).

Schiffrin, Andre, *The Business of Books: How International Conglomerates Took Over Publishing and Changed the Way We Read* (London: Verso, 2000).

Sen, Asok, *Iswar Chandra Vidyasagar and His Elusive Milestones* (Calcutta: Riddhi India, 1977).

Shaw, Graham, 'On the Wrong End of the Raj: Some Aspects of Censorship in British India and its Circumvention, 1920s–1940', in Abhijit Gupta and Swapan Chakravorty (eds), *Moveable Type: Book History in India* (Ranikhet: Permanent Black, 2008).

———, 'South Asia', in Simon Eliot Jonathan Rose (ed.), *A Companion to the History of the Book* (Malden, M.A.: Blackwell, 2007).

Shulman, D.D., 'Poets and Patrons in Tamil Literature and Literary Legend', in Barbara Miller (ed.), *The Powers of Art* (Delhi: Oxford University Press, 1992).

Spufford, Margaret, *Small Books and Pleasant Histories* (London: Methuen, 1981).

Sriram, V., *The Devadasi and the Saint: The Life and Times of Bangalore Nagarathnamma* (Chennai: EastWest Books, 2007).

Stark, Ulrike, *An Empire of Books: The Naval Kishore Press and the Diffusion of the Printed Word in Colonial India* (Ranikhet: Permanent Black, 2007).

Suntherlingam, R., *Politics and Nationalist Awakening in South India* (Tucson: University of Arizona Press, 1974).

Tamizhnaadan, *Tamil Mozhiyin Muthal Achu Puthakam* (Salem: Salem District Contemporary Painters and Writers Association, 1995).

Thani Nayagam, Xavier S., 'The First Books Printed in Tamil', *Tamil Culture* VII (3), July 1958.

*The Hindu Speaks: On Libraries* (Madras: Kasturi & Sons, 1992).

Thomas, Keith, 'The Meaning of Literacy in Early Modern England', in G. Bauman (ed.), *The Written Word* (Oxford: Oxford University Press, 1986).

Thompson, E.P., *The Making of the English Working Class* (New York: Vintage, 1968).

Thompson, John B., *Books in the Digital Age: The Transformation of Academic and Higher Education Publishing in Britain and the United States* (Cambridge: Polity, 2005).

Trautmann, Thomas, *Languages and Nations: The Dravidian Proof in Colonial Madras* (New Delhi: Yoda Books, 2006).

Venkatachalapathy, A.R., 'Almanacs and Railway Timetables: A Brief History of Tamil Book-Publishing', in *Gum and Calico: Libraries of India* (New Delhi: Alliances Francaises, 1998).

———, 'Art in the Type Foundry: The Cultural Uses of Typemade Blocks in Colonial Tamilnadu', *Nunkalai*, March 1999.

———, 'Caricaturing the Political: A Brief History of the Cartoon in Tamil Journalism', *Art India*, 8 (4), 2003.

———, 'Domesticating the Novel: Society and Culture in Inter-War Tamilnadu', *The Indian Economic and Social History Review*, 34 (1), January–April 1997.

———, 'Exaggerated Obituaries: The Tamil Book in the Age of Electronic Reproduction', in Nalini Rajan (ed.), *Digital Culture Unplugged: Probing the Native Cyborg's Multiple Locations* (London: Routledge, 2007).

———, 'Fiction and the Tamil Reading Public', in Meenakshi Mukherjee (ed.), *Early Novels in India* (New Delhi: Sahitya Akademi, 2002).

———, 'Grammar, the Frame of language: Tamil Pandits at the College of Fort St George', in Thomas R. Trautmann (ed.), *The Madras School of Orientalism: Producing Knowledge in Colonial South India* (New Delhi: Oxford University Press, 2009).

———, *In Those Days There Was No Coffee: Writings in Cultural History* (New Delhi: Yoda Press, 2006).

———, '*Kalaikkalanjiyam*: The Making of the Tamil Encyclopaedia, 1947–1968', in Swapan Chakravorty and Abhijit Gupta (ed.), *Moveable Type: Book History in India* (Ranikhet: Permanent Black, 2008).

———, 'Reading Practices and Modes of Reading in Colonial Tamilnadu', *Studies in History*, X (2), July–December, 1994.

———, 'Songsters of the Crossroads: Popular Literature in Colonial Tamilnadu', *South Indian Folklorist*, 3 (1), 1999.

———, 'Written on Leaves in the Malabarian Manner: Print Culture in Eighteenth-Century Tranquebar', *Review of Development and Change*, XIV (1–2), January–December 2009.

Warren, W.H., *Author and Printer* (Madras: Christian Literature Society, 1925).

Webb, R.K., *The British Working Class Reader, 1790–1848* (London: Allen & Unwin, 1971).

Williams, Raymond, *Culture* (London: Fontana, 1983).

———, *The Long Revolution* (Harmondsworth: Penguin, 1965).

Winslow, *A Comprehensive Tamil and English Dictionary* (1862, rpnt. New Delhi : Asian Educational Services, 1979).

Wood, Ananda E., *Knowledge Before Printing and After* (Delhi: Oxford University Press, 1985).

### (viii) Unpublished Manuscripts and Dissertations

Pothi Reddy, S., 'Dhanukkodi Nattuppura Puyarpadalgal', Unpublished M.Phil. dissertation, Madurai–Kamaraj University, 1981.

Raman, Bhavani, 'Document Raj: Writing and Scribes in Early Colonial South India', Unpublished manuscript, 2010.

Srinivasan, V., 'Amarajothi Alliance Iyer', Unpublished manuscript, no date.

Veeraraghavan, D., 'The Rise and Growth of the Labour Movement in the City of Madras and its Environs, 1918–1939', Unpublished Ph.D. thesis, I.I.T., Madras, 1987.

Trivedi, Harish, 'The "Book" in India: Orality, Manuscript, Print (post)colonialism', Unpublished paper.

# Index